TEACHING ENGLISH
CREATIVELY

TEACHING ENGLISH CREATIVELY

SECOND EDITION

By

JOHN H. BUSHMAN

University of Kansas
Lawrence, Kansas

and

KAY PARKS BUSHMAN

Ottawa High School
Ottawa, Kansas

C H A R L E S   C   T H O M A S • P U B L I S H E R
Springfield • Illinois • U.S.A.

Published and Distributed Throughout the World by

CHARLES C THOMAS • PUBLISHER
2600 South First Street
Springfield, Illinois 62794-9265

© *1994 by* CHARLES C THOMAS • PUBLISHER

ISBN 0-398-05911-X

Library of Congress Catalog Card Number: 94-7062

First Edition 1986
Second Edition 1994

Printed in the United States of America
SC-R-3

Library of Congress Cataloging-in-Publication Data

Bushman, John H.
    Teaching English creatively / by John H. Bushman and Kay Parks
Bushman.—2nd ed.
      p.   cm.
    Includes bibliographical references and index.
    ISBN 0-398-05911-X
    1. English language—Study and teaching (Secondary)—United
States.   2. Language arts—United States.   3. Activity programs in
education—United States.   I. Bushman, Kay Parks. II. Title.
LB1631.B797   1994
428'.007'12—dc20   94-7069
                                             CIP

PREFACE

With this second edition of *Teaching English Creatively*, it is still our intent to provide inservice and preservice teachers of English practical activities derived from sound educational theory and research to help make their job in the classroom effective and enjoyable. So often teachers hear "English is boring," "Why do we have to do this?" and "What's this got to do with me?" It is our hope that if teachers use the activities in *Teaching English Creatively, Second Edition,* they will not hear those expressions.

This second book keeps the activities we included in the first book; however, we have added much so that now this book represents the current research and effective practice in English education. Our chapter on Teaching Writing now includes the latest on assessment and using portfolios in the classrooms, the Teaching Literature chapter has been broadened to include much more on the teaching of young adult literature, and we have included more background on the grammar issue, since it simply refuses to go away. We have also added a new chapter about middle and secondary schools. In addition, we have updated all the "Additional Readings" sections at the end of each chapter so that resources with the latest theory, research, and practice are noted for your use.

Again, we have made every effort to be as informal in our presentation as possible. We empathize with you, the busy English teacher; therefore, we want you to be able to read this book quickly and easily. *Teaching English Creatively, Second Edition* is informal in language, tone, and style although it reflects, we think, much scholarly thinking. We hope it is an easy-to-read and useful source for teaching English.

J.H.B.
K.P.B.

CONTENTS

TEACHING ENGLISH
CREATIVELY

Chapter 1

MIDDLE AND HIGH SCHOOLS IN AMERICA

We begin our book with an overview of middle and high schools in America because, we believe, it will serve as a threshold from which to begin the process of thinking creatively, teaching creatively, and, in particular, teaching English creatively. What we are about to suggest throughout this book is somewhat different from the traditional programs often found in middle and high schools. The theory and research clearly suggests a different way—a new way—of teaching English. Before we delve into the specific areas of English that will be addressed in the forthcoming pages, we feel it is important to know about the context in which teachers place this creative approach. Now before going any further, we should note that many excellent teachers are already using many, if not all, of the curricula and instructional suggestions that we make. And we say BRAVO!! Lead on! Just when we begin to think that there are more of those who do than don't practice these creative approaches, we hear of the new grammar program instituted at a middle school or we hear of the excessive report writing that is taking place in the 5th and 6th grades. That revelation knocks us back to reality, and we once again know that there are many teachers who simply are not teaching creatively or effectively as the research and theory suggests.

THE MIDDLE SCHOOL

The organization of schools in America has changed significantly since the early schools of many years ago. Traditionally, young people attending school spent eight years in the elementary school, often called the "grammar" school; and then spent four years in what we have commonly called the high school. While the junior high movement began and was the dominant pattern in the 1900s, it was not until the 1980s that almost all students attended a school system that had a three-level organizational pattern. Specifically, the junior high pattern, which was dominant by 1970, included grades seven, eight, and nine. It was in

3

the mid-1980s that a shift took place to the middle school concept which emphasized grades six, seven, eight, and sometimes nine (McEwin & Alexander, 1987).

As the shift to an elementary, middle, and high school organization began, it was evident that the program for the middle level should be different from that of the upper level. Early in the junior high movement, middle level students were to explore a variety of subject matter, primarily job opportunities, which could be studied in more detail later at the high school level. Specifically, the intended program for the junior high school can best be described by Gruhn and Douglass (1947) in *The Modern Junior High School.* In this text, the authors suggest that the optimal educational program for the early adolescents should be built around the following six functions of the junior high school: integration, exploration, guidance, differentiation, socialization, and articulation (pps. 59–60). In reality, as the junior high school developed and matured, the educational program for the early adolescents was far from the optimal program suggested by Gruhn and Douglass. What developed was an organizational unit containing grades seven, eight, and nine with an educational program almost identical to the program found in the high school. Very little integration occurred; one could almost say there was none. Very few exploratory courses existed which resulted in very little differentiation of curricula and instruction to meet the diverse needs that were apparent in the early adolescents. To say the least, the junior high did not meet the high expectations that educational leaders had for the early adolescents.

As a result of the inadequacies found in the junior high schools, the notion of middle schools as an alternative emerged. Interestingly, the notion of the middle schools came about not as a protest of the *concept* of the junior high but a protest against the *program* that was found in the junior highs. Therefore, the middle school folks wanted to build on the program that had been delineated when the junior highs were established. These concepts served as the theoretical foundation for the middle schools. In addition, the new middle school was to serve as the transition between elementary and high school and there was to be a blend of the child-centered nurturing that has been traditionally found in the elementary school with the subject-centered high school.

The recommended practices which serve as the foundation for the middle school included the following:

1. Interdisciplinary organization with flexible scheduling
2. Adequate guidance program, including a teacher advisory plan
3. Exploratory program including many offerings for students
4. Curriculum which includes personal development programs, continued learning skills, and basic knowledge areas
5. Varied instructional methodology to the needs of a diverse student body
6. Orientation and articulation for students, parents, and teachers

(Alexander, 1987)

Are these concepts actually found in middle schools or are they just a part of the philosophical base but not found in reality? A study by Binko and Lawlor (1986), while a survey of a small number of middle schools, seems to indicate that middle schools are a mixed bag. While they found some differentiation of teaching methods according to ability levels, some utilization of media by students and teachers, and creative ideas developed by students, there was not much interdisciplinary cooperation among staff members, there was little personal guidance for students, and there were very few exploratory programs.

The data of Binko and Lawlor (1986) mentioned above and the findings of Richard Arlington (1990) seem to agree with our experience looking at and working with middle schools. Teachers frequently rely on worksheets and textbooks to teach. Instruction rarely occurs unless it is in the form of corrective feedback after students have responded incorrectly. Many students work alone and are asked to read the text and respond to worksheets about the text. Students are often required to locate or remember literal information. The instruction in one class rarely is linked to that of another class. Specifically, spelling tasks are unrelated to any curriculum area, writing tasks are unrelated to authentic content, and vocabulary study is given without instruction. According to Arlington (1990), all of this is done with worksheets after worksheets after worksheets.

THE HIGH SCHOOL

In *A Place Called School* (1984) Goodlad writes of the similarities of schools in general and the high school in particular. He suggests that while some schools have their unique programs that may or may not be beneficial to students, most schools are quite consistent in regard to their physical appearances and educational programs. He suggests that most classrooms are

> ... devoid of amenities likely to provide comfort, unattractive or at least aesthetically bland, and cramped for space (just a few square feet per person). They [classrooms] lacked, commonly, decoration in the form of wall hangings, prints of good paintings, contrasting colors on walls, doors, and cupboards, and the like (p. 226).

The academic program, as described by Goodlad, seems to parallel the description just noted of junior high/middle schools.

> Students in the classes we observed made scarcely any decisions about their learning ... Nearly 100% of the elementary classes were almost entirely teacher dominated with respect to seating, grouping, content, materials, use of space, time utilization, and learning activities. A similar situation prevailed in 90% of the junior high and 80% of the senior high classes, and the increase in student decision-making was in only one or two areas, usually somewhat removed from the learning activity itself, and more in the arts, physical education, and vocational education than in the academic subjects (p. 229).

As we read Goodlad and others and reflect on our own experiences in high schools, it becomes apparent that the high school is generally a place in which students are lectured to, sit passively as they hear those lectures or read from the text, or work at worksheets—all of which have been generated by the teacher.

In addition, students and teachers work with a fragmented curriculum. Crowell (1989) suggests that our schools "have separate subjects, separate skills, separate objectives, separate evaluations, segmented continuums, linear methods, behavioral techniques, and isolated classrooms. Moreover, these practices convey to students a world of knowledge unrelated to meaning and a world in which outcome is independent of process" (p. 61).

Nancy Atwell (1987) says it well:

> Our junior—and senior—high classrooms too often function as holding tanks. We separate the big fish and the little fish into their homogeneous groupings, and we provide the minimum environment required for survival. The tanks are drably furnished, the effect is flat, and the inhabitants have little say about what they'll do while they while away six years of their lives. The American secondary school status quo presents a bleak picture, revealing little evidence of the collaboration, involvement, and excitement in acquiring knowledge that our students crave—that all humans crave (p. 36).

Many times the creative teacher with student-centered approaches in hand finds it somewhat difficult at first to be successful in this authoritarian climate. This is especially true in language arts. For in the Goodlad study it is clear that emphasis in the English classroom is given to mechanical correctness: a correct form of mechanics and grammar, a study of a formal expository composition type usually in the form of the five-paragraph theme, and a reading of the literary forms usually consisting of reading what is in the anthology and what is on the prescribed reading list taken from a menu consisting of the classics. We have found, however, that if teachers are well-grounded in theory and knowledgeable of the research that has been done in English curriculum and pedagogy, they are more likely to be successful in using and communicating their creative approaches to those who are in control.

MIDDLE AND HIGH SCHOOL STUDENTS

Pre-adolescents are people in transition. They are no longer children nor are they adults. Thornburg (1974) calls this period the "bubble gum years." The journey they take through their "growing up" period may be the most frustrating time of their lives. It is for this reason that we must understand the 10- to 17-year-olds, not only so that we can better relate to them, but also so that we can build a curriculum and use effective strategies that will meet their needs and interests. It is vitally important to know that the curriculum for the pre-adolescent is not the same curriculum for the older adolescent. In addition, it is imperative that teachers know that the middle school student is not, and can not be, the high school student. They are two distinct beings and must be thought of in that way.

Of all the changes that do occur during this period between childhood and adult, the physical growth may be the most noticeable. Tremendous growth-spurts and sexual development may cause these young people embarrassment as their bodies make such drastic changes. It is during this period that the pituitary gland increases production of two hormones. One hormone stimulates growth of bones and tissues, causing tremendous growth spurts. This rapid change in growth causes a drastic change in the pre-adolescent: Height often increases 25 percent, and weight many times doubles. The young people have a craving for food, and they have frequent periods of fatigue. The second hormone influences sexual development and is responsible for the appearance of secondary sexual characteristics such as change of voice and the appearance of the beard for the males and breast growth for the females.

Klinglele (1979), a scholar in the field of middle-level education, suggests ten factors that teachers ought to consider:

1. Girls generally are approximately two years ahead of boys in growth.
2. Muscular development and body framework are often disproportionate.
3. Minor accidents become common because of rapid growth, high activity, and awareness.
4. Alertness, excess energy, and high activity levels are often followed by fatigue and a stoop in posture.
5. Girls often have less stamina than boys.
6. Because of peer competitiveness, physical conditions such as heart abnormalities are often first discovered.
7. Through peer pressure to improve personal appearance, fads become important to youngsters.
8. A seemingly increasing capacity to wriggle and squirm becomes apparent.
9. Inquisitiveness and curiosity about their bodies follow internal and external bodily changes.
10. Girls begin their menstrual cycles, and their bodies experience rounding of the hips and development of the breasts (p. 21).

Emotionally, the young people, especially the pre-adolescent, are quite unstable. In any given 30-minute period, they can be creative, then dull; cooperative, then obnoxious; energetic, then lifeless; and childlike, then adult! In addition, the group is very important for the young people and they often turn to it for some stability in their unstable world. We are not sure that school people in general really understand what all of this means for our track record for working with these young people is not good. It seems that our main concern is control: tracking groups; holding to a minimum, if indeed any, student initiative in curriculum matters; and keeping students in seats—5 rows across, 6 desks deep—with little group work. Perhaps one of the best things that teachers can do for pre-adolescents and adolescents is acknowledge that the problems associated with adolescents are real and may cause tremendous unrest.

In the cognitive area, the pre-adolescents and adolescents reflect a variety of thinking levels. Most of the pre-adolescents (10–12 years) are still in the concrete operational period, while most adolescents (13–19 years) are into the formal operational period. The cognitive development of young people is of primary concern as we think about curriculum and teaching strategies over grades five through twelve.

Jean Piaget (1958, 1969), perhaps more than anyone else, has helped us understand how young people think. Piaget argues that the cognitive changes from infant to adult are the result of a developmental process—a process that occurs in four stages: the sensorimotor period (0–2 years), the preoperational period (2–7 years), the concrete operational period (7–12 years), and the formal operational period (12 years to adult). While these stages give the appearance of start-and-stop operations, they are not meant to be. The theory suggests a gradual movement from any one period to another. Certainly the age classification is not without movement. These categories are meant to give only a general time frame for any particular stage. These stages have other characteristics as well: (1) Different reasoning takes place at different stages, with the reasoning occurring at later stages being superior to the reasoning in the previous stage; (2) the reasoning in each stage is inclusive rather than particular; (3) what has been learned in a previous stage is incorporated into the new knowledge at the later stage; and (4) each operational level is developed from the previous stage (i.e., formal reasoning cannot develop before concrete reasoning is developed).

Generally, during the concrete operational stage, children become more independent in their thinking. They can think logically, they can classify, and they can show relationships. Real experience is very important to middle level students. Their thinking revolves around immediate and concrete objects rather than concepts and abstractions. As adolescents move into formal operations, they are able to apply logical operations to all classes of problems. These adolescents are able to reason about abstract objects and concepts that they have not directly experienced.

While Piaget did not apply his theories to education, many have made that relationship. Furth (1970), Elkind (1981), Wadsworth (1978), and Thornburg (1970, 1981) suggest interpretations of Piaget's theories and offer applications to teaching. All emphasize the importance to thinking, the development of learning capacities, the relationship of reasoning, and the active involvement of students in their learning at various levels. Elkind (1981) makes the case for the Piagetian theories in building curriculum. He says the following:

Each stage of cognitive development has its own set of mental operations and these provide the analytical tools for that stage. If curriculum materials for children at that stage are consistent with mental operations of that stage, then they are appropriate. If they are too simple or too complex, then they are not appropriate (p. 227).

While this is very brief overview of a very broad, complex theory of cognitive development, it does offer a basis for teaching the English skills and choosing the English curriculum for the middle and high school level students.

FOR ADDITIONAL READING

Alexander, William M. "Toward Schools in the Middle: Progress and Problems." *Journal of Curriculum and Supervision,* 2, 314–329, 1987.

Arlington, Richard L. "What Have We Done with the Middle?" in *Reading in the Middle School.* ed. Gerald Duffy. Newark, DE: International Reading Association. 32–40, 1990.

Atwell, Nancie. *In the Middle: Writing, Reading, and Learning with Adolescents.* Portsmouth, NH: Heinemann, 1987.

Binko, James & Lawlor, James. "Middle Schools: A Review of Current Practices— How Evident Are They?" *NASSP Bulletin,* 70, 81–87, 1986.

Crowell, Sam. "A New Way of Thinking: The Challenge of the Future." *Educational Leadership,* 47 (September, 1989), 60–63.

Elkind, David. *Children and Adolescents.* New York: Oxford University Press, 1981.

Furth, Hans G. *Piaget for Teachers.* Englewood Cliffs, NJ: Prentice-Hall, 1970.

Goodlad, John. *A Place Called School.* New York: McGraw-Hill, 1984.

Gruhn, William T. & Douglas, Harl R. *The Modern Junior High School.* New York: Ronald Press, 1947.

Inhelder, Barbel and Piaget, Jean. *Growth of Logical Thinking in Childhood and Adolescence.* New York: Basic Books, 1958.

Klingele, William E. *Teaching in Middle Schools.* Boston: Allyn & Bacon, 1979.

McEwin, C. Kenneth & Alexander, William M. *Report of Middle Level Teacher Education Programs: A Second Survey (1986–1987).* Boone, NC: Appalachian State University Media Service, 1987.

Piaget, Jean and Inhelder, Barbel. *The Psychology of the Child.* New York: Basic Books, 1969.

Thornburg, Hershel D. "Developmental Characteristics of Middle Schoolers and Middle School Organization." *Contemporary Education,* 52 (Spring, 1981), 134–137.

Thornburg, Hershel D. "Learning and Maturation in Middle School Age Youth." *Clearing House,* 45 (November, 1970), 150–155.

Thornburg, Hershel D. *Pre-adolescent Development.* Tucson, Arizona: University of Arizona Press, 1974.

Wadsworth, Barry J. *Piaget for the Classroom Teacher.* New York: Longman, 1978.

Chapter 2

CREATING AN EFFECTIVE
CLASSROOM CLIMATE

As each summer comes to a close and the first day of school gets closer and closer, most teachers think more seriously about readying themselves for the coming nine months. As they do, many evaluation questions are posed: How will my program this year differ from the one I followed last year? Do I need to make any changes to fit different goals I want to accomplish? Should I change the appearance of my classroom? In other words, what preparations can I make to insure that there will be a classroom climate that is both comfortable and effective for the goals that I want my students to achieve this year?

Needless to say, there would be as many different answers to these questions as there are English teachers. And that's the way it should be because for all teachers to do their best, they must design their classroom and methods so that they feel comfortable with them and personally assured that the desired curriculum goals will be attained. At the same time, however, there are some basic components to the English classroom situation that teachers need to consider when planning an effective classroom climate.

ROOM DECOR

First, the decor of the room should be considered. Many times, what the students see as they enter the classroom forms their first impression and expectations of curriculum, the approach, and the teacher. Is your room ready to make the impression you want it to? Is it livable? At the same time, does it foster learning, or does it prevent it? How about the bulletin boards? You don't have to be an artist to make them interesting and attractive. It's always a good idea to keep a bulletin board file with folders for each unit or skill you want to tackle during the school year. Pictures from magazines and students' papers and projects from previous years may serve as good bulletin board material. Fairly inexpensive letter stencils can be purchased in a number of different styles from a local art supply store or, again, perhaps a particularly talented student can make a unique letter set for your use. Wall space can also be used to display a wide variety of English-oriented materials. You might include posters of punctuation marks, figures of speech, and specific literary works, to mention a few. Again, if students create these, it not only cuts down on costs but also provides more meaningful learning experiences for them, too.

To further contribute to the interests and education of the class, you could provide "pick-up corners" displaying items of current emphasis areas. Such a corner might include literature works on a current thematic unit, student work, cassette tapes, etc. These corner displays may also serve as previews for a future unit to stir interest a week or so in advance.

Another pre-September consideration is the seating arrangement. All teachers, of course, need to decide what's best for their needs and goals for the students. But, if the English classroom's purpose is to promote the further acquisition of communication skills, we strongly suggest an arrangement that enables the students to easily see and hear one another. For the teacher who has experienced nothing but teaching to straight rows, a circle may be in order. You might be surprised how successful a different arrangement can be in terms of providing a warm and meaningful atmosphere. And, there's no reason that one arrangement must be followed for the entire year. Perhaps a number of different formats can be set up throughout the year to meet specific educational goals and objectives and the needs of the various activities. Sometimes, simply changing for the sake of changing helps to keep the atmosphere fresh, alive, and innovative to foster a continuous flow of learning.

ROOM ATMOSPHERE

Now that the room is ready, how about you? How prepared you are and how you act toward your students the first few days may be a big determinant in the type of climate established. Some teachers take on a "don't-smile-'til-Christmas" approach, while others promote a "be-their-best-friend" method. Whatever the approach, for each extreme has its disadvantages, there are certain components that each of us needs to consider. One major attitude we need to convey to our students is that we do care about them; we are there to help them grow both educationally and personally. To do this, we need to convey a feeling of warmth and interest in them as people. One way to begin this is to check on their names before the first day of school. Find out how to pronounce their names and if they go by a particular nickname. For example is it *Elizabeth* or *Liz* or *Beth,* or does she go by her middle name *Sue?* One way to find out this information is to check the preceding year's yearbook. Not only will the yearbook prove helpful in this matter, but it will also help to identify names with faces and give you a hint as to which students are new to the school.

After you have the names down, don't stop there. We all know that with a pupil load of 90 to 180 students it's impossible to connect names with faces overnight, not to mention getting further acquainted with them. To facilitate this long process, you might want to make use of a student "Personal Interest Inventory" (Fig. 1). This is basic information regarding family, hobbies, reading interests, travel experiences, etc. As an alternative, you might prefer that the students include this information in a "Letter to the Teacher." This approach is very informative; in addition, it gives you an indication of the students' present writing skills. No matter which technique you use to get to know your new students, remember that this is a two-way street. Whatever information you ask of them, you should, in turn, be willing to answer yourself. After all, it is important for them to know that you're also a unique individual with interests and experiences outside the classroom.

In addition to becoming acquainted, there are two components to the classroom operation that the students need to know and understand at the very beginning. One is your expectations for them in terms of supplies needed, grading procedures, general behavior, etc. Whether you operate best in a tightly run or a flexible atmosphere, the students need to know what is expected of them and why. Whether or not students are included in the actual policy-planning procedure, all policies should be fully discussed with them to give them an understanding of the justification behind each one. One consideration of policy planning is to be flexible enough to fit the needs of the students as well as the goals of the activities. Again, if changes occur, they should be fully explained. The explanations and discussions of policies not only provide students with guides for behavior but also provide them with a responsibility for offering input into classroom procedures.

Secondly, at the beginning you should provide your students with the

Figure 1
Personal Interest Inventory

Complete the following.

Name _____ Nickname _____
Parents' Name _____
Father's Occupation _____
Mother's Occupation _____
Brothers and Sisters (names & ages) 1._____ 2._____
                                    3._____ 4._____ 5._____
Hobbies _____
Out-of-school Organizations or Groups (YMCA, athletics, Scouts, church, Candy
    Stripers, etc.) _____
Outside Job and Hours Each Week _____
Summer Activities (vacation, sports, camp, work, school) _____
_____
Places you've lived other than this area _____
Other countries you've visited _____
Subject(s) most liked _____
    Why? _____
Subject(s) least liked _____
    Why? _____
What books have you read recently? _____
What magazines do you read regularly? _____
List the parts of the newspaper in the order in which you read them. _____
_____
Favorite Television Shows _____
Favorite Movies _____
What man or woman do you most admire? _____ Why? _____
What do you expect to gain in this class this year? _____
_____
Who was your last year's English teacher? _____
In the space provided below, copy your schedule of classes for this semester.

goals of the class curriculum. If the students know what direction the class will lead, they will probably have a warmer feeling of security about the class. This may include discussions on such items as English skills to be tackled, approaches to be used, the extent of group work, major projects, and major literature works to be covered.

No matter what type of classroom climate you want to create, you should keep in mind that the key component is to establish a climate that will promote effective learning. Elements that might come into consideration are creative and interesting displays of learning materials and flexible seating arrangements. An atmosphere of interest and concern for the students should be displayed from the beginning as the teacher is also setting up personal and educational goals and directions to serve as guidelines throughout the school year.

Chapter 3

GETTING READY FOR GROUP INTERACTION

Establishing an atmosphere that is conducive to effective group inter-action is often a problem in secondary school classes. The activities suggested in Chapter 2 help a great deal to alleviate the problem, but there is still much to be done. One of the major goals (objectives, if you will) of English teachers is to help young people function effectively in groups, large and small. For it is this oral competency that will enable students to share ideas, offer criticism, relate personal experiences, and take stands on issues—processes that are absolutely necessary for a com-munity to be healthy, alive, and productive.

In the school community, this is important. If students do not have the necessary desire and skill to communicate well, their performance in many areas may suffer. Students who do not talk much may not develop language facility. That they may not have as many ideas to share will affect their desire and ability to compose in speech and in writing. Lack of skill in conversation and group talk in early grades, and in the later grades as well, may contribute to poor reading skills.

In the social community it is important for young people to become independent citizens who can participate effectively with their peers; therefore, schools must provide skills so that students can experience self-discipline and self-direction but, at the same time, learn the process of a group, which is the process of how people talk together.

These skills must be taught and learned. The process of effective group interaction does not just happen by chance. Teachers should provide a sequence of activities that will enable students to acquire these effective discussion techniques. We believe that group participants won't share their ideas and feelings until specific classroom conditions are met. Students must know and trust each other well and they must see a need to participate in groups. Once these human relations conditions are met, teachers can then provide additional skills. These include listening skills, roles that are found in group interaction, and techniques to enable

16

participants to interact in a discussion extensively so that they can discuss a problem in depth.

BUILDING RELATIONSHIPS

For students to feel comfortable contributing in groups, they must first know and trust the people with whom they are interacting. To know each other helps to build the relationships that are needed for open and honest responses. However, to know names is not enough. Unless people understand each other and feel good about each other, they will not share their feelings and ideas in a group discussion.

The following are some activities that we have tried on our classrooms; they work very well for us.

Activities

1. Create a Twenty-Five Questions Sheet similar to Figure 2. Instruct students to secure signatures from students who meet the requirements listed on the sheet. No more than two signatures should be obtained from any one student. Remind students that they should not volunteer information; they should wait until they are asked the question. After the activity, discuss with the students the process. Did everyone get around to ask questions of everyone else? How many signatures did they get? Discuss the use of this activity as an "icebreaker."

2. Pin a name tag to the back of each student. Instruct students to seek their identities by asking each classmate no more than three questions which can be answered with a "yes" or "no." Make the tags by cutting 3-inch circles out of multicolored construction paper. Select names that are popular with the students: musicians, government officials, television personalities.

3. Put the group in a circle. Have participants fit their names and an item which begins with the same initial sound as their first name in an introduction? "I'm Tom; I'm going backpacking; and I'm going to bring a tent." Susan, the next person in the circle, introduces herself in a similar way: "My name is Susan and I'm going on a backpacking trip with Tom. I'm going to take a sleeping bag." The process continues around the circle until all have participated.

4. This activity has as its major purpose to break the ice of the group. It is fun and certainly helps to reduce the inhibitions that frequently

Figure 2
Twenty-Five Questions

Directions: Obtain signatures from your classmates who meet the descriptors listed. Please do not obtain more than two signatures from any one student. You should not volunteer information; wait until you are asked the question.

1. A person who is an only child _____
2. A person who has always lived in this city _____
3. A person who has visited a foreign country _____
4. A person whose favorite subject is English _____
5. A person whose family owns a station wagon _____
6. A person who lives on a dead end street _____
7. A person who has the same number of letters in his/her first name as you do _____
8. A person whose birthday is in the same month as yours _____
9. A person who can play a musical instrument _____
10. A person who has caught a fish _____
11. A person who has lived on a farm _____
12. A person who has never had the chicken pox _____
13. A person who likes spinach _____
14. A person who has all four grandparents living _____
15. A person who has been on television _____
16. A person who has a cocker spaniel _____
17. A person who has been snow skiing _____
18. A person whose initials spell a word _____
19. A person who can bake bread _____
20. A person who owns a gold fish, hamster, or gerbil _____
21. A person who has been in the hospital in the past year _____
22. A person who has a niece or nephew _____
23. A person who wants to be a professional actor/actress _____
24. A person who has read four books in the past year _____
25. A person who works after school _____

occur as groups get together. It is assumed that by this point students know each other fairly well. In addition, the activity serves to provide a structure for interaction among the group. Students will need to talk to one another. Place students in a sub-group according to one of the following criteria:

- Shoes that they are wearing—types, colors, ages, etc.
- Number of letters in first name, last name
- Color of hair
- Sibling information: oldest child, youngest child, middle child, only child

After the sub-groups are together, members discuss within each group to determine what the central element is that is shared by each of them. The activity is non-threatening; participants simply have an open, free discussion in which they seek the thread that holds them together.

5. This activity can be used effectively after students are acquainted. It serves as a beginning activity to help get the group functioning as a group. Read several *Answers* and ask students to write them down on a sheet of paper. Possible answers: revenge, anger, a smile. Then ask the group to list possible questions that could go with the answers that they have written before them.

Possible questions: What do I feel when someone hurts me?
What do I feel when someone abuses an animal?
What should you give a sad person?

To begin the sharing, read an answer and have the students share their questions that they have written down. A discussion of the responses follows.

6. Have students create a two-part time line of their lives. The first part is to include special events or occurrences that have happened thus far. These events can take on any nature. For example, the students may list a happening that had a particular influence on them, goals that they achieved, or something remembered as being particularly fun, exciting, or sad. The events may be explained in writing or represented by a symbol of some type. When possible, a date should accompany the event. The second part of the time line consists of the students predicting future events of goals that they either want to happen or that realistically they can see as occurring at some time. Again, they may be represented by symbols or descriptions and should be accompanied by a date. After time lines have been completed, put students in pairs for sharing. After the sharing, all students go back to the large group. Each student then introduces his/her partner to the large group on the basis of what he/she has learned through the time line explanation. After the introductions, display the time lines around the room for a closer examination by the students.

7. Use a Personal Inventories Sheet similar to Figure 3. Have students place their names in the proper space and fill in the information that is requested: at the top, three books read, movies seen, or TV shows enjoyed; on the bottom, three things they have to do but must do; on the

left, three things they want to learn to do; on the right, three things they do poorly; and in the middle, three things they do well. When completed, have students display their Personal Inventories around the room for sharing and discussion.

8. Group students in a circle around a stack of multicolored construction paper. Have students select two colors: one that reminds them of a positive experience and one that is negative. For example, a student might choose a black piece of paper, which usually has a negative connotation, but because a special person was wearing black the first time this student saw him/her, the experience was very positive; therefore, black was chosen for that reason. The students share their choices and the reasons for them.

9. Have students draw a map of their rooms. They should include furniture, windows, closets, etc. Then, have them answer questions or give a response concerning their room by marking on the map. Some possible questions/statements to which the students may respond:

- Place yourself in the room.
- Mark your favorite spot.
- Mark your least favorite spot.
- Rate from 1 to 10 the cleanliness of the room.
- Mark your favorite poster or picture.
- Where and what is your favorite object in the room?
- What color is the room? What emotional color is it?
- Draw a clock in the room. Put on it the time you like to be in your room.

Have students discuss their rooms.

10. Have students create a Value Continuum Sheet similar to Figure 4. Instruct them to mark the appropriate place on the continuum indicating their responses to statements that you read to them. "A" represents "strongly agree"; "Z" represents "strongly disagree." Statements that you choose should be slightly controversial and of interest to students. The following is a partial list of possible statements:

- The movie rating system should be informative but not restrictive.
- The government should use money to clean up rivers and pollution before feeding indigent families.
- If a person is starving, it is justifiable for that person to steal.
- Young people run away from home to prove their maturity.

Figure 3
PERSONAL INVENTORIES

Directions: Complete the following with the appropriate information.

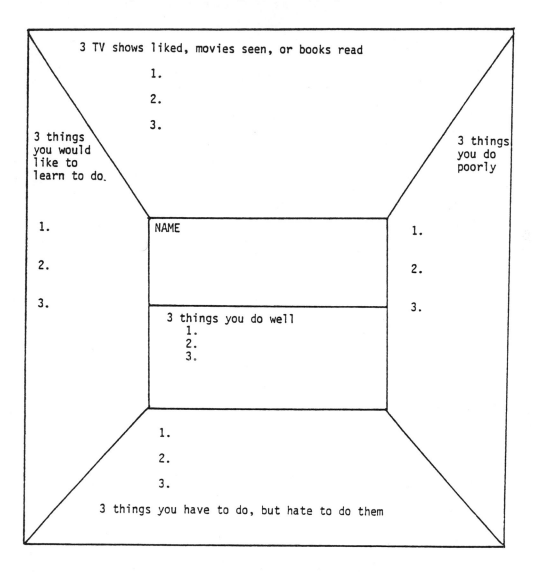

Figure 4
Value Continuum

Directions: On each of the continuum (horizontal) lines indicate your position on the statements read to you by your teacher by marking an X on the appropriate place.

AGREE   DISAGREE

  1. A_____Z

  2. A_____Z

  3. A_____Z

  4. A_____Z

  5. A_____Z

  6. A_____Z

  7. A_____Z

  8. A_____Z

  9. A_____Z

10. A_____Z

Students' responses to this activity test the degree to which trust has been established. In addition, these statements require participants to commit themselves to a position which in itself helps to establish trust. Students may wish to discuss some or all of the statements and their positions on them.

11. Create a 111 Adjectives Sheet similar to Figure 5. Each student

Figure 5
111 Adjectives

Directions: Circle five adjectives which you feel best describe your personality. You may add a sixth adjective at the bottom of the sheet if you think of one more appropriate than those that are on the list.

aggressive	introverted	refined
ambitious	jealous	relaxed
assertive	jubilant	religious
awkward	kind	reserved
brave	lavish	respectful
bright	lazy	responsible
busy	liberal	rigid
calm	lively	sad
capable	logical	secure
carefree	loud	self-conscious
clever	loving	selfish
concise	mature	sensible
confident	mean	sensitive
crazy	mediocre	sharp
creative	mellow	shy
defensive	modest	sociable
delicate	musical	solemn
dependable	naughty	solitary
dependent	noisy	stubborn
determined	nervous	talented
domineering	objective	talkative
dreamy	onerous	tender
emotional	original	thoughtful
enthusiastic	overemotional	timid
extravagant	peaceful	tough
extroverted	perceptive	unaffected
fiery	perfectionist	understanding
foolhardy	physical	unorganized
free	playful	unpredictable
friendly	powerful	vain
gentle	proud	violent
glum	questioning	warm
happy	quiet	withdrawn
harsh	quick	witty
impetuous	rash	worried
independent	realistic	yielding
intelligent	rebellious	zestful

Sixth Adjective _____

circles five adjectives that he/she feels best describes him/her. The student may add a sixth adjective if he/she doesn't find the best descriptive adjective of him or her in the list. Have students share their lists. The activity may be repeated later after additional trust activities have been done. At this time, students can choose adjectives that best describe other students. This new list is then shared.

12. Instruct students to list ten descriptive words about themselves. Then have them find ten pictures in magazines, one to illustrate each word; have them glue the picture to a single sheet of paper with the descriptive word printed on it. These pages are then fastened into a booklet, and the student designs a cover for the book with something special or unique about himself/herself on it. Have students share their books. Much of the value of this activity lies in the interaction that takes place as the students find pictures for each other and discover the interests they have in common.

13. Using a coat of arms similar to Figure 6, have students complete the sections by drawing and/or writing their responses to the following statements:

1. The thing that makes you the most angry.
2. The goal you most want to achieve.
3. The one gift you would give the world.
4. Something you are good at/something you would like to be good at.
5. A favorite literature character.
6. A word you would like others to use to describe you.
7. A color that represents you.
8. A favorite food.

Share and display coat of arms.

BUILDING THE INTERACTIVE PROCESS

Three important areas to consider when building the group cohesiveness are participating, listening, and role playing. There are many activities that teachers can use to help build these skills.

Even after students have experienced some of the activities which build relationships, they still often need a gentle nudge to contribute to the discussion. This nudge in the form of skill-building activities helps students to see a need to share with their peers. They become aware of

Figure 6
Coat of Arms

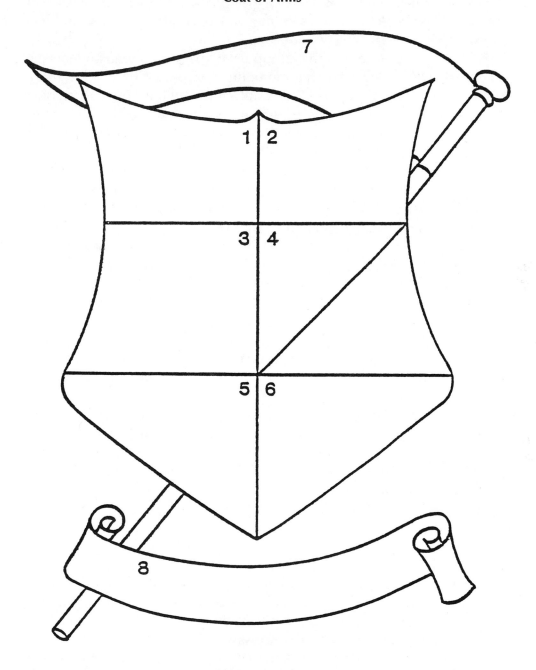

the responsibility that goes with membership in a discussion group. There are times when members of a group talk too much: the reverse of the previous problem. As a result, many groups suffer with the problem of excessive talk rather than not enough.

Listening is vital to effective group participation. Often, students get so excited about their participation point of view that they fail to listen carefully to others' thoughts. As a result, much time is lost in discussion because arguing usually begins. There are times when the interactive process breaks down because people are developing rebuttal statements rather than listening to the contributions.

In order for the interactive process to succeed, students should be aware of the many varied roles that they play. Teachers will recognize, we're sure, these roles as they are found in their classes: diplomat, dominator/monopolizer, humanitarian, yes-man. The following illustrates our concern: Sam talks most of the time and monopolizes the discussion. Helen is quite aggressive and doesn't mind stepping on a few toes to get her point across. Jim, on the other hand, tends to agree with whoever is doing the talking; he simply doesn't have an original thought. Beth, the mediator of the group, tries to help bring the discussion together by being very diplomatic; then there is Joe. He talks to hear himself talk. He pokes fun; he makes irrelevant comments; he's simply a cutup. These and other roles frequently make their way into discussion groups, and if students are not aware of their existence, the group suffers.

The emergence of a leader can also be a concern. Groups may wish to spend some time talking about the qualities of leadership and how leaders emerge.

The following, then, are activities that teachers may use to help build effective discussion groups.

Activities

14. To help the group see the need to participate, select a topic for discussion and ask the group to discuss it using the following guidelines: During the discussion, each person must contribute at least once and at random. No person can participate twice until all have participated once. Discuss with students the process.

15. Have each student use a copy of the following crossword puzzle (without the words). Instruct students to fill in the puzzles using as many different letters as possible to form words. Score one point for each

different letter used for the individual score (perfect score is 21 points). Divide the class into groups of five to seven each. Have students compare individual puzzles as they work as a team to complete one puzzle. Score the group puzzle to arrive at a team grand total. Compare these scores with other teams. A discussion should follow concerning the need for full participation in this activity. Discuss how this is important in other discussions, as well.

One possible key for the puzzle is as follows:

16. Have each student use a copy of Figure 7, "What Is A Teacher?" Instruct them to complete the ranking by following the directions on the top of the page. Then, divide the class into groups of five to seven each. Have students work as a team to make a group ranking using the same sheet. Then, have students complete the observation questionnaire, "Response to Group Interaction" (See Fig. 8). After filling out the questionnaire, students should discuss this information first in the small groups and then discuss it as an entire class.

17. This activity helps in the listening process. Ask each person in the group of five to seven to discuss a topic using the following patterns: (1) summarize the preceding person's statement; (2) state points with which he/she agrees; and (3) give his/her own opinion.

18. Place people in a circle. Have one student begin a story. The story develops as each person repeats the story and adds to it. This activity encourages creativity and is dependent upon listening for a unified story line. You may wish to have the student who began the story relate the whole story from beginning to end.

Figure 7
What Is A Teacher?

Directions: The following is a list of characteristics that frequently are used to describe a teacher. First as an individual and second in a group, rank each of the ten statements. To indicate your decisions, place a "1" in front of the statement that is the most important characteristic of a good teacher, a "2" in front of the next most important characteristic, etc. Place a "10" in front of the statement least descriptive of a good teacher.

Individual   Group

_____ _____ He/She has no favorite students.

_____ _____ He/She develops a warm and friendly relationship.

_____ _____ He/She speaks with a strong, clear voice.

_____ _____ He/She understands how students grow, develop, and learn.

_____ _____ He/She encourages oral interaction.

_____ _____ He/She is aware of individual differences in his/her students.

_____ _____ He/She sponsors extracurricular activities.

_____ _____ He/She has a thorough understanding of the subject matter.

_____ _____ He/She fosters critical thinking.

_____ _____ He/She knows how to enforce discipline.

19. Divide the class into groups of five to seven each. Have each group calculate the average number of brothers and sisters of the members of the group. The first to finish should stand up. Discuss how leadership evolved in the group.

20. This activity can be very enjoyable as well as educational. As a result of the activity, students have a better idea of the numerous roles that are played in groups. Create cards with the name of a specific role on them. Roles to use: diplomat, yes-man, silent member, clown, hostile agressor, dominator/monopolizer, humanitarian, logical reasoner. Distribute the cards to people in the groups at random, give the groups a topic to discuss, and tell them to discuss the subject from the point of view and in the manner of the role suggested on the cards. Discuss the activity following the role playing. Have the group point out the advantages and disadvantages when discussion groups are made up of people with a variety of these traits or just one.

21. This activity is similar to the previous one, as it emphasizes the roles that are found when a group is attempting to solve a particular

Figure 8
Response to Group Interaction

Directions: After completing the "What Is A Teacher?" activity, respond to the following questions. Be honest and fair as you evaluate the group interaction.

1. Did everyone in the group participate? Were there some who simply were not involved.

2. Did everyone feel comfortable with each other? Did you feel comfortable to say what you wanted to say?

3. Was there any particular organization to the group? Did a leader emerge?

4. To what extent did group members try to involve those who chose not to participate? Were their efforts successful?

5. To what extent did the tension level of the group change? Why do you think this happened?

problem. Create cards with the following roles on them and have the group discuss a particular problem.

1. Initiator—Suggests new ideas, suggests changes
2. Information seeker—Asks for factual clarifications
3. Opinion seeker—Asks for values clarification
4. Information giver—Offers facts
5. Opinion giver—Offers opinions or values
6. Elaborator—Develops meanings; gives examples
7. Coordinator—Clarifies relationships between various ideas
8. Evaluator—Questions the logic or facts of an idea

EXTENDING THE INTERACTIVE PROCESS

Many discussion groups develop a rapport conducive to much group interaction after participating in the sequence of discussion skills activities just described. One problem, however, is that these discussion groups fail to discuss topics in any depth. The group members know each other;

they feel comfortable expressing their ideas and feelings; they use effective discussion techniques; but they fail to get to the core of the problem under discussion. The following activity helps groups to go beyond the surface level.

Activity

22. Discuss with students the various processes that may be used to help groups discuss topics in depth. These processes include, but are not limited to, the following: elaboration, clarification, justification, comparison, contrast, and evaluation. Brainstorm with students questions and/or statements using these processes that may be given in a discussion to force the speakers to move beyond the surface level. After statements/questions have been generated, have students discuss a topic of interest and use these statements/questions at appropriate times. For example, in a discussion of *Huckleberry Finn,* Sara says, "It is illogical for Huck to be helping Jim escape." Ted, wanting Sara to justify her position asks, "What assumptions are you basing that on?" Sara, in responding, will be extending the discussion beyond the surface level through justification.

FOR ADDITIONAL READING

Beacham, Melissa. "Encouraging Participation from All Students." *Education Digest,* 56 (April, 1991), 44–46.

Bormann, Ernest and Bormann, Nancy. *Effective Small Group Communication.* Minneapolis: Burgess, 1972.

Bushman, John H. "Achieving Student Interaction in Creative Junior High/Middle School Programs." *English Journal,* 66 (April, 1977), 67–72.

Bushman, John H., and Jones, Sandra. *Effective Communication: A Handbook of Discussion Skills.* Buffalo, NY: D.O.K. Publishers, 1977.

Cintorino, Margaret. "Getting Together, Getting Along, Getting to the Business of Teaching and Learning." *English Journal,* 82 (January, 1993), 23–32.

"Designing Classrooms with Students in Mind." *English Journal,* 82 (February, 1993), 81–83.

Gorman, Alfred. *Teachers and Learners: The Interactive Process of Education.* Boston: Allyn & Bacon, 1974.

Heyman, Mack. "Places and Spaces: Environmental Psychology in Education." *Fastback.* Bloomington, Indiana: Phi Delta Kappa Foundation, 1978.

Kirby, Dan and Liner, Tom. *Inside Out: Developmental Strategies for Teaching Writing* (Chapter 3). Portsmouth, NH: Heinemann, 1988.

Rief, Linda. "Immersion: Writing and Reading" in *Seeking Diversity: Language Arts with Adolescents.* Portsmouth, NH: Heinemann, 1992, 35–51.

Ruff, T. P. "Middle School Students at Risk: What Do We Do with the Most Vulnerable Children in American Education?" *Middle School Journal,* 24 (1993), 10–12.

Stanford, Gene. "Taming Restless Cats: Alternatives to the Whip." *English Journal,* 62 (November, 1973), 1127–1132.

Stanford, Gene. *Developing Effective Classroom Groups.* New York: Hart, 1977.

Stanford, Gene and Roark, Albert E. *Human Interaction in Education.* Boston: Allyn & Bacon, 1974.

Chapter 4

TEACHING ORAL ENGLISH

Oral communication occupies an important place in the classroom because it ties together activities which too often remain unrelated in the English class. Although these oral activities are often labeled "speech," the usual definition of oral communication actually includes all areas of classroom verbalization—from the simple teacher question-student response to formal speechmaking and drama. Because such activities serve as aids to learning in each of the other language arts—composition, literature, language, and media—oral communication should be an integral part of every English class if students are to find meaning in the material and ideas they encounter.

Generally, there are two major categories of oral communication: speech and drama. Speech activities may include, but not be limited to, platform speaking, discussion, conversation, and interviewing, while drama emphasizes pantomiming, role playing, and improvisation.

SPEECH

As we see it, the general purpose for speech study in the English class is to develop citizens who can participate satisfactorily in everyday situations that demand oral work. For most people, these situations include conversations, discussions, and introductions. For some, it may extend into interviews, panels, and platform speaking. No matter what students decide to do with their lives, a competence in some or all of these speech areas is essential. It is important not only to be able to carry on intelligent conversations, but also to express their thoughts and to establish their own identities by what they do and say.

Speech activities are most valuable not only in helping students to express their thoughts and develop their confidence but also in helping them to practice their language usage. James Moffett (1967) points out:

Although a student might come to use connectors, expand modifiers, subordinate clauses, and embed sentences just by sheer imprinting stylistic imitation —I think it is safe to say that such learning would never go far without the functional need for qualification and elaboration arising in dialogue. This is why I do not think exercises with dummy sentences, no matter how superior the grammar, will teach students how to use various linguistic constructions appropriately and habitually. The expatiation process of dialogue adjusts a speaker's verbal and cognitive instruments at just the moment when he cares the most and in just the way that he, individually, needs this adjustment (pps. 19–20).

The various activities usually associated with oral work can also be as sterile and as ineffective as the dummy sentences to which Moffett refers if developed solely for the purpose of memorizing language patterns. Group discussions, impromptu speeches, and interviewing are rewarding activities when dealing with particular literature and linguistic themes. Speech activities should evolve in response to reading, writing, and viewing. At the same time students are becoming familiar with particular structures of the language, they may find new insights into a character they only knew on a surface level in their reading.

Activities

1. Divide the class into groups of two to three to talk about a topic. One person is assigned to observe the process of conversation, looking for who speaks the most, what they say, reactions to statements, nonverbal communication, etc. In addition, it is important to note the extent to which the discussion skills suggested in Chapter 3 of this book were implemented. When the groups return to the entire class, these observers report their findings. A class discussion may then evolve to decide what qualities exist in good conversations and group communication processes.

2. Select a group of students (or ask for volunteers) who have different feelings about the literature they are reading in class and encourage them to discuss several aspects of the work. For example, students may be reading *A Separate Peace* and may have differing views concerning the guilt Gene feels in the book. Included in this activity is the discovery of the difference between a discussion and a debate. There should be a genuine effort by group members to listen, consider, and even concur. The objective of the group members is to make a joint effort to reach a solution, whereas debaters are concerned more with persuading the audience to accept their points of view. These activities are easily and

eagerly presented when such topics as current events and school policies are selected for discussion.

3. While giving announcements to the class may not seem an important activity in the development of speaking competency, it can be beneficial both as a listening exercise as well as a method for improving one's self-confidence as a speaker. For example, have a student give a list of announcements that you may usually give concerning assignments and coming events. After the novelty of students giving announcements wears off, quiz the students on what was just announced. If the students are normal, they will probably be amazed that, although they remember hearing the announcements, they did not really listen to what was said. Following a discussion of specific listening skills, have the class discuss what a speaker and/or a listener can do to bring about effective communication. Perhaps some of the listening skill-building activities in Chapter 3 would be useful as reinforcers.

4. At some time, students will certainly be interviewed and may also have the chance to interview. Divide the class into pairs and have students interview each other. This activity works especially well at the beginning of the year when the class is not yet well acquainted. Suggest that students interview each other to find out three new things about that person they did not know previously. Interesting items (e.g. countries lived in, unusual pets, hobbies, and talents) are discussed.

5. For a second activity in interviewing, have each student identify someone in the community whom he/she would like to interview. Through class discussion identify items that would be important to ask in the interview situation. Discuss the entire sequence of the interview—making the appointment, the questions to ask, and any follow up that may be desirable. Prepare an evaluation for the interviewee to complete. This may be taken to the interview by the student, but it should be returned by mail.

6. Impromptu speaking may not be included in some English classes if speech courses are offered. Impromptus, however, are valuable in the English classroom, especially if there is a need to eliminate self-consciousness and to break down speaking inhibitions. In addition, the ability to compose quickly and to express readily is certainly important in oral communication. Students discover that impromptu speaking occurs daily in their lives as they relate experiences and express ideas in discussions. Have students draw from a box of current headlines or pictures and have them use these for impromptu speeches. After a

minute or so to collect their thoughts, they present their minute or minute-and-a-half speech on the topic. Taping these, especially on videotape, can add a greater dimension to the exercise.

We have not said much about formal platform or podium speaking, primarily because we feel this formal speechmaking should be left to the speech class. We feel that the more informal, more practical approaches in oral English would benefit the student in the English class. However, it can be included, especially if there are students who you feel would benefit from this experience. If you decide to include the formal speech, make it as enjoyable and meaningful as possible by having students speak on subjects relating to their interests. Our concern is that these speeches be as relevant and meaningful as possible; having students give an after-dinner speech seems to be a bit inappropriate for ninth graders.

CREATIVE DRAMA

This second classification of oral communication is one of the most popular teaching instruments in England and is becoming popular in English classrooms across this country. It is a natural element of language-arts courses, since drama can be used most effectively in bringing about the integration of the subject areas in English. By its nature, drama deals with the whole person and may involve at various stages all the aspects of the human being. Drama in the English classroom, however, needs to be defined apart from that which is taught in a course concentrating on performance. Anthony Adams (quoted in Barnes, 1968), Chairman of Churchfields Comprehensive School, England, clarifies this point

> It is important to distinguish between drama, theatre, and the literary study of dramatic texts. The first is our main concern here and represents a particular form of classroom drama growing largely out of improvisation; we are interested in the education of children in English through drama, not in the production of trained actors and actresses. The concept of "playing to an audience" is irrelevant to a large part of our concerns, and there may indeed be times in classroom drama where an audience may be a hindrance or a danger. Thus, it is drama at the level of the individual or the group rather than primarily at the level of public presentation which we call theatre, with which we are concerned (p. 9).

Douglas Barnes (1968) concurs:

> Drama should be seen as part of this classroom talk. Like all task it may arise from a topic proposed by the teacher, from a shared experience, or from a work

of literature. Drama, however, differs from other talk in three ways: movement and gesture play a larger part in the expression of meaning; a group working together upon an improvisation needs more deliberately and consciously to collaborate; the narrative framework allows for repetition and provides unity that enables the action more easily to take on symbolic status—to have meaning beyond the immediate situation in which it occurs (p. 8).

An objective in the use of drama in the English class, then, is to expand the boundaries of experiences for students so that they may develop a more complete understanding of themselves, their work, and their relationships to other people. As Barnes suggests:

All secondary teachers know pupils who, although able to perform written tasks in the explicit and general language required by schools, cannot join in a free discussion of the same topic [and] . . . they cannot think aloud in the role. Students so deprived . . . need urgently an education directed by dramatic methods in which they are not presented with final certainties, but are required to face the uncertainties involved in discussing and planning their work . . . (p. 12).

Drama in this sense can be used freely within any English class. It is as effective with composition and language as it is with literature. It adds a more exciting dimension to learning and it helps to bring about that effective communication that was described earlier. It is difficult, however, to attempt pantomime, role playing, and improvisation with a class that has never experienced this level of participation. It is imperative to precede the actual creative drama activities with warm-ups.

Nonverbal Warm-Ups

Creative drama will be most effective when the teacher establishes an atmosphere conducive to mental, emotional, and physical expression. The classroom, for example, must lend itself to freedom of movement and, therefore, should be free of desk clutter. Arranging desks in a large circle or around the walls of the room provides a clear central space. Or, desks can be clustered at different areas of the room for props. The teacher's desk should melt into the rest of the classroom structure to emphasize that participation is aimed at everyone, for everyone. However, prior to moving the desks entirely out of the picture, students may need the physical shielding that a desk provides to "protect them" from criticism during warm-up exercises. At this point it is best to begin with activities that each student performs at his/her desk, or at least directly behind it. These activities are usually in response to directions given by the teacher. This retains a one-to-one, student-to-teacher relationship while students build confidence in their ability to control movement. Some exercises to use involve the class in nonverbal warm-ups:

- bending to pick up objects of varying weight, size, and shape
- getting ready for school in the morning
- buttoning a shirt or blouse
- sewing on buttons
- hunting for keys in a purse or pocket

More expressive tasks, still nonverbal:

- walking barefoot across asphalt
- walking on pebbles, in mud, through water
- approaching a growling dog
- groping through a dark tunnel
- walking along a narrow ledge

After some of the individual barriers begin to fade, desks may be removed and activities involving two or more people are introduced:

- tossing an imaginary ball back and forth
- handing a wounded bird from student to student
- thumb wrestling
- pushing palms against palms
- sawing down a tree with a long two-handled saw
- pushing a child on a swing
- pushing a log through a door to force it open
- moving furniture
- playing tug-of-war

To improve control in their movement, students can repeat some of these exercises in slow motion. To practice responding to another person, pairs of students stand facing each other. Each takes his/her turn mirroring the other's image. The pace of the movements begins slowly, increasing in speed as competence improves. Following these activities most students are ready to begin their experiences in creative drama. The first we recommend is pantomime.

Pantomime

7. Before using pantomime with literature, have students practice with additional warm-ups specific to pantomime. Working in a circle, students respond to words which represent different emotions. For example, students hearing the word "fear" may draw back, raise hands and have a grimace on their faces. You can suggest other words such as hate, disgust, sorrow, surprise, joy. The same words are used as the students take the activity a bit further. After hearing the word, students individually step forward from the circle and show their interpretation of the given emotion. The final warm-up activity has five or six students stepping forward one at a time and, by touching one another, creating a "collage" which represents a combined interpretation of the particular emotion.

8. This activity involves a particular use of pantomime; you can create many more. In this activity, students respond to the literature they hear much the same as they respond to the words in the previous warm-up activity. As you read a short poem or a portion of a larger work, have students, five or six at a time, individually respond to the work by stepping from the circle and, by touching one another, create an interpretation in the form of a "collage" to that particular piece of literature. The following works have been used quite successfully:

"Invictus"	Henley
"Harlem"	Hughes
"The Leaden-Eyed"	Lindsay
"Women"	Swenson
"At A Window"	Sandburg
"John and Jane"	Hardy
"Loneliness"	Jenkins
"Yes, It Hurts"	Boye
"Life for My Child"	Brooks
"The Buck in the Snow"	Millay
"The Pardon"	Wilbur
"I am Cherry Alive"	Schwartz
"The Young Ones, Flip Side"	Emanuel
"Learn to Be Water"	Marcus
"Will I Remember?"	Margolis
"The Hangman"	Ogden
"No Man Is an Island"	Donne

(Meditation XVII)

"Mother and Daughter"	Sexton
"Morning Song"	Plath
"The Invisible Woman"	Morgan

These are but a few of the many pieces of literature that can be used effectively with pantomime. Portions of short stories, essays, and novels should also be considered. After completing the "collage" response to a given piece of literature, students discuss the various interpretations and respond to alternative interpretations. It may be that a second or even third reading of the poem is necessary in order for other students to show their interpretations. The important point is that students should discuss the responses before going on to additional study of that particular work.

As you can see, students have experienced a piece of literature. They have done more than just read and discuss; they have become personally involved with the work.

Pantomime with Vocabulary

9. After students have studied the definition of selected words from the dictionary, they pantomime to their peers their understanding of that definition. In this way, they do not only receive the formal definition but also make a personal response to it.

Pantomime with Language

To help students realize the importance of nonverbal communication, use pantomime in a series of settings that will emphasize gestures and facial expression.

10. Ask students to work in pairs. One person draws a slip of paper from a box and tries to communicate the message written on it to the other person without speaking. Continue the activity until all students have participated.

The following are examples of the messages:

1. I'm broke. Will you lend me a dollar?
2. I have a headache. Do you have an aspirin?
3. I have a flat tire. Will you help me fix it?
4. I ran out of gas. Will you give me a lift to the gas station?
5. I don't have my homework done. May I copy yours?

Pantomime in Writing

11. Have students do the suggested warm-ups as described on the previous pages. Then have them continue to walk in the circle and have them respond to your verbal suggestions: They are walking in a snowstorm. How deep is it? How can they walk? Can they see? What is the temperature? Are they cold? Are their fingers and toes cold? Are their noses cold? What are they wearing? Are they happy? Tired? Depressed? Weary? Now, have students sit down and begin to write. They draw upon their pantomime experience for the direction of their writing.

Verbal Warm-Ups

Since the warm-ups that we suggested earlier are nonverbal, you should have students practice verbal interaction before using improvisation and role playing.

12. Working in pairs, students engage in a word-association format. One student says one word; the other responds with the first word that comes to mind. They continue for 1–3 minutes.

13. In pairs, they extend the warm-ups. They make up a weather forecast, one word at a time. They tell a story, one sentence at a time. For the last warm-up, one student creates the story while the partner pantomimes it. They reverse roles after 1–3 minutes.

Improvisation

By this time many of the barriers of self-consciousness have been removed, but it may still be necessary to begin improvisations in groups working simultaneously while you move from group to group offering assistance where needed. For early improvisation it is best to work with simple, familiar situations. For example, the groups can create a scene around a young man bringing his wife-to-be home to meet his parents; a father meeting his 15-year-old daughter in the hall at midnight on her return from a party that ended at 10:30; or a student trying to write in a diary or read a forbidden piece of literature as the privacy of his or her room is constantly invaded by the family. Some groups may be so pleased with their improvisations that they may wish to present them in front of the class. If not, the entire class can work together on a scene where they all respond to each other. In a cafe or restaurant situation, students can either (1) take the part of waitresses, truck drivers, preachers, policemen, businessmen, students, secretaries, as a fight breaks out or (2) be passengers on a plane as it is hijacked or is about to crash. Smaller groups can depict a crowd in an elevator as it stalls. The possibilities are limited only by the imaginations of the class.

With these improvisational warm-ups or pre-improvs finished, students can use improvisations with their study of the language arts.

Improvisation in Literature

14. Students bring so much more to the reading of Frost's "The Road Not Taken" after having improvised the following situation before reading the poem:

> Four students play a mother, father, 10-year-old daughter and a 16-year-old son. The father has the opportunity to leave his present job and move to another state to accept a new position. The new job involves an advancement, new responsibilities, financial rewards, but little security at this time, since the position is new and has no track record. The four discuss the situation and reach a decision as to what the family should do.

After discussing various aspects of the improvisation, suggest that another individual (Frost?) had perhaps struggled over a similar decision. While not exactly the same, it may have been as important and critical to those involved. Students are now ready for their adventure with "The Road Not Taken."

15. The following improvisational activity is created before the reading of two of Mark Twain's stories.

> Students, working in pairs, enter into a Liar's Contest. Each takes his/her turn telling an imaginary story in which he/she includes the most outrageous characters, fabulous events, impossible situations, and unbelievable endings. As the students are telling their tales to each other, the teacher randomly selects a pair to tell a portion of their tale to the entire class.

This improvisational activity serves as an introduction to the reading of "Tom Quartz, the Cat" and "Buck Fanshaw's Funeral."

Improvisation in Language

The following is a continuation of the non-verbal communication activity suggested on page 39. This time you use improvisation.

16. After a discussion of the pantomime activity, ask for five or six volunteers. Give the following directions:

> You are a troup of cave people. You are sitting around a campfire having supper. You are trying to communicate but you lack a single verbal language. How would you act?

> After a few minutes, freeze the action:

> You have reached a point where you need a verbal language. Continue to improvise until you have one word that you all recognize.

> Again, freeze the action:

> A stranger enters. He wants to communicate. Teach him the word. Complete the activity with a discussion about the improvisation as it relates to the study of non-verbal communication. This would be a good activity to begin your study of "the silent language."

Improvisation with Vocabulary

Improvisation can be used effectively to increase the understanding of vocabulary words. Traditionally, students are given words to memorize, but often they never have a complete understanding of their meaning or use. Improvisation help students to feel the meaning and to make use of the word immediately.

17. The following are some examples of how you might effectively use improvisation with vocabulary after students have studied the dictionary meaning.

Belligerent Have a student stand in front of an imaginary bank vault. No matter what happens, he/she is not to move. Have another student approach and try to persuade him/her to move. The resulting behavior of the "belligerent" person does the rest. Simply restate the term and apply the work to the situation. Encourage the use of the word in the interaction.

Empathy One student must explain a particular problem to another student (they don't have the money to go to a party, death of a pet or friend, illness of parent, etc.) A second person attempts to find out how that feels from the first person. Results are discussed.

Ridicule One student is working on an assignment. A second student constantly makes fun of him/her. Discuss results. Again, use the term in the discussion.

Role Playing

Role playing can begin as simple variations of speaking activities. For example, it may be appropriate for students to examine persuasive techniques through role playing and platform speaking. Students portray a motorcycle rider speaking on the attributes of life on the road, or a revolutionary leading a rally compared to his/her addressing a policemen's convention.

Next, students can assume the roles of characters in the literature they are reading to gain a deeper understanding.

18. Arrange a press conference with several characters in the book with the rest of the class acting as reporters. The students assuming the roles of the characters must answer all the questions completely in character. If there is a disagreement on interpretation, the action may be stopped anytime, discussed, and then roles exchanged.

19. Six students are used in this activity. You give each student a name and a character description which parallels the six major characters in the novel, *Ox Bow Incident:* Canby, Gil, Croft, Davies, Osgood, Tetley. You then give the students the following problem and have them try to reach a solution. They speak from the point of view of and in the manner of the characters assigned to them.

> Each of you in this room is a citizen of a very small western community. Recently, your community has been plagued by a number of burglaries and everyone is a little bit jittery. Your community is known for taking care of its problems quickly, even if it means taking matters into your own hands. Your sheriff is out of town on business and two hours ago the six of you decided to gather at the local meeting house to decide on a course of action. Now you have been interrupted by Fred Daws, a new member of the community, who has heard that Pete Moss, who lives on the outskirts of town, has been beaten to death and robbed. Fred also mentioned that a black '57 Chevy was seen leaving the Moss house and almost everyone in the community knows that the only black '57 Chevy belongs to Harry Dickson.

After the role playing, discuss with the students the experience. You then introduce the novel to the students. As they read the work, they find it interesting to compare attitudes and actions of characters with those presented in the role-playing activity. Too, students compare and contrast the conflicts and solutions reached in the novel and by the role-play group.

20. Students have finished reading Shakespeare's *Romeo and Juliet.* Four volunteers are seated in the front of the room to role play the following alternative situation which might have occurred.

> Romeo has been exiled to Mantua after having killed Tybalt, Juliet's cousin. Juliet's grief for her exiled husband is beyond words; yet, her parents think that she cries over the death of her cousin. To hopefully ease her pain, they call for the immediate marriage of Juliet to the noble count Paris; in fact, they strongly insist that the wedding occur within the week. To seek advice in her unimaginable situation (Juliet is already secretly married to Romeo), she goes to see Friar Laurence. The Friar insists that the only answer is to tell her parents the truth.

The four take the parts of Juliet, Friar Laurence, Lord Capulet, and Lady Capulet. After ten minutes or so the role playing should come to a stop, with all conflicts being resolved. A discussion of the role play should now occur.

Role Playing with Language

21. The major objective of this activity is to make students aware of the effects of age, education, and socioeconomic situations on how we use our language. Ask for five volunteers. Instruct them to role play a group of 16-year-olds talking about a friend's new car. Freeze the action. Instruct them that they are now a group of clergy trying to pick a date for their interdenominational retreat. Freeze again. Now they are a group of English teachers discussing the decorations for the new English office. Freeze again. They are now a group of truck drivers discussing which is the best place along the highway to eat. After this, discuss the roles that were developed. How did each group differ? Did the students play the roles effectively? How did they talk? What words were used? Did they sound different? What determines what and how we say what we do?

Creative drama creates a bond between the students and literature, language, and composition. It enables the reader and writer to become personally involved with their language.

FOR ADDITIONAL READING

Barnes, Douglas. *Drama in the English Classroom.* Champaign, Ill.: NCTE, 1968.

Bowser, June. "Structuring the Middle-School Classroom for Spoken Language." *English Journal,* 82 (January, 1993) 38–41.

Bushman, John H. "Creative Drama: Personalizing Literature." *Statement, The Journal of the Colorado Language Arts Society,* XIV (October, 1978), 1–5.

Dixon, John. *Growth Through English.* Reading, England: National Association for the Teaching of English, 1967.

Duke, Charles R. *Creative Dramatics and English Teaching.* Urbana, IL: NCTE, 1974.

Ecroyd, Catherine. "Motivating Students through Reading Aloud." *English Journal,* 80 (October, 1991), 76–78.

Hoetker, James. *Theatre Games: One Way into Drama.* Urbana, IL: NCTE, 1975.

Johnson, David W. "Teaching Students to be Peer Mediators." *Educational Leadership,* 50 (September, 1992), 10–12.

Koziol, Stephen and Massey, Julie. "Research on Creative Dramatics," *English Journal,* 67 (February, 1978), 92–95.

Moffett, James. *Drama: What Is Happening.* Urbana, IL: NCTE, 1967.

Sorenson, Margo. "Teach Each other: Connecting, Talking and Writing." *English Journal,* 82 (January, 1993), 42–47.

Spolin, Viola. *Improvisation for the Theatre.* Evanston, IL: Northwestern University Press, 1963.

Wagoner, B.J. *Dorothy Heathcote: Drama as a Learning Medium.* Washington, D.C.: NEA Press, 1976.

Way, Brian. *Development through Drama.* New York: Humanities Press, 1967.

Chapter 5

THE TEACHING OF WRITING

During the recent years, critics of education in general and English programs in particular have come down hard on the writing skills of students. Many have interpreted test scores to indicate a declining writing ability; others have looked to performance out of the school setting to make their criticism. The question of why Johnny and Janie can't write is not an easy one to answer; there are many, many variables that must be evaluated before jumping on any one reason for such a decline, if indeed there is one. Certainly, some of the concern must be shared by those who teach the English skills in the classroom. Many schools do not have writing programs, and those that do often lack a most important element: a writing sequence. Many times, too, teachers have students spend a great amount of time on grammatical study preparing students so that they can get ready to write; and when all is said and done, little time is actually spent on writing. When students do write, too often the writing activities at the beginning of the year are the same as those at the end. Students are asked to perform the same task—write a well-developed, structurally sound, clearly and concisely expressed theme—at both ends of the semester or year. The problem, of course, is that products are emphasized exclusively and students have had little opportunity to participate in a *process* of writing. Most teachers agree that students have little success.

The National Writing Project, an outgrowth of the Bay Area Writing Project, has done much to further the understanding of and experience in the writing process. That program in and of itself has done more to affect writing curricula in schools. There have been other programs and many people, too, who have contributed to this awareness of process writing. The books by Ken Macrorie, Donald Murray, Donald Graves, Janet Emig, James Moffett, Peter Elbow, to mention only a few, have made giant contributions to how kids are taught to write in elementary, junior high/middle, and high school.

THE WRITING PROCESS

Generally speaking, the three major components of the composing process are prewriting, writing and rewriting. There are other facets of the process that are frequently found in writing programs but most, if not all, educators have come to use these three words to describe the process of writing. It is these three steps in the process that occur when students write.

When students are in the prewriting stage, they are doing just what the name implies: they are involved in an activity prior to the act of writing. During prewriting, students may talk in large or small groups or with a partner about the subject that is to be written. They may even be exploring the possible subject, if one has not already been decided upon. It is during this time that students are, as Donald Graves suggests, in rehearsal. They are talking out the topic, finding a direction that the writing might take. Teachers may also structure other activities to help students in their prewriting. Brainstorming a topic using the entire class or a small group enables students to flood the classroom with ideas that may possibly be used in the writing. It is during this time that students make lists, gather data, and create a tentative focus for a piece of writing that is about to take place. Suggestions for prewriting prior to writing the initial draft occur in the sections of "Focused Writing" and "Structured Writing" found on pages 65 and 91.

Students equipped with ideas about which to write begin the act of writing. Depending on the objective of the writing that is to be done, students may write many drafts. In any event, students should be encouraged to get the ideas down first, then to revise if revision is applicable for the piece of writing. Some practice writing, in which the establishment of fluency is the main objective, would not be revised. Since most writing of any consequence will be revised, it is imperative that student writers get their ideas down without concern for grammatical, mechanical, or stylistic conventions. We have used the following expression many times to encourage student writers to engage in this process: "Feel free to make a mess, then clean it up." It is because of the revision stage that students can emphasize ideas and content when they first begin to write. They know they will have a chance, perhaps many chances, to revise their writing. They realize that they do not have to get it right the first time.

Revision, then, is the third component of the three-stage writing process. Student writers "clean up" their writing through a variety of means. Some use interaction with a partner, discussion in small support groups, and dialogue in a conference with the teacher to find out how others view their writing. Students take this advice along with specific guidance from the teacher to review their writing and to make necessary changes in order to create their finished product. Specific suggestions in revision are included on page 73.

THE WRITING SEQUENCE

We have had the concern about the *what* and *how* of teaching writing and our current programs take care of that quite well. We are *now* quite concerned with the *when* of teaching writing—in other words, how much, when and to whom. What we are suggesting is that many of us who have been involved with teaching teachers the process of teaching writing are now concerned that some of the parts of the writing process may be started too soon in the elementary and middle schools. It is evident that we must have a clear-cut sequence of teaching writing that parallels the cognitive development of students so that pre-adolescents in the middle grades are not expected to complete the same writing tasks that adolescents in the upper grades are asked to complete. We believe that teachers intellectually know that these two sets of students should not be expected to do the same level and skill development and, therefore, should not be expected to do the same tasks; however, something breaks down between the "knowing" and the "doing."

Two major changes in how we view curriculum development and the teaching of writing have contributed to making sequencing in the writing program a reality. These changes are (1) a shift in a knowledge-based philosophy of curriculum development to a philosophy based on human growth and development and (2) a shift from a product-based to a process-based approach to teaching writing. We will address each of these very briefly.

In a knowledge-based curriculum, the subject matter is simply assigned to certain grade levels and taught at the level regardless of the ability of the students to comprehend the subject matter. For example, the topic sentence, the thesis statement, or a three-paragraph theme may be assigned to the eighth grade as curriculum to be taught and mastered before students are allowed to go on to the next grade level. A strong case can be made that there are many eighth graders in many schools who are not intellectually ready to learn and to use those particular writing components. The grammar program is a classic example of content which is divided among grade levels regardless of students' ability to learn the concepts. In the approach based on human growth and development, the writing activities are presented consistent with the students' abilities to understand and to do them. As a result, teachers are able to offer a variety of activities to younger students which will provide a solid foundation for more structured, sophisticated writing that follows in later years.

The shift from product to process orientation in teaching writing enables teachers to focus on various parts of the process, thereby creating more freedom for students to experiment with their language. In this way, students are able to practice their writing, develop confidence, and establish fluency before they are concerned with a finished product. As we have said previously, the fear of having to "get it right" the first time is removed. The prewrite, write, rewrite model, which was discussed in the previous section, encourages the writer to gather ideas, to play with the most effective ways of expressing those ideas, to write first and second drafts, and to revise writing—all before creating the final product.

So the chance for sequencing in the writing program is strengthened by this shift in philosophy. Teachers are now able to take what they know about the writing process and to provide experiences that are based on what young people can learn and do at any given age. In doing this, teachers have become more aware of the physical, emotional, and cognitive characteristics of pre-adolescents and adolescents and how these characteristics affect the teaching of writing.

It seems to us that teaching writing in secondary schools should reflect what we know about pre-adolescents and adolescents. Readers are reminded of the physical, emotional, and cognitive characteristics of adolescents that are presented in Chapter 1. In that way, the writing curriculum takes into account these intellectual and experiential levels of young people, in that students are asked to perform consistently with what we know, or at least think we know, about the pre-adolescent and the adolescent.

We suggest this approach so that English teachers can structure their writing program so that it offers different experiences for young people in the middle grades than it offers to students in the upper grades. This has not always been the case. Writing assignments that call for rather sophisticated writing and abstract reasoning frequently are found in the middle level. We have heard of horror stories of fifth, sixth, and seventh graders having to write full-fledged "term papers" with all the component parts. Ample research exists to suggest that these ten- eleven- and twelve-year-olds are still at the concrete operational level and are using thinking processes that involve mostly categorizing and labeling as well as depending greatly on direct observation for the generation of ideas. They are simply not ready—not intellectually nor experientially—for the formal language manipulation as well as the confrontation with such tightly woven structures that come with such writing tasks.

When middle level and high school level teachers differ in their expectations concerning the writing that is done, growth in writing has a chance of taking place. Students find success when given the opportunity to produce work that is appropriate for their level. The success helps in the growth in which students use language to express themselves and growth in the kinds of writing that takes place. Early in the writing program, students play with their language, making it fresh and alive: they write frequently without concern for grammatical or mechanical conventions as they reinforce the fluency that they began in the elementary level. This frequently occurs as journal writing. As fluency is further developed, students zero in on one idea as they write. They put aside the practice writing and work to develop one idea well. As the writing progresses, students rework their writing. They get feedback about what they have written from their peers as well as from the teacher. They take this criticism, evaluate it, and decide how they will revise what they have written. As students mature in their writing, they move to a more sophisticated type of writing in which the student must join content and structure effectively. While this sequence frequently occurs in a single writing/English class, it best suits students if it is also spread throughout the secondary grades.

THE MIDDLE LEVEL

One of the major concerns of teachers at this level is the negative attitude that students have toward writing. Because of previous unsuccessful writing experiences, many students despise putting pencil to paper. For this reason, the writing sequence starts with much time spent on prewriting activities to help remove these inhibitions toward writing that have been established. Students spend substantial amounts of time collecting effective uses of language from a variety of sources. They work, too, at creating their own effective language. They create bumper stickers, book titles, license plates, word puzzles, and hink pinks in an attempt to make their language fresh and alive and, at the same time, to help them see that working with language can be fun. Emphasis at this time is on what is right and exciting about language, not what is wrong with language. There is much verbal interaction during this time, as well. Students need time for structured talk which generates ideas for use when they begin writing. The time spent at this time varies with the needs and abilities of students. Perhaps the best way to know when to have students move on and to begin writing is when they are comfortable creating language, securing examples of effective language and sharing these examples with their peers.

The middle-level students must have the opportunity to communicate about self in an atmosphere that is built around respect for each others' ideas and feelings. The writing here is personal and usually related to real-life experiences. The writing flows without regard to structure or form. During this time, students work in small groups to find qualities of good writing that they are using. The writing in this stage is not qualitatively evaluated. Students are free to express themselves in any way that seems appropriate to them at that time. They explore their feelings and emotions through this writing. A major characteristic of middle-level students is that they are primarily interested in themselves. Many agree that this egocentrism should be explored in the classroom.

The journal is also a part of this stage and is appropriate for the middle-level student. It encourages fluency in writing, emphasizes nonevaluative writing and offers a place to share ideas and feelings. Because of these factors, the journal frequently becomes an important part of the middle-level students' writing program.

The research on the pre-adolescent clearly reflects the need for peer approval. In light of that research, teachers should be aware of the usefulness of groups of the middle-level students. Small support groups can be an integral part of the writing program. The group can provide an audience for students' writing, a source for generating ideas, a support team to aid in revision, and a place for critical thinking, the latter primarily at the higher grade levels in the middle range.

Focusing in on one idea is also found in the middle-level writing curriculum. It can also be thought of as a transitional stage since it meets the needs of two sets of students: those at the upper end of the middle-level range and those at the lower end of the upper level range. Focused writing is personal and is usually in the narrative mode. Again activities draw upon the experiences of the writers. At this time students are asked to write with excitement, to continue to experiment with their language, and to develop their authentic voice; but to do it while focusing on specific ideas. The intent is to use what has been gained in previous writing as students emphasize the selection, organization, and presentation of their ideas. The emphasis now is to help students to be more selective in what they write, to determine the "hook" or "angle" they wish to use to organize their ideas, and to suggest alternatives in effective presentations.

THE SECONDARY LEVEL

The research, especially that from Piaget, seems to indicate that students in the upper grades or in what we commonly call the high school can reason at the formal operational level. The writing program should reflect that intellectual ability. In general, these students have reached intellectual maturity and are able to think in a systematic way, to reason by implication at the abstract level, and to bring together variables through synthesis.

Revision plays an important part in these students' writing program. While students in the middle level do begin revising their work, the bulk of the revision takes place in the upper grades. It seems to be more effective if students spend most of their writing time at the middle level just simply practicing writing by writing as many different pieces as possible without spending much time with one particular piece of writing. This approach changes considerably in the upper grades when the emphasis is shifted to revision. While some of the concrete-level editing (e.g. capitalization, terminal punctuation, commas in a series, use of the hyphen, use of italics, use of quotation marks) occurs at the middle level, most of the revision (e.g. use of phrases, concept of subordination, fragments and run-ons, sentence variety, parallel construction, patterns of organization, paraphrasing) is tackled by upper-level students.

Because of the sequential nature of this writing curriculum and because of the cognitive development of adolescents, senior high students are ready for more structured writing. The final stage completes the sequence and gives balance to the total writing program. We strongly believe, based on what we know about the development of students' thinking processes and what we know about the writing process, that structured or expository writing cannot and should not be taught earlier in the writing program. The hypothetical reasoning which is usually found in the adolescent who has moved into the formal operational stage is a vital part of this more formal writing. Therefore, students who have not attained this reasoning power may be frustrated with and usually unsuccessful in the writing if this expository writing is begun too early.

Structured writing demands a rather high degree of sophistication. The difficulty arises as students struggle with the manipulation of two important components: content and form. Through the earlier writing experiences, students have been more at ease with their writing because much of the content has come from experience, or at least general knowledge of the subject matter, and the form has not been a restrictive force. It is because of this relationship of form and content that this structured writing should be handled by upper-level students.

There are many creative, useful writing activities that help students to come to grips with content and form. Formal letters, reports, reviews, letters to the editor, formal speeches, and news articles emphasize logical thinking processes as do the more traditional formulaic structures (e.g. research papers, general themes, and the five-paragraph essay) but the creative approaches are much more interesting and relevant to high school students.

To write literary responses from a selection read is also a normal part of the senior high writing curriculum. Students should be able to make a statement or pose a problem about a work and defend or solve that particular response showing the level of reasoning or writing skill appropriate for students who have moved into the formal operational level. These literary responses are important and appropriate as long as they are balanced with other writing activities.

We believe that this writing sequence is important in order for students to be successful writers. But one teacher cannot do it alone. There must be a collective effort by teachers, administrators, and curriculum directors. Middle- and secondary-level educators must see a need for cooperation so that both levels are actively involved in teaching young people to write. The benefit from this writing sequence, in addition to producing better writers, is that each level has certain, clearly stated responsibilities in the total writing program. As a result, learning to write does not have to be completed by grade 9, 7, or 6 but it occurs step by step in a process that takes many years, with each grade level making very important contributions to the process.

Activities

Language Fluency

1. Spend 5–7 minutes each day or as often as is possible discussing a current topic of interest with the students. This topic should be as common as a school problem or a community and national concern. Try to get as many different ideas about this concern out in the classroom discussion. One of the major complaints that students offer is that they have nothing to write about. This activity, if followed regularly, will help take care of this problem.

2. Suggest several topics that would be popular with students: cars, money, relationships, home life, school, sports. Put students into groups of 3 to 7 to work on the topic that has been assigned to that group. Have students list as many words, or phrases as possible that would be related to their particular topic. Each group should choose a recorder to write down the words and phrases for later use. When the groups are finished brainstorming these topics have the group together write a few lines/thoughts expressing some of the ideas that were mentioned in the groups. Each group should decide on a reporter who will read some of the ideas to the entire class. As the lines/thoughts/sentences are presented, discuss them in terms of descriptive value, conciseness, and clarity.

3. Just for the fun of it and to help students to be creative with their language, have students create Hink Pinks, Hinky Pinkies, and Hinkety Pinketies. Students should find two words that rhyme and mean the same as the descriptors given. Hink Pinks: one-syllable words; Hinky Pinkies: two-syllable words; Hinkety Pinketies: three-syllable words. Some examples are given; students should fill in the rest. You and your students can create many more.

> HINK PINKS
>   drink for pigs—hog nog
>   dark shelf—black rack
>   big boat—large barge
>   wet light—_____
>   insect in a carpet—_____
>   overweight lion—_____
>
> HINKY PINKIES
>   positive drape—certain curtain
>   flirty cucumber—fickle pickle

royal bird—regal eagle
overweight taxi driver—_____
super big elephant—_____
war on cows—_____

HINKETY PINKETIES
list of candidates—election selection
frozen two-wheeler—icicle bicycle
advice from Santa—remember December
faithfulness to a king—_____
container for stairway railing—_____

4. The objective of the following activities is not just to pass the time away having fun but to help students see that playing with language can be enjoyable, and that working with words and phrases creatively can enable them to express their ideas with language that is fresh and alive, yet precise.

Clarifying Abstractions/Existential Sentences. The existential sentence connects in abstraction such as "happiness" to something in the concrete world such as "a warm puppy"; the connection is made with a form of the verb, "to be."

a. It quite often is humorous.
 Exhaustion is overchewing your bubble gum.
 Happiness is 5 green lights in a row.
b. It can appeal to the senses.
 Courage is eating a raw oyster.
 Pity is a kitten in a rainstorm.
c. It can be tragic.
 Courage is telling your dad you have had an accident.
 Sadness is not having a date on Saturday night.
d. It can be profound.
 Sadness is a well between two gardens.
 Hope is a flower in a junkyard.

The following are a few abstract ideas that may be appropriate for your students to use:

Death	Panic
Misery	Hate
Honor	Confusion
Suffering	Anxiety

Humiliation   Happiness
Love   Despair

Bumper Stickers. Bumper stickers are used primarily to imply a broad meaning with just a few words. Such writing frequently makes use of figurative language. Clarity and conciseness are supreme. Some examples are given here:

Race is a different colored face.
Don't be fuelish—drive 55.
Crime doesn't pay; neither does farming.
Don't complain about the price of food with your mouth full.

If you think education is expensive, try ignorance.
Adam was a rough draft.
God is back—and is he mad!
Illiterate? Write now for free help.

Have students make up some bumper stickers of their own. Use school events, local news, or special interest as sources.

Book Titles. Some examples:

Learning our ABC's	by Al Pha Bet
The Doctors	by Bill MeLater
The Day At the Fair	by Mary Go Round
The Short People	by Midge Et
The Diary of a Chinese Avon Lady	by Ding Dong

Have students create some of their own.

Visual Expressions. Have students write the common expression for the following visual expressions:

Standing	ham	fish	Dofootor
mis	rye	water	
	T	pants	Your hat
B	O	pants	Keep it
T Bush e	U		
A	C		
	H		

		One kind	another	
R		One kind	another	
G Rosie I	KDI	One kind	another	BE
N		One kind	another	BE
		One kind	another	B̶E̶
		One kind	another	B̶E̶

Have students create their own.

5. Use the pictures in Figures 9 through 17 for additional practice. Have students list as many creative expressions describing or responding to the pictures. Encourage the use of fresh, alive language that may describe in a special way. Students may wish simply to record lists of words or phrases that come to mind as they react to the pictures. The pictures were created by Steve Crum, English teacher, J.C. Harmon High School, Kansas City, Kansas.

Writing Fluency

Many people find it much easier to express their thoughts in speech rather than in writing. Perhaps this feeling of inadequacy in writing has come about as the result of the constant critical evaluation with little reinforcement that is received in writing programs. These people see proof of their ability to communicate orally when those who listen to them appear to understand. From the time children first begin to speak, they experiment with the sounds they hear until they stumble on to the right combination to make themselves understood. Most parents react excitedly, praising children and encouraging them to repeat that success. Other noises, jabbering, and nonsense sounds are simply labeled "baby talk," not necessarily discouraged, yet more quickly forgotten as children build on those sounds which successfully communicate for them. Therefore, children learn to speak in an atmosphere of encouraged experimentation which leads to successful building of meaningful language through positive reinforcement. The same procedure, then, can be used to develop the writing process.

After exploring the various word combinations and sounds, students need an opportunity to "experiment" with this language to develop successful ways to communicate their ideas through writing, just as they did when developing their oral communication. They should be allowed to build on their successes, gradually leaving behind the awkward broken phrases which parallel their vocal "baby talk." Those around them just encourage their written successes through positive reinforcement just as their parents once did.

Students must write as much as they want, as freely as they want, about what they want, without fear of failure. They must know that they will not be criticized or "graded down" for their attempts, but that their successes will be rewarded along the way.

6. Give students the opportunity to write whatever comes into their

Figure 9

Figure 10

Figure 11

Figure 12

Figure 13

Figure 14

Figure 15

Figure 16

Figure 17

minds for a short period of time—3 to 5 minutes. Tell students to put pencil to paper and start writing—nonstop.

In addition to this experimental, timed writing, stimuli can be included to create an atmosphere conducive to writing. Figures 9 through 17 can be used as additional stimuli for experimental writing.

7. Have students write thoughts of their childhood. Students are free to skip to different phases of childhood. They may desire to write about an experience, or they may simply wish to list words or phrases they associate with this period of their lives. They may wish to bring in childhood snapshots to act as stimuli.

Students need an audience for their writing. Just as people find limited growth in discussion with themselves, writers need feedback from an audience of readers. Students share their writings with each other in pairs or in small groups. At first, only positive comments are given. Students look for qualities of good writing—words or phrases that sound good together, vivid images, effective descriptive words and lively verbs. After receiving this response, students are more likely to remember what was successful and forget about the other items that received no response. Therefore, through reinforcement, students learn what is effective in their writing and build on it. We suggest that the qualities of good writing that students find as they read their writing be listed on poster board or the chalkboard. We think this approach is most appropriate since it shows students that the qualities do indeed exist in their writing. After many qualities are found over a week's time, you can establish a writing worksheet similar to the one shown in Figure 18. As students read additional writing, they can use this writing-revision worksheet to help them note the writing qualities and to aid them in preparing their revisions.

Journal Writing

Having students write in journals is most appropriate, as it can be an integral part of attaining fluency. Journal writing is important, as it helps the beginning writer to establish fluency—an important facet of the writing process. Fluency is established as students test out their ideas and their writing techniques without concern for correctness. The concept is to write freely without fear of penalty. In one sense, we see the journal as a place to practice writing, practice much like one would practice a musical instrument or a particular play in an athletic activity.

Even though the writing is less formal than some of the other writing done in class, we do see the use of the journal as having a writing objective. It is not only a place for sharing ideas and feelings but also a place to practice writing techniques. It seems to us that the journal is public or at least having the potential of being public if it is carried out in the classroom. Some entries may simply be written and nothing done with them; on the contrary, some may be read in support groups in the classroom. Therefore, our general rule is: "Don't write anything that can't be read in class." For those students who wish to write more intimate, personal entries, the diary that is kept at home may be just the answer. Perhaps the best idea is to recommend both: the diary at home and the journal at school. In this way, students are doing more and more of what is important: writing.

We caution teachers about the use of the journal. It has become a very popular vehicle in teaching writing and has been used extensively by many teachers. As a result, some students may get burned out with its use. Therefore, we urge moderation in the use of the journal. Frequently, teachers have students write in their journals at the end of the hour. Others have found that journal writing is effective when it occurs at the beginning of the period. Whenever the writing occurs, we urge teachers

Figure 18
Writing Revision Worksheet

Title of Writing _____

QUALITIES IN WRITING	Editorial	Advice
Stimulating Vocabulary		
Variety of Sentence Types		
Good Description		
Metaphor		
Simile		
Imagery		
Modifying Words		
Good Detail		
Putting the Reader There		
Suspense		
Good Use of Repetition		
Use of Dialogue		
Effective Word Play		
Humor		
Effective Beginning		
Effective Ending		
Organization		
Rhythm		
Clarity of Expression		
LANGUAGE CONVENTIONS		
Mechanics		
Spelling		
Grammaticalness		

On the back of this sheet provide positive comments concerning qualities of the writing not mentioned above as well as suggestions for improvement.

to respond to the writing that is done. Simple comments such as "Interesting point of view," "Good point," or "I've been there, too" help to create the motivation for additional journal writing.

Journal writing should vary. Sometimes the emphasis is given to a writing strategy—repetition, verb choice, etc.; other times the emphasis is given to the exploration of an idea. The writing strategies are governed primarily by what is being emphasized in the writing program or by particular problems that students may be having. Topics are limited only to the creativity of the students and teacher. We remind teachers of a publication from the National Council of Teachers of English, entitled *What Can I Write About?* (1981). That publication can be very useful when choosing topics for writing.

Focused Writing

Students move now from the general prewriting experiences to the selection, organization, and presentation of a particular idea. The fresh, honest style of writing emphasized earlier continues as students are encouraged to write with excitement, to experiment with their language, and to develop their authentic voice, but to do it while focusing on a specific idea they wish to express.

As in other parts of the writing program, sharing and criticizing play an important role. Positive comments about the quality of writing from peers in small groups are continued throughout phe writing program. However, after a few writing experiences, students begin to receive negative comments. Because students feel comfortable about their writing and their sharing in groups, suggestions to change their writing are now accepted more easily.

The following were but a few of the many activities that help students to focus their writing:

8. Prewrite: Have students brainstorm on a subject for 5–7 minutes. After recording all responses on the chalkboard, have students organize the points into 3 or 4 general areas.

Write: Have students write a story focusing their thoughts and feelings on one of the areas.

9. Prewrite: Have students respond to the pictures in Figures 9 through 17. Talk about the characters: what they were doing before the picture was taken, how they got where they are, what they are doing, what they are saying, feeling, and what kind of lives they live.

Write: Students can include these concerns and thoughts in a creative story. In addition to detail and point of view, students have experience in writing dialogue.

10. Prewrite: A dialogue with hats stimulates much excitement and interest in writing. All that are needed are hats and a hat rack! Have students discuss what a hat might include in a conversation: what it looks like, its texture, size, color, firmness, shape, place of birth, schooling, parents, siblings, hobbies, religious preference, and medical history.

Write: The writing activity occurs after hats have been placed on the rack. Each hat starts a conversation with the hat next to it. Hats might discuss a topic of general interest to hats: their relative position on the rack, their likes and dislikes, and their concerns and frustrations.

Write: The second writing is a narrative in which students tell the origin and description of their hats . . . from the hat's point of view, of course!

11. Prewrite: Have students think of a special place. This place could be an outdoor or indoor setting. In either case, students should have this place in mind before you start the process. Use the following questions/ statements, and more that you can create, to stimulate descriptive thought.

Sense of Sight:
   What objects can you distinguish?
   Are they stationary or moving?
   What is the relationship of the objects to one another?
   What are the shapes and sizes of these objects?
   Are there any striking colors to these objects?
   What are the colors to the setting as a whole?
   Is there any color that stands out above the rest?
   What is the source of light?
   How can the quality of light be described?

Sense of Hearing:
   Is this setting relatively quiet or noisy?
   What specific sounds can you hear? Note three.
   What is the quality of the sounds? Harsh? Mellow? Shrill?
   What do these sounds remind you of?
   Is there any one sound that stands out?
   Are there any interrupting sounds?
   What are the sources of the sounds in your setting? People? Machinery? Nature?

Sense of Smell:
Is there a particular odor?
What is its source?
What are the distinct qualities of the odor(s)? Fresh? Stale?
What do these odor(s) remind you of?

Sense of Taste:
Are there objects that can be tasted?
What kinds of taste sensations do they suggest?

Sense of Touch:
Can you touch any of the objects?
What is the texture of the objects that you can touch?
What can you learn from touching that didn't come from seeing, smelling, and hearing?

Write: Have students put the reader at this place through a story in which the writer relates a personal experience. After the writing, have students share in small groups.

12. Prewrite: An interesting activity which emphasizes point of view involves the retelling of a story. This helps students to see that different situations may appear completely different when viewed by different people. Have students choose an inanimate object which writes a story on "How I Changed (name of object's owner) Life." Some examples: a book that changed their philosophy, a record that inspired them to some action, or a car which almost caused them to have an accident.

Write: Have students choose an object and write a story from that object's point of view.

Write: As a follow-up and a second activity, have students choose a well-known story and retell it from a different point of view, e.g. a section from *Call of the Wild* —retold by a different person or by a different dog in the pack.

13. Prewrite: Have students bring to class a snapshot of their childhood. If a snapshot is not available, students may simply use their memory of this childhood experience. Discuss with students the incident or time that this snapshot represents.

Write: Have students focus in on this incident out of their childhood by developing a story around it.

14. Prewrite: Have students focus their discussion around a character description. Perhaps they could create and describe "an intelligent creature from space."

Write: Have students choose a character to describe. In their writing, students focus their attention on colorful and explosive verbs and descriptive modifiers. This activity works very well in a science fiction unit.

15. Prewrite: Students working in groups of five create ideas for each of the following categories: heroes, villains, problems, situations, and settings. They place these ideas in paper bags.

Write: Individual students draw an idea from each bag and create a story using the five elements.

16. Prewrite: Students discuss the following unfinished sentences as possible beginnings of their writings.

- She had gone as far as she could go; the door at the end of the hall was locked.
- The perfect parent should take on the responsibility to . . .
- I'll never forget the time when . . .
- He couldn't believe his eyes as the figure approached.
- The score was tied, the count was 3–2, and the pitcher released the ball.
- It was an ordinary book of matches, but in the hands of the four-year-old it was disastrous.

Write: After discussion, students choose one unfinished sentence to complete in a narrative. Encourage students to make their writing fresh, alive, and honest.

17. Prewrite: Use the following missing-person's report. Have students read it carefully; then discuss the importance of detail in the report and in other kinds of writing, as well.

> Johnny Axehandle was reported missing at 5 A.M. from the State Penitentiary in Scooterville. Axehandle, convicted for armed robbery, is tall and weighs approximately 195 pounds. The 42-year-old Caucasian has dark brown hair cut close to his head. His hair is thinning on top and he has a slight bald spot at the crown of his head. His eyes are brown and are overshadowed by bushy eyebrows. A noticeable two-inch scar is located just below his right eye. The lanky escapee is described as a desperate, somewhat irrational man. Members in nearby communities should be cautious of any unfamiliar people in the area. Axehandle, alias John Shovel, may be armed and dangerous.

Write: Give students a potato (they may bring one from home) and ask them to create a Missing-Potato Report. Encourage the use of detail to give specific information. Put all potatoes in the center of the room. Exchange Potato Reports and have students find the potato that is described in the Potato Report that they have been given.

18. Prewrite: Encourage students to use their imagination by completing the following UFO Report. Discuss when completed.

THE UFO REPORT

Directions: For 3–5 minutes, brainstorm on the topic "UFO." Put down every word or phrase that comes into your mind.

Now, go back and examine your UFO ideas. Place your words and phrases under the following appropriate categories.

Appearance   Sounds   Movements
Emotions   Misc.

Write: Have students focus in on their ideas concerning UFO's and have them use their imagination to describe a possible sighting. Be creative! Have them put their ideas in a story.

19. Prewrite: The age-old saying, "When life gives you lemons, make lemonade" is appropriate for this writing activity. Give students lemons and have them do the lemon activity. Work with them through the first prewriting warm-ups then let them finish the activity by writing on one of the topics listed. In the prewriting section, have students jot down descriptive words or phrases about their lemons in the following areas: sense of sight—movement, surface texture, color, shape; sense of touch—texture, temperature, weight, firmness; sense of smell; sense of hearing; and the sense of taste.

Write: Have students choose one of the following topics (they may wish to choose one of their own) and respond. These writings should be shared and criticized in groups.

- Write a personal history of your lemon.
- Write a letter of introduction.
- Write a drama with your lemon as one of the characters.
- Write a politician's speech as he/she/it campaigns for office.

20. Prewrite: Have students use the pertinent facts that are included in the following newspaper stories—plot, characters, setting—and discuss possible stories. Students would, of course, greatly expand the information.

Write: Have students write stories which might include background information of the characters, other possible characters that could be involved, motivation of the people involved, and many additional fictitious items not included in the original newspaper item but appropriate to the newly created fictitious story. These newspaper clippings actually appeared; however, the names and places have been changed to insure the anonymity of the subjects.

HIGH RISE, Kan. (AP)—The High Rise Bureau of Investigation and local authorities continued Friday to investigate Sooner County's first homicide since 1977.

Mary Doe, 23, was found shot to death Thursday night in her home east of High Rise. She had been wounded at least nine times with a small-caliber weapon, Sooner County Sheriff said.

A .22-caliber pistol was found in the house, he said, but investigators still had no suspect or motive in the slaying which they believe occurred between 9 A.M. and 1 P.M. Thursday.

LOW PROFILE, Neb.—It's not the most glamorous stakeout Sam Spade has ever been on.

But the Happy County undersheriff believes he can outwait a burglary suspect, who authorities believe swallowed a $100,000 diamond ring after his arrest for a weekend burglary.

"We're just going to let nature take its course," Spade said Thursday as officers continued to wait for the stolen ring to pass through the suspect's digestive tract.

GOLDSPOOF, South Africa (AP)—Three black gunmen seized 25 hostages at a suburban bank Friday in a holdup attempt to win the release of political prisoners, but the bid ended in the deaths of all the gunmen and two of the hostages.

It was the first time blacks in this tightly controlled white minority-ruled country have taken hostages to try to win the release of political prisoners.

Police stormed the bank after the gunmen started shooting the hostages.

GREEN TUB, N.H.—A 6-year-old boy who apparently was stabbed by intruders in his house identified a photograph of his neighbor, leading to the arrest of the neighbor and two other men in the slayings of the child's mother and half brother, authorities said Thursday.

"He broke the case wide open for us," Load County District Attorney said of the boy. He is in satisfactory condition under police guard at Mooney Hospital in Green Tub.

GOLD MUD, Colo (AP)—A blizzard pushed south through eastern Colorado Friday, causing traffic pileups and closing parts of the network of highways connecting the industrial and commercial cities along the eastern edge of the Rockies.

Between 450 and 500 cars were involved in a series of major traffic pileups on a snowbound, 20-mile stretch of Interstate 25 between the northern suburbs of Gold Mud and Gold Sand, the Colorado State Patrol said.

No deaths were reported in the accidents, but a paramedic set out on foot from Gold Sand in response to reports of injuries at a pileup south of the city, officials said.

HAPPENSTANCE, Nevada—Law and order has come to this community 73 miles southeast of Riley—and the town is divided over its application.

At the center of the controversy is Norman Krude, a 27-year-old former Navy military policeman hired as the city's first full-time marshal.

But rather unconventional tactics at enforcing the law have brought Krude's defenders and detractors among the fewer than 400 persons living in the community.

As suggested earlier, after each writing experience, students share their writing in small groups. During this time students relate positive and negative criticisms about the quality of the writing. The use of the Writing Revision Worksheet (See Fig. 18) is very helpful. At this stage of the writing, students do not consider the writing as a complete paper, or a finished product, but a piece of writing that has many good points as well as some that need revision. The group criticizes the writing as it appears in that stage knowing that it will be revised as it moves through the process to an eventual product. It is during this time of group interaction that students prepare for their revisions.

Structured Writing

It is at this time in the sequence that a more structured form of writing be introduced to students. The kind of writing that is suggested here requires much confidence, discipline, and sophistication—qualities that are developed gradually and with practice. They are attained after a comfortably paced building process.

Research papers, general "themes," and the essay forms are often included in schools because the educational system requires them. Exposure to these structures is beneficial for academic but probably has little other use; however, other structured writing such as formal letters, reports, reviews, letters to the editor, speeches, and news articles emphasize the same logical thinking processes but are much more relevant to the students' lives. Therefore, they may be more useful to students when they finish their formal education.

The essential point to remember is that in any form of writing, success is achieved through a careful but creative expression of an idea. Effective writing is practiced and developed; it is rarely instinctive. Even a letter to the editor can be ineffective, and therefore not read, if it does not incorporate elements of good writing. Structured writing should be attempted only after students mature in the composing process. It is for this reason that the sequence described in the previous few pages has been suggested.

21. Prewrite: Have students discuss the possible content that would go into a speech for a person announcing to their community his/her candidacy for mayor of their city (or some other appropriate office). The speech includes qualifications, reasons for running, goals for the administration, etc.

Write: Have students write that speech.

22. Prewrite: Have students discuss the characteristics of a review of a film, story, poem, or a novel. Possible items to include are evaluation of character development, plot, theme, setting, the author's mood, and tone.

Write: Have students write a review of a work they have read or seen. In it they should rate its effectiveness in dealing with the general theme and recommend for or against it based on their opinion of the work.

23. Prewrite: Students frequently question many decisions that are made by school, community, state, and national leaders. They often spend a great deal of time "griping" but fail to follow through with the courage of their convictions i.e. they don't share with those leaders their concerns. The letter to the editor provides a relevant and meaningful avenue for students to develop and support a position on a particular issue. It also is a way for students to see their efforts in print. Discuss with students the characteristics of a letter to the editor.

Write: Have students choose an item of concern and have them write a letter to the editor. Whether students submit their letters to the community newspaper, the school publication, or just an in-class dittoed collection which can be exchanged with other classes, they can reap the benefits of having their ideas shared with many people. Too, through this medium, students write more formally in a very meaningful way.

24. Prewrite: Discuss with students the various kinds of letters that are written: friendly letter, business letters, application letters. Compare and contrast the characters of these letters. Discuss the content of each, as well.

Write: Ask students to write a letter of each kind to three people whom they know in the school or community.

25. Prewrite: Work with students on how to paraphrase—a very important technique used in research writing. Have students practice with well-known speeches, poems, or citations from books.

Write: Have students select a portion of writing and paraphrase it.

26. Prewrite: Discuss the characteristics of a biographical essay with students. Also, discuss the importance of the interview as a means of gathering information, the main source for this activity. Discuss with students the people available in the community that would be appropriate for the source of a biographical essay. Also, discuss the general characteristics of the interview and the protocol in setting one up. Have students practice interviewing by working in pairs with their classmates.

Write: Have students write a biographical essay after collecting information from an interview.

27. Prewrite: Have students find information about a public figure (politician, news reporter, television personality, film star, or school official) with whom they disagree on one or more issues. Discuss with students the issues and the point of view expressed by that public figure.

Write: Have students write an essay in which they express that public figure's position on an issue from that person's point of view.

28. Writing in response to reading literature is appropriate in the Structured writing stage as long as it is kept in balance with other kinds of writing. It would be impossible to list all of the literature that is taught in high schools so that writing activities could be suggested; therefore, our recommendation is for teachers to create prewriting activities related to the literature read before students are asked to respond to that literature. Common responses include writing analyses of plot, setting, theme, character; character sketches; and critical essays.

Revision

The revision process is so important to the writer. It is at this time that the writer takes a second or third look at the ideas that are down on paper and decides what changes are to be made. Students should be encouraged to follow this procedure. This can only happen if the writing program reflects a process orientation rather than one that emphasizes products. It is during the revision stage that the tentative writing moves another step closer to a product.

During the preceding sequence, students have written a great deal and shared this writing with their peers and the teacher. They have reached much positive criticism as well as some suggestions as to what can be done to improve the writing. It is not necessarily wise for students to completely accept all negative criticism as best. If they do, they may simply be writing someone else's ideas. It will become something which is not theirs and they will lose interest in the project. On the other hand, students should not totally disregard changes that have been suggested. Therefore, students must consider suggested changes carefully. Will this change still convey the original idea? Will it, in their opinion, strengthen or weaken the image? Is it more clear, more vivid, or could it work better somewhere else in the paper? After a careful analysis, students can make honest and justified decisions on how to use the criticism they have received. Students must retain confidence in their own ability to create.

Students should not only reflect on these peer comments but also consider how they have used elements of good writing which have been discussed in class.

- They analyze their beginnings and endings. Teachers can be very helpful in this process by bringing in 3 or 4 selections of published writing and by reading a short excerpt from the beginnings and endings.
- They check for effective repetition.
- They tighten and strengthen their writing by removing unnecessary words.
- They look at description, detail, and the general clarity of expression.

SPELLING

We include the teaching of spelling in this book since we firmly believe that we teach spelling in the middle and upper grades most effectively through our teaching of writing. To teach spelling in isolation simply is not successful. We have all been through the spelling list approach at one time or another—list on board on Monday, pretest on Wednesday, and final spelling test on Friday. The words are usually taken from a spelling book; they are in alphabetical order. An interesting problem usually arises: Students never get to words beginning with *R* or the remaining part of the alphabet because time runs out in the school year.

However, that really isn't the main concern. The effect that this method has on overall spelling improvement is at best minimal. Students may do well on the Friday test because they can memorize well, but the overall effect on how students spell is nil, primarily because students have very little, if any, ownership of the words that they are asked to spell. The words are seldom used since they are not part of the students' regular vocabularies. Interestingly enough, some of the words that they are asked to spell will never be a part of their working vocabulary. Students in the middle and upper grades need to learn how to spell the words that they regularly use.

That is not to say that students need not be nudged a bit into incorporating new words into their writing and speaking vocabularies. They should. However, the effective way to accomplish this task is through discussion of words as they read literature selections in class and as they talk about each other's writing in support groups. New words are added to our vocabularies as we are actively involved in the study of the language arts, not by learning words through isolated lists. Many teachers find the spelling approach suggested here to be quite useful and effective.

Spelling in the middle and upper levels should be primarily an individual matter. However, before describing how this individual approach to spelling is incorporated into the English classroom, mention of some general considerations in the spelling program is in order.

A Spelling Guide

A few guidelines for helping students with their spelling problems may be helpful. Frequently students have no process through which they can increase their spelling accuracy. It may be helpful for teachers to suggest the following steps for students to use when they are learning to spell a new word. Teachers should have students:

1. say the word aloud and distinguish each syllable as the word is spoken.
2. try to visualize how the word appears with eyes closed, in other words, see the word spelled correctly as they "think" the word.
3. look at the word again on paper to see if their visual impression was accurate.
4. write the word on paper and check its spelling.
5. repeat step number four twice.
6. write a short piece of discourse in which this word is used frequently.

While this method may not turn everyone into excellent spellers, it does help increase spelling accuracy, and it can be used by the individual writer most any time and any place. It is a process that students can use by themselves.

Spelling Rules

While we mentioned earlier that teachers in the middle and upper grades should not emphasize the rules of spelling, a few very common spelling rules that have few exceptions may be reinforced at this time. Because the English language is so cosmopolitan, there is little consistency in the spelling; therefore, most spelling rules have many exceptions. Because of this, most of the time it is safer simply to learn the word itself without relying on a rule. However, the following list may be helpful:

1. Nouns ending in *y* preceded by a vowel add *s* when making the plural form. Those ending in *y* preceded by a consonant change the *y* to *i* and add *es.*
2. Words ending with a silent *e* drop the *e* before a suffix beginning with a vowel and retain it before a suffix beginning with a consonant.
3. Words of one syllable that end in a consonant preceded by a single vowel double the consonant before adding *ing* or *ed.* If the word has more than one syllable, the same process occurs if the accent is on the last syllable.
4. Place *i* before *e* when the sound is long *e,* except after *c;* after *c,* the spelling is *ei.*

An Individual Spelling Program

To begin this spelling program, teachers should secure a list of spelling demons. Many lists are available: twenty-five most misspelled words, 100 spelling demons, etc. Lists also exist for particular grade levels as well. We recommend that teachers use the list as a basis for students' individual spelling lists. Students spell the words as they are dictated. Those words misspelled go on each student's list. Students do not receive a grade on this first spelling activity; it is for diagnostic purposes only. Words that are misspelled from that point on are placed on the students' individual list. These words come from a variety of sources: revised writings, essay examinations, and daily written lessons. Students are responsible for spelling words correctly. If words are misspelled, they show up on the list of words to be studied and eventually to be tested.

Periodically throughout the semester, teachers test students over the words that appear on their individual spelling list. This testing may occur weekly, every two weeks, or monthly. Teachers should devise a method for this testing that best suits their program. We offer two possibilities: (1) Teachers place students in pairs and have each student test the other student on his/her words. The spelling tests may be evaluated by the students at that time, or they may be turned in for teacher evaluation. If this approach is used, teachers may need to move about the room during the testing to see that students are remaining on task and are following the appropriate procedure. (2) Teachers have students individually come to the teacher's desk for the evaluation session. This approach is workable if teachers periodically plan a lesson on which students can be working by themselves, so that the teacher is free to test individual students. This may be a free reading time, journal-writing time, or general study time. If this approach is selected, teachers dictate the words to the students for correct spelling. This second approach may demand more of the teacher's time but may be more beneficial due to the quality control that prevails.

Whichever approach is considered, the following comments about the spelling program may be useful:

1. Students should be tested over only ten words or fewer at a time. Some students may have as many as forty-five words on their lists; some may have only four. Students with only four should not be penalized because they are good spellers; therefore, they are tested over just four. Students with many words should be given every chance to succeed; therefore, they should be expected to have ten words ready for any given test.

2. Students should be encouraged to keep their word lists in a place that will be safe and secure. The journal works well for this purpose. It is frequently kept in the classroom and, therefore, is readily accessible. Teachers may find that they want to keep these lists as well. One teacher who uses this approach to teaching spelling has a small three-ringed notebook in which she keeps the spelling list for each student in her classes. While she agrees that it takes more of her time to do this clerical recording, she believes it is the best procedure to use for her students. As she evaluates assignments from which misspelled words are taken, she adds these words to the appropriate lists in the notebook. When the periodic tests are completed, she removes the appropriate words from the lists. This approach works particularly well for students who fail to keep an up-to-date list. These students are still held responsible for the words that they have failed to place on their lists. They may have to check with the teacher's notebook!

Teachers who use this individual spelling program find that it works. Students are held accountable for the correct spelling of words that they use. Students find relevancy in that they are concerned with words that they write rather than with words from a spelling list that may not be in their working vocabulary. Teachers also find that the lists get shorter and shorter as the year progresses. Students are more concerned with spelling because they know that they will meet the word again if they misspell it in their writing.

ASSESSMENT

Evaluation of student writing may prove to be the most difficult problem that teachers face as they teach the language arts. On the one hand, teachers want to encourage students as much as possible; therefore, they do not want the evaluation to be a negative influence on students; on the other hand, teachers certainly want the evaluation to be an honest reflection of the student's work. Arriving at this fine line that separates these two concerns will help both the teacher and the students as they participate in the writing program.

Making evaluations is important to both students and teachers. Students do need to receive some indication of how they are doing. To what degree is growth in writing ability to take place? Students need evaluation of skill development. How well did they use a particular technique or strategy? Teachers, too, feel the need to make evaluations. They not only feel the responsibility to give students feedback regarding their growth but also need in a more practical way some indication of student progress for the grade book.

The key to all of this evaluation is that it can come in many different forms. Teachers must remember that the foremost reason for giving evaluations is to help students to become better writers. Secondarily, it seems to us, is the need for the mark in the grade book even though we do realize the pressures from many sources in that matter. The evaluations that are given can be in the form of student oral or written comments, teacher oral or written comments, or letter or number grades. This last type, perhaps, is the least effective if used alone. Of course, we realize that the most effective evaluation probably will be a combination of all of these types of feedback. The general rule to follow, it seems to us, is that evaluation, in order to be useful for students, must tell the students something specific about their writing. To simply place a letter or number grade at the top of the paper without further comment does the student little good.

We have found that a point system works quite well in combination with peer evaluation and teacher assessment when the writing is to be judged qualitatively. Some writing or writing activities, however, need not be evaluated in that way. There are many prewriting and even experimental and practice writing experiences that should not be given a quality grade. Since many teachers feel the need to record some grade, they are implementing a system of participation points. In this way, teachers are able to give credit for a task completed without making a quality judgment that an A, B, or C reflects.

The writing that is to be evaluated qualitatively (i.e. it is to become a finished product) usually is read and discussed in support groups. After that process, the students revise the writing and it is then ready for a evaluation by the teacher. At this time the final grade is placed on the paper. Points are still used at this time, as well. So, when the teachers use participation points, students receive the same number of points (the number that the activity is worth) if the task is completed; when teachers use quality points, students receive points in a range from the least to the best, consistent with the quality of the product submitted. It seems to us that this system offers the best hope for consistency and effective feedback in the evaluation process, as well as for addressing the realities of what should and should not be evaluated qualitatively in the writing program.

Six-Trait Analytic Scale

While there are many measurement instruments that are helpful in the assessment of writing (holistic evaluation, Kirrie, 1979; analytic evaluation, Diedrich, P., 1974; primary trait scoring, Lloyd-Jones, R. 1977; standardized tests, ETS, 1975; T-unit analysis, Mellon, J., 1969, Cooper, 1987; attitude scales, Schuessler, B., A. Gere, and R. Abbot, 1981 and Daly, J. and M. Miller, 1975), we believe one of the most effective instruments available is the Six-Trait Analytic Scale developed by teachers from the Beaverton (Oregon) School District #48 (Spandel and Stiggins, 1990, p. 29). The use of this instrument allows teachers to center attention on specific traits found in writing. These traits are Ideas and Content, Organization, Voice, Word Choice, Sentence Fluency, and Conventions. In using these traits, teachers and students are well aware of strengths and weaknesses in writing. The Six-Trait Model also enables students and teachers to have a common language when discussing writing. The following are descriptors used with each of the traits:

Ideas and Content
Has a clear in purpose
Is original in presentation
Puts the reader in the writing
Uses effective detail
Has original ideas
Displays knowledge from experience
Is insightful
Has a controlled topic

Organization
Enhances reading
Has a central theme
Has a sense of fluency
Has beginning, middle and end
Shows unity and cohesion

Voice
Portrays a sense of the individual writer
Displays a commitment to the topic
Displays honest, natural writing
Engages the reader

Sentence Structure
Displays fluid writing with effective rhythm
Conveys clear meaning
Has a variety of sentence types
Has a variety of sentence beginnings
Makes effective use of fragments

Word Choice
Uses precise language
Has a sense of imagery
Portrays clear, colorful expression
Incorporates effective figurative language

Writing Conventions
Uses grammar and usage that are appropriate for audience, occasion, and writer
Uses punctuation that enhances meaning

Uses generally acceptable spelling
Uses conventions that generally enhance readability

When used for assessment purposes, educators can make generalizations about the quality of writing for a large number of students at any given time. These students may be a part of a state, multi-district, district, school, or classroom assessment. When assessed, each paper is read usually twice and is given a score from 5 to 1 in each of the traits; therefore, each paper has six scores showing the strengths with some writing traits and, perhaps, weaknesses in others. For example, a score of 3 on any given trait represents a balance of strengths and weaknesses; a score of 2 or 1 represents more weaknesses than strengths; a score of 4 or 5 represents more strengths than weaknesses. At the completion of the assessment, school officials know the writing abilities as measured by the Six-Trait Analytic Scale at the various levels. What we think is important is that teachers have very specific information about students' writing to share with their student writers.

While using the instrument for assessment provides diagnostic information about writing, it is equally beneficial as an instrument for use in instruction (Bushman, Goodson, Ketter, 1992). After teachers have assessed students' writing and have determined the strengths and weaknesses, they can use activities (many in this chapter) to help students improve writing skills in general and the writing traits in particular. Kay Kassem, English teacher at Shawnee Mission Northwest High School (Kansas), has created a series of activities for use with the Six-Trait Model (see Figure 19). When teachers find that their students have weaknesses in organization, for example, they can use specific activities to help students overcome those weaknesses. Students can work together in groups to talk about the traits and help each other improve their writing. Figure 20 can be most helpful when students use it with each other's writing, whether it be in groups, with partners, or just as individual writers.

We strongly believe that the Six-Trait Analytic Scale is best used when incorporated into the revision process within the writing program. It is not a knowledge base that is taught in isolation; nor do we believe it is taught trait by trait and then practiced in writing emphasizing one trait at a time. If it takes 10 weeks or so to get through the traits, the emphasis has been wrong. We think that the traits may be mentioned while students are involved with WRITING but emphasized in detail when students are REVISING. Inexperienced writers do not learn about

Figure 19
Selected Activities for the Six-Trait Model

Ideas and Content

Observations: To increase details in writing have students observe some area and record their observations. Have writers use these observations to create a very detailed piece of writing.

Logic Skills: Discuss with students fact versus opinion, inductive reasoning, and deductive reasoning. Search newspapers and magazine editorials and essays to determine which logic skills are used. Generate ideas: To help students see that they do have ideas about which to write, have them in a whole class activity brainstorm ideas about which they have opinions.

Unusual angle: A new perspective on writing may be found by having students find stories that have taken on a different angle. One such writing is Rubin's (1982) "The Dog Whose Bite Was Worse Than Its Bark." Rubin writes not about the loved family pet, but about the ugly, hated animal that was part of her childhood.

Organization

Patterns: Work with students in their use of various patterns of organization: chronological, spatial, importance, comparison and contrast, and analogy. Discuss with students when one organizational pattern may be more useful and more effective than another.

Voice

Point of view: To help students find a fresh, expressive voice, suggest they write from a new point of view. Choose literature as examples: Scieszka's *The True Story of the 3 Little Pigs by A. Wolf* (1989).

Audiences: Have students write for the school newspaper about an issue of importance to them; then have them write about the same issue to the school principal or district superintendent.

Writer's identity: Choose a selection in which the voice is strong. Ask students to respond to various questions about the writer: what is the writer like? Is the voice hot? cold? loud? soft? If the voice were a dog, what kind would it be? why? Have students tell which words help them to give their answers.

Figure 19
Continued

Word Choice

Vocabulary: Choose words from literature that students are reading. Have students discuss the words. Have students work with the words through creative drama and writing.

Changing words: Have students work through their writing finding words that are vague, overused, and ineffective. Have students substitute with more effective choices.

Weak words: Work with students in their use of weak nouns and verbs. Students should look through their writing to see if they can identify words that need to be replaced. The over use of the "to be" verb is of primary concern in most student writing.

Forbidden
words: Make a list with your students of forbidden words—words that are overused and ineffective. Place these words on the chalkboard or poster board to keep as a reminder for students.

Sentence Fluency

Combinations: Sentence combining practice can be an effective method of showing students how to vary sentence structure. Prepare a worksheet with many simple sentences and ask students to combine into longer more complex sentences.

Parallelism: Parallel structure is an important concept to understand when creating clear, rhythmic sentences. Students should examine their writing to make sure that structures in their writing are parallel.

Beginnings: To show students that all sentences need not begin in the same way, read aloud or show on the overhead a paragraph from a piece of literature that students are reading emphasizing how the sentences vary in their beginnings. Discuss how sentence beginnings may be varied effectively.

Writing Conventions

Grammar, usage: Help students to revise and edit while involved in the writing process. To do isolated activities with grammar, usage, and mechanics will not be successful. Students need to work with their own writing.

Peer Groups: Revising writing works very well when incorporated into small group work. Grammar, usage, mechanics, and spelling can be corrected and discussed while students are working with each other's writing.

Figure 19
Continued

Read aloud: Emphasize to students that reading writing aloud helps in the editing process.

Spelling: Creating a personal list of misspelled words can be an effective tool for students. These words may be marked by the teacher or identified by peers. Working in pairs, students can quiz each other.

sentence fluency, for example, and then write with a variety of sentences. They write and then rewrite looking at their sentences. It is more effective if students have their own writing before them as they analyze it in terms of writing qualities. Students should think in terms of getting their ideas down on paper; then, they can think in terms of organizational patterns, effective voice, sentence variety, word choices, and the writing conventions.

Some concern is expressed by teachers after the Six-Trait Model has been used concerning the assigning a grade for the paper. As we have discussed earlier in this chapter, grading is a necessary evil and will not go away. While the Six-Trait Model gives needed information for the student writer, it does not, in and of itself, become accessible for the determination of a grade. Some argue that the 1–5 score on each of the traits is sufficient; others believe that the paper deserves an A–F grade. While we believe that the student is best served by using the scoring of the various traits, we can see the need for some flexibility for those who need that letter grade. Therefore, some teachers have weighted the traits and have arrived at a total number which then can be given a letter grade. This process, however, is not recommended by those who created the Six-Trait Model. The following is an example of this approach:

Ideas and Content	$1\,2\,3\,4\,5 \times 5 = $ _____
Organization	$1\,2\,3\,4\,5 \times 5 = $ _____
Voice	$1\,2\,3\,4\,5 \times 3 = $ _____
Word Choice	$1\,2\,3\,4\,5 \times 3 = $ _____
Sentence Fluency	$1\,2\,3\,4\,5 \times 3 = $ _____
Conventions	$1\,2\,3\,4\,5 \times 1 = $ _____
	Total = _____

Teachers can determine a range for the grade from the number attained using this approach. The reader will note that Ideas and Content and

Figure 20
Six-Trait Student Checklist

Ideas and Content

The ideas presented are clear in purpose Examples:	Yes	No
The paper has original ideas Examples:	Yes	No
An attempt has been made to involve the reader Examples:	Yes	No
Writer makes use of detail effectively Examples:	Yes	No

Organization

There is a central point to the writing Example:	Yes	No
Ideas move smoothly through the paper Examples:	Yes	No
Paper has strong beginning and ending Examples:	Yes	No
There is a sense of cohesion in the paper Examples:	Yes	No

Voice

Strong sense of the individual writer is present Examples:	Yes	No
Writing is very natural and honest Examples:	Yes	No
The reader is engaged Examples:	Yes	No

Sentence Fluency

An effective rhythm is present Examples:	Yes	No
Sentence beginnings vary Examples:	Yes	No
A variety of sentence types are included Examples:	Yes	No

Figure 20
Continued

Word Choice

Figurative language is effectively incorporated Examples:	Yes	No
Imagery is present. Examples:	Yes	No
Accurate, strong, specific words are chosen Examples:	Yes	No

Writing Conventions

Acceptable grammar/usage is apparent Examples:	Yes	No
Spelling is generally acceptable	Yes	No
Punctuation enhances meaning	Yes	No

Organization are thought of as most important; Voice, Word Choice, and Sentence Fluency are next importance. Writing Conventions receive the least weight. Teachers would be advised if using this method to weigh the traits as they feel best meets their needs. We have created a method (see Figure 21) by which the Six-Trait scoring can be retained but combined with other rubrics that are used in the assessment of portfolios (see next section). In this way, student writers are able to compare their scores with the six traits from paper to paper, and the teacher is able to use the rubric which may have other important information to be assessed on a particular paper. You will note that there is space for notation about self reflection (SR) and peer editing and conferencing (PE/C). This figure can be duplicated a number of times on a sheet of paper and can, therefore, be used to keep track of the writing progress of individual students.

Portfolio Assessment

Portfolios have been used for many years in the art and business world. Artists have put the best that they can do into a portfolio and have used this means for showing their quality of work to prospective employers, educational institutions, or any other agency that would need to know what the artist was able to do. Now, portfolios are making their way into education; teachers are finding them most useful to help students show

Figure 21

Title _____	I/C	O	V	S	WC	C
Type _____						
Date _____						
Comments:	SR			PE/C		

Grade _____

what they know and are able to do. Variety is perhaps the best way to describe the use of portfolios in education. No two seem to be alike. But, it is apparent that the objective in using them is similar: show over time what students are able to do. Portfolios are found in math, social studies, English, and other classes at the middle and junior high schools. They are also widely used at the elementary level. While teachers in all content classes do use portfolios, most use the portfolio in connection with the writing programs. So even if the science teacher may use portfolios, often they are used in connection with writing in the science classroom. This, of course, is not always the case, but we find writing as the connecting link to portfolios. We suppose the reason for this is the emphasis given to the teaching of writing in the English class, the use of writing in all content classes, and the need for authentic writing assessment.

The testing/evaluation program before portfolios did not provide the necessary information to show how students are doing in their writing development. So often the tests were the norm-referenced, nationally standardized tests that measure some things but do not speak to how well writers write. Judy Gilbert in her book *Portfolio Resource Guide: Creating and Using Portfolios in the Classroom* (1993) shows graphically the new paradigm in teaching and assessment. The attention, she states, "has turned from a focus on what is taught (subject matter content) to what is learned (student outcomes)" (p. 3).

What we have come to believe about writing and how well students can write can now be assessed more accurately. For example, we believe that by the time students finish high school they should be able to write a well-developed essay to an appropriate audience with a high degree of accuracy (outcome). We would expect that students would need to know and use writing techniques, perhaps the six traits mentioned earlier (what they need to know and be able to do). To find out if students did indeed write what we wanted them to write, we would ask them to write

Figure 22

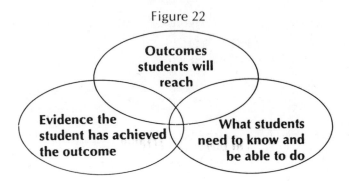

(authentic evidence). This is a far cry from what is often found in the middle and high school English classes. Frequently, teachers may still have the same outcomes; however, teachers believe that grammar is what students need to know; and the evidence that the student has achieved the outcome is in the form of a grammar test or the standardized test mentioned earlier. It is evident that what students need to be able to do and the evidence to show that it has been accomplished do not follow from the outcome that has been expressed. The position that teachers take who use portfolios is that the evidence should be writing and that writing is best displayed in a portfolio since that evidence does show growth of writing skills over time.

While no two writing portfolios are identical, some general characteristics are common among them:

1). Students keep their work in folders throughout the period of the portfoliio (5 weeks, 9 weeks, a semester, etc.).
2). At the time that the portfolio is to be created, students review their work and choose certain pieces (usually three) to put into their portfolio. Teachers and students develop criteria on which to base the choices that are made.
3. Students write a reflection on their portfolio as well as on the writing that is included.
4. Students choose a "best piece" and write a reflection on why that is the best piece of writing. Teachers usually assess that piece of writing. Some will assess the whole portfolio.
5. Often students, teachers, parents, or friends respond to the portfolio.
6. The assessment instrument (rubric) that will be used to assess the writing and/or the portfolio is made available to students as they begin the portfolio process.

The following (Figure 23) is a portfolio design created by Mary-Kris Roberson, a sophomore English teacher at Manhattan High School in

Manhattan, Kansas. She has developed a Human Rights Unit and in doing so assesses students growth in this unit through the portfolio. While the unit includes work in literature, the emphasis is given to developing writing skills.

As Figure 23 indicates, Roberson shares with her students what the portfolio will include by listing the items. These are general categories; students will select the particular items from a working folder that each student keeps in the classroom. You will also note that three rubrics (Figures 24, 25, and 26) will be used for assessment purposes.

During the Human Rights Unit, students will be involved in a variety of classroom activities:

Response papers: informal directed responses to in-class readings, speakers, audio recordings, videos, etc.

Learning Log Entries: written responses which illustrate new or enhanced understanding gained from literary concept mini-lessons, language workshops, oral presentations made by the teacher, or guest speakers.

Options for Learning: options presented to the students after a piece of literature has been read to encourage them to do further independent reading, research of a related topic, and/or to create: sketches, blueprints, research reports, role-play situations, interviews of community or family members, collages, time lines, etc.

Writing Workshops: provides a concentrated writing setting in which more formal methods of writing are addressed. This unit focuses specifically on three: persuasive essay, comparison/contrast essay, and opinion essay.

Students will select a most satisfying piece to include in the portfolio. As students do this, they will also complete a Most Satisfying Piece Reflection (Figure 27). Reflection is a key element in a portfolio as it enables students to think about the process that they used in creating their writing and reflect on it. Students think about how they generated their topic, how they feel about the writing now that they are done, what problems they had, and just why they think this is their best piece. The figure ends with the students creating their goals of writing for the next unit. A similar reflection is done for the Oral Presentation (Figure 28).

A key element of this portfolio and of many portfolios is the sharing of it to others. Sometimes this is done to other classmates, school personnel, but often to family members. The objective for the activity is for students

Figure 23
Human Rights Unit Portfolio

Level: 10th Grade
Purpose: To illustrate growth in written and oral work
Contents: Title Page
                Table of Contents
                Preface
                Three Reading Responses
                Three Learning Log Entries
                Two Writing Options
                One Option for Learning Activity
                One Oral Presentation of Writing Option or Option of Learning
                Reflection of Oral Presentation
                Photographs and Audio or Video Tape of Oral Presentation
                Most Satisfying Essay
                Reflection of Most Satisfying Essay
                Reflective Essay
Process: Students will be asked to keep all materials in a working folder
                during the unit and, as the end of the unit, pull items from their
                working folder to be placed in their portfolio.
Forms: Unit Portfolio form, Portfolio Sharing form, Reflection forms
Assessment: For assessment, three rubrics will be used for the Reflective
                Essay, Most Satisfying Piece, and the Oral Presentation.

to take responsibility for their learning and the communication of that learning to someone else. Roberson uses the sharing concepts in two ways. First, she has students share their portfolio with their parents and has the students and their parents complete a form entitled Portfolio Sharing (Figure 29). Using this form enables parents to interact with their students about what they are doing in school, to make a direct response to their students about the material found in the portfolio, and to sign the form for its return to school. They also have an opportunity to ask the teacher questions about the material.

Three items are assessed through the use of rubrics: the Reflective Essay (Figure 24), Most Satisfying Piece (Figure 25), and Options for Learning Oral Project (Figure 26). Roberson is able to indicate the assessment on each of the rubrics, using a range of descriptors and points to show level of evaluation. She also is able to show levels of concerns. HOC, MOC, LOC are abbreviations that are used to indicate that certain writing traits have High Order Concern, Medium Order Concern, or Low Order Concern. Figure 26 indicates that the content, organization,

Figure 24
Reflective Essay Assessment

_____ Evidence of reflection on growth as a communicator (30 points)
 _____ Strong evidence of improvement in content, word choice, sentence fluency, and risk taking within the portfolio.
 _____ Some evidence of improvement in content, word choice, sentence fluency, and risk taking within the portfolio.
 _____ Little/No evidence of improvement in content, word choice, sentence fluency, and risk taking within the portfolio.
_____ Effective organization of reflective essay (10 points)
 _____ Clear sense of beginning and ending, logical and effective sequencing, controlled pacing, and smooth transitions.
 _____ Some sense of beginning and ending, logical and effective sequencing, controlled pacing, and smooth transitions.
 _____ Little/No sense of beginning and ending, logical and effective sequencing, controlled pacing, and smooth transitions.
_____ Effective documentation of growth (10 points).
 _____ Strong use of supporting quotes from personal work.
 _____ Some use of supporting quotes from personal work.
 _____ Little/No use of supporting quotes from personal work.

and sentence fluency are of high concern, while voice and word choice have medium concern and conventions are of low concern for this paper. A similar rubric is devised for the Oral Project. The arrangement of traits for this activity have been rearranged to meet the needs of this particular assignment.

The final assessment is on the Human Rights Portfolio itself (Figure 30). A total of 400 points are used in this portfolio. These points are distributed by giving the major parts of the portfolio the greater number of points, while the less important components receive the smaller number.

You will find many of the qualities that we have come to believe are necessary for good portfolio assessment. A careful examination will find the following:

Active student, teacher, parent involvement
Metacognition skills
 self-reflection
 self-assessment
 goal-setting
 Choices
 Ownership
 Conferencing

Figure 25
Most Satisfying Piece Assessment

HOC (50%)

Content:

Organization:

Sentence Fluency:

MOC (40%)

Voice:

Word Choice:

LOC (10%)

Conventions:

Comments:

    Responsibility
    Sharing
    Growth over time

Teachers and students are finding the portfolio assessment enables students to take more of the responsibility in their education; it enables teachers to assess authentic student work showing how the student has grown over a period of time, and it enables parents to have a better understanding of the strengths and weaknesses of what their young people know and are able to do.

Figure 26
Options for Learning Oral Assessment

HOC (50%)

Preparation:

Presentation:

MOC (40%)

Organization:

Word Choice:

LOC (10%)

Creativity:

Comments:

The Writing/Reading Connection

We have throughout this chapter urged teachers to use the most creative measures to help students become the best writers that they can be. We have suggested, for example, that when students are having problems with beginnings that teachers show how published writers begin their works. Teachers bring to class 4 or 5 young adult novels and read the first 2 or 3 paragraphs showing students how some writers begin. We would go further and suggest that young adult literature is a

Figure 27
Most Satisfying Piece Reflection

1. Why did you choose this as your most satisfying piece of writing?

2. How did you come up with this topic?

3. How did you feel when you completed this piece?

4. Did you encounter any problems when writing this piece? If so, how did you solve them?

5. If you could have done something differently, what would it have been?

6. What are your writing goals for the next unit?

tremendous source for young writers. While writing in isolation may produce quality writers, but at some time, inexperienced writers need the visual model. Young writers need to interact with "real" authors. As students interact with these writers, they get a sense of what writers do. Writing a long, extended piece or a short poem takes time. It is not something that is done in a 50-minute class period. Students also realize that authors struggle to use just the right word; they work and rework their sentence beginnings so that the appropriate impression is made; and they think and write, both at the same time, in order to generate the best writing that they can create.

It is obvious that students are able to learn many of the writing techniques and strategies by reading literature to which they can relate. Students need not have the grammar book to learn language conventions for the literature itself provides students with effectively used metaphors,

Figure 28
**Options for Learning
Oral Presentation Reflection**

1. Why did you choose this oral presentation for your portfolio?

2. What steps did you take in research and/or in your written preparation that made this presentation your best?

3. What were your goals for improving your oral language skills in this unit?

4. Did you successfully reach those goals? If so, how? If not, what prevented you from reaching them?

5. What are your oral language goals for the next unit?

   1.

   2.

   3.

similes, dialogue, imagery, rhythm, humor and other such conventions. The important connection comes when students see the use of these strategies in the literature, and they begin to incorporate these techniques in their own writing. Students may learn of effective beginnings from Robert Cormier (*The Chocolate War*) or Lois Duncan (*Killing Mr. Griffin*); the unsent letter from Chris Crutcher (*Chinese Handcuffs*); symbolism from Mildred Taylor (*Roll of Thunder, Hear My Cry*); description and characterization from Sue Ellen Bridgers (*All Together Now*); setting from Robert Lipsyte (*The Contender*) or Gary Paulsen (*The Island*); flashback from S.E. Hinton (*The Outsiders*); or point of view from Gloria Miklowitz (*Good-Bye Tomorrow*) and Alice Childress (*A Hero Ain't Nothin' But a Sandwich*).

Perhaps most of all, literature gives students a source for written response. If used correctly, literature can inspire students to create original, thought-provoking writing. As students respond to literature, they are able to make connections between the universal themes found in litera-

Figure 29
Portfolio Sharing

The things I would like for you to look at tonight:

Parent Response

Three stars for you: * * *

*

*

*

One wish for you:

The most important thing I would like to say to you now is the following:

Parent's Signature _____ Date _____

Questions for the teacher:

ture and their own goals, visions, values, and morals. They are able to have vicarious experiences through their reading and compare these experiences with their own. In other writing, we have suggested that "writing that ties the literature and the student's world together helps students formulate answers to their personal dilemmas" (Bushman and Bushman, 1993, p. 65).

Writing Models

Many well-crafted young adult novels can serve young writers well as they read about writers at work. In Gary Paulsen's novel *The Island,* Wil

Figure 30
Human Rights Portfolio
Assessment

_____ Essay (100 points)

_____ Option for Learning oral presentation (100 points)

_____ Portfolio Contents (100 points)

_____ reflective essay (50 points)

_____ introduction to final products (20 points)

_____ preface (10 points)

_____ title page

_____ three reading responses

_____ three learning log entries

_____ two writing options   (20 points)

_____ photographs and audio or video tape of option for learning

_____ assignment form

uses writing to learn more about himself. He reflects on his surroundings and how he is interacting with his environment. S. E. Hinton's *Taming the Star Runner* includes Travis who has finished his first novel and has sent it off to be published. Important to young writers is Travis' attitude about his writing, the audience to whom he had thought he had written, and his overall concern about changing any part of this "finished" novel. Herb Karl's *The Toom County Mud Race* takes the form of a story written by Jackie, the main character. Jackie turns in his story one chapter at a time to Ms. Hartwell, his English teacher, who returns each chapter with her comments. Other books that would be useful to student writers include *The Man Who Was Poe*, Avi; *Chapters: My Growth as a Writer*, Duncan; and *Author! Author!* by Susan Terris.

Other forms of writing are found in many other young adult works. Writing is used for therapy and reflection in Chris Crutcher's novel *Chinese Handcuffs* and Jenny Davis' novel *Sex Education*. Journalism is found in Sandy Asher's *Summer Smith Begins,* William Bell's *Forbidden City,* and Dallin Malmgren's *The Ninth Issue.* Journals and diaries play important parts to many young adult novels. A few are mentioned here: *Alicia: My Story,* Alicia Appleman-Jurman; *Stotan,* Chris Crutcher; *Robyn's Book: A True Diary,* Robyn Miller; *A Haunting in Williamsburg,* Lou Kassem; and *A Begonia for Miss Applebaum,* Paul Zindel.

The connection of writing and literature is very strong. Reading leads to writing, and writing leads to reading. Richard Peck, a prominent young adult author, perhaps says it best: "Nobody but a reader ever became a writer." By using the reading/writing connection in the classroom, students are better able to incorporate much of what they read and learn about the writer's craft to their own writing.

Publishing Writing

Many avenues are open to teachers and students for publishing student writing—from the simple classroom collection in which everyone contributes a piece of writing to the more sophisticated national journal which publishes writing which has been selected by an editor or review committee. Whatever the source may be, it is imperative that teachers encourage students to publish their writing for it is evident that one type of publishing or another should be the goal of writing. Within the range of publishing sources mentioned above, students can find the appropriate place to have their pieces open to be read by others. A few of the sources are mentioned here:

In-class collection: Teachers simply collect writing at any given time and create a collection for the entire class to have. There is no selection process as all writing from all students is included. The collection remains in the class.

Collection exchange: Teachers collect writing as described above but exchange the class collections with other teachers and other classes.

School Publications: With this source for student publication, teachers move beyond the collection procedure in which everyone participates to a selective process in which a panel composed of students and teachers select writing that will be included. These are often called literary journals and represent the best writing in the school.

District Publications: If the school district is large enough in that there are many schools in the district, a similar process to the school publication can occur only at the district level. Students from across the district submit writing to be published in a district publication.

State Publications: State organizations such as the state affiliate of the National Education Association or the National Council of Teachers of English and others often publish student writing. Due to space limitations here, names of state journals can not be listed, but teachers can solicit information from state affiliates about the availability of journals that publish student writing.

National Publications: Many organizations publish student writing at the national level. Competition is keen since journals are limited to the amount of writing that can be published. A leader in the field of national publications is *Meryln's Pen*. Two editions are now available: the Intermediate Edition for grades 7–10 and the Senior Edition for grades 11 and 12. The address for information is P.O. Box 1058, East Greenwich, RI 02818. A second journal with national distribution is *The Writers' Slate*. It publishes student writing from grades K–12 and has three issues per year. Information may be obtained by writing P.O. Box 664, Ottawa, KS 66067. There are other sources as well: *Scholastic Voice*, 730 Broadway, New York, NY 10003; *Stone Soup*, Box 83, Santa Cruz, CA 95063 to mention just a few. The best source for publications for young writers is, perhaps, the *Market Guide for Young Writers* published by Shoe Tree Press of White Hall, Virginia.

FOR ADDITIONAL READING

Andrasick, Kathleen D. "Independent Repatterning: Developing Self-Editing Competence." *English Journal,* 82, 2, February, 1993

Antorino, Margaret. "Writing for the Public." *English Journal,* 82, 3, March, 1993.

Atwell, Nancy. *In the Middle: Reading and Writing with Adolescents.* Portsmouth, NH: Boynton/Cook, 1987.

Axelrod, Rise B. and Cooper, Charles. *The Concise Guide to Writing.* New York: St. Martin's Press, 1993.

Balderman, Jack; Grant, Cheryl; and O'Grady, Eileen. "Public Letters: Discover the Power of Good Writing." *English Journal,* 82, 3, March, 1993.

Belanoff, Pat and Dickson, Marcia. *Portfolios: Process and Product.* Portsmouth, NH: Boynton/Cook, 1991.

Bushman, John H. and Bushman, Kay P. *Using Young Adult Literature in the English Classroom.* New York: Macmillan, 1993.

Bushman, John H.; Goodson, F. Todd; and Ketter, Jean. *Using the 6-Trait Analytic Scale for Instruction: Activities for the Classroom—6-12.* Ottawa, KS: The Writing Conference, Inc., 1992.

Christiansen, Mark. "The Importance of Revision in Writing Composition." *The Education Digest*, 56, 2, 1990.

College Entrance Examination Board. *The Test of Standard Written English*. Princeton, NJ: Educational Testing Service, 1975.

Cooper, Charles. *Writing Assessment Handbook, Grade 8* (Revised Edition). Sacramento: California State Department of Education, 1987.

Daly, John and Miller, Michael. "The Empirical Development of an Instrument to Measure Writing Apprehension." *Research in the Teaching of English*, 9, 3, Winter, 1975.

Diedrich, Paul. *Measuring Growth in English*. Urbana, IL: NCTE, 1974.

Elbow, Peter. *Writing with Power*. New York: Oxford University Press, 1981.

Elbow, Peter. *Writing Without Teachers*. London: Oxford University Press, 1973

Emig, Janet. *The Composing Process of Twelfth Graders*. Urbana, IL: NCTE, 1971

Fulwiler, Toby. *The Journal Book*. Portsmouth, NH: Boynton/Cook, 1987.

Graves, Donald H. "An Examination of the Writing Processes of Seven-year-Old Children." *Research in the Teaching of English*, 9, 1975.

Graves, Donald H. *Teachers and Children at Work*. Portsmouth, NH: Heinemann, 1983.

Gilbert, Judith. *Portfolio Resource Guide: Creating and Using Portfolios in the Classroom*. Ottawa, KS: The Writing Conference, Inc., 1993.

Gill, Kent (ed). *Process and Portfolios in Writing Instruction*. Urbana, IL: NCTE, 1993.

Guth, Sheryl. "Publishing Student Writing." *English Journal*, 82, 2, February, 1993.

Hillocks, George. *Research on Written Composition*. Urbana, IL: ERIC Clearinghouse on Reading and Communication Skills and National Institute of Education, 1986.

Keim, Marybell C. "Creative Alternatives to the Term Paper." *The Education Digest*, 57, 4, 1991.

Killgallon, Dorothy. *Sentence Composing: The Complete Course*. Portsmouth, NH: Heinemann, 1987.

Kirby, Dan and Liner, Tom. *Inside Out*, 2nd Edition. Portsmouth, NH: Boynton/Cook, 1988.

Kirrie, M. *The English Composition Test with Essay*. New York: College Entrance Examination Board, 1979.

Lloyd-Jones, R. "Primary Trait Scoring" in C. Cooper & L. Odell (eds.) *Evaluating Writing*. Urbana, IL: NCTE, 1977.

Macrorie, Ken. *The I-Search Paper*, 2nd Ed. of *Searching Writing*. Portsmouth, NH: Boynton/Cook, 1988

Macrorie, Ken. *Writing to be Read*, 3rd. Ed. Portsmouth, NH: Boynton/Cook, 1984.

Madraso, Jan. "Proofreading: The Skill We've Neglected to Teach." *English Journal*, 82, 2, February, 1993.

Moffett, James. *Active Voice*. Portsmouth, NH: Boynton/Cook, 1981.

Murray, Donald. *The Craft of Revision*. Orlando, FL: Harcourt Brace Jovanovich, 1991.

Murray, Donald. *A Writer Teaches Writing*. Boston, Houghton Mifflin, 1985.

Murray, Donald. *Write to Learn*. New York, CBS College Publishing, 1984.

Olson, C. *Practical Ideas.* Sacramento, CA: California State Dept. of Education, 1987.

Paulson, F. L., Paulson, P.R., and Meyer, C.A. "What Makes a Portfolio a Portfolio?" *Educational Leadership,* 48, 5, 1991.

Powell, David. *What Can I Write About?* Urbana, IL: NCTE, 1981.

Rico, Gabrielle. *Writing the Natural Way.* Los Angeles: J.P. Tarcher, 1983.

Routman, Regie. *Invitations: Changing as Teachers and Learners K–12.* Portsmouth, NH: Heinemann, 1991.

Schuessler, Brian; Gere, Ann; and Abbot, Robert. "The Development of Scales Measuring Teacher Attitudes Toward Instruction in Written Composition: A Preliminary Investigation." *Research in the Teaching of English,* 15, 1, February, 1981.

Spandel, Vicki and Stiggins, Richard. *Creating Writers.* New York: Longman, 1990.

Stillman, Peter. *Writing Your Way.* Portsmouth, NH: Boynton/Cook, 1984.

Strong, William. *Sentence Combining: A Composing Book.* New York: Random House, 1983.

Tierney, R. J.; Carter, M.A.; Desai. L.E., *Portfolio Assessment in the Reading-Writing Classroom.* Norwood, MA: Christopher-Gordon, 1991.

Tompkins, Gail. *Teaching Writing: Balancing Process and Product.* Columbus, OH: Merrill, 1990.

Walling, Donovan R. *A Model for Teaching Writing: Process and Product.* (Fastback #256). Bloomington, IN: Phi Delta Kappa Educational Foundation, 1987.

Wilson, David E. "Teaching Writing: Middle Level Teachers Change their Focus." *Schools in the Middle,* 1, 2, Winter, 1991.

Wolf, Dennie Palmer. "Portfolio Assessment: Sampling Student Work. *Educational Leadership,* 46, 7, 1989.

Zemelmann, S. & Daniels, H. *A Community of Writers: Teaching Writing in the Junior and Senior High School.* Portsmouth, NH: Heinemann, 1988.

Chapter 6

TEACHING LITERATURE

We are sure that most teachers would agree that literature plays a most important role in the English curriculum. In fact, more emphasis is given to the study of literature than any other of the language arts. Certainly, we would agree that literature is an important component for students. The extent to which this emphasis is found may be open for discussion but we certainly do not discount the importance. For it is through literature that students can see themselves as well as others, but more on that in the next section.

There are a number of reasons for this popularity. Some feel more comfortable in teaching literature than in teaching language and composition; others really do believe that the study of literature is much more important than the other language arts and therefore should have more time spent on it in the curriculum. Too, we believe one of the major reasons for this emphasis is the model that is found in college teaching. English departments at colleges and universities offer far more literature courses than any other kinds. Rarely do students in a 36-hour English major have more than two or three courses in other areas. As we see it, the amount of literature included is not of primary importance but how we as teachers have our students relate to this literature.

RESPONDING TO LITERATURE

It seems to us that the primary goal for English teachers is to have their students become personally involved with the literature that they read. If we as English teachers can foster this personal involvement, students may develop more confidence in responding to what they read and relying less on the literary critics. All too often the voice of the critic has become the voice of authority, and students with less experience and knowledge have felt that their own responses are unacceptable. Students have rejected their own responses and accepted those of the critics.

That is not to say that the critics have no place in the English classroom.

They do. However, their place should be kept in perspective to the goals of the class. The critics' responses are to be considered not as better or worse than those of the students but as equals. They have other points of view, of course, distinguished with more experience and maturity, but their positions do not supersede the responses of the students.

All of this is to say that students should become actively involved with literature that they read. The experience should be enjoyable and successful. Teachers must be very careful not to become too analytical in their approach. If we stress the historical point of view, if we emphasize the particular genre, or if we center our attention on the literary techniques that the author may or may not have used, we may find many students with this attitude suggested by one ninth grade student: "I love to read but I hate literature." Our approach, then, must be to foster a different attitude, one that might result in students enjoying literature and reading voluntarily and not regarding reading as a task to be avoided if at all possible. While it is important to note these more technical characteristics of literature in classroom study, they do not command primary attention. The attention is given to the work itself, what the authors have to say, how they say it, and the students' personal responses to it. To help students to do this, teachers may wish to have students respond to a few of the following questions:

What is your first reaction to the work?
What feelings and/or emotions does the work evoke in you?
What character(s) do you particularly like? Dislike?
Do any of the characters remind you of people that you know?
What memory does the work help you recall? Have you been in a similar situation?

Of course, at some point in the activity, teachers will want to move students to perception, interpretation, and evaluation of what they have read:

Would you change the ending of the work? If so, how?
What do you consider to be the most important word, phrase, or quote in the work?
What reaction or explanation of the title do you have?
What fears and/or concerns do you have for the characters?
What is the major point of the work?
Does this work remind you of any other literary work?

What is your final reaction to the work? (Bushman and Bushman, p. 78).

To continue with a further example, students reading Harper Lee's *To Kill a Mockingbird* in a thematic unit entitled "Who is My Brother?" have as their primary concern investigation of such general questions as: How do the students feel about the apparent discrimination presented in the book? How does this discrimination affect them? Was Scout able to relate to the minority in the book? Can the reader relate in the same ways? Another way? How does each character affect the reader? Why is (or is not) Lee's story believable? It is at this point in the study of the Lee book that the teacher may turn from this *emotional* response to what we call the *intellectual* level of response. Now is the time to help students see that their responses occur not by accident but by design—the design of the author. They have these responses primarily because the author structured her work in such a way that the readers responded as they did. Now is the time for students to investigate the use of symbol, tone, figures of speech, and other important tools of writing.

We (Bushman & Bushman, 1993) have written of the struggle that teachers have when they work with literature in the classroom:

> The enjoyment of reading must be an integral part of the classroom to foster the positive attitude toward literature that is necessary for life-long reading. We want our students to enjoy the literature now, but we also want them to continue this enjoyment as they proceed to higher education or become productive members of society.
>
> The role, then, of the classroom teacher is to walk that fine line between having students read for the pleasurable act that it is and read to increase their powers of literary analysis and, thus, become members of an educated, literate society. To this end, teachers will want to make decisions carefully concerning the literature curriculum: its design and how it is delivered to students. In addition, teachers will want to structure lessons that will enable students to independently evaluate the quality of the literature they are reading. To know that we like a work is great; to know why we like it is even better (p. 27).

Although written in 1967, John Dixon's *Growth Through English* still seems to offer a point of view on reader response theory important to the contemporary classroom:

> On the other hand, response is a word of our making, an activity in which we are our own interpretive artist. The dryness of schematic analysis of imagery, symbols, myth, structural relations, et al., should be avoided passionately at school and often at college. It is literature, not literary criticism, which is the subject. It is vividly plain that it is much easier to teach literary criticism

than to teach literature, just as it is much easier to teach children to write according to abstract models of correctness than it is to teach them to use their own voices (p. 60).

Activities

There are a number of activities that you can structure for your students so that they may make a personal response to what they are reading. The following are but a few.

1. Certainly one of the most important ways for students to share their personal response to something they have read is by talking about it with others. Therefore, have many large and small group discussions skills before attempting group work. We have discussed this in Chapter 3. Many times you will wish to have specific tasks for students to explore in small groups. Then, follow this small group activity with reports of their findings to the entire group. It is important, too, that the discussions emphasize application, analysis, synthesis, and evaluation rather than just the memory or rote level of learning. Careful questioning of students will help them make these important personal responses.

2. Have students respond to Value Sheets. A value sheet consists of thought-provoking statements duplicated on a sheet of paper accompanied by a series of questions. You distribute these sheets to the students for their response. A Value Sheet can present literature and connect it to the students' lives. The sheet contains directed questions which help students to clarify their thinking. There are no right or wrong answers. For example, the following questions might be selected for a values sheet on Robert Frost's poem "The Road Not Taken." What was an important choice you have made in your life? What influence has your decision had? To what extent are you (not) proud of the choice that you made? Have the students responded to the questions? Be sure that their responses are related to the piece of literature.

An alternative approach is to pose a moral dilemma having to do with the literature that they have read. On the values sheet have students suggest how they think a character would solve a problem, how would they (the students) solve the problem, and in what ways are they and the character similar or different?

3. Help students to make their personal response to literature by structuring a creative drama experience for them. For a brief review of the process, reread Chapter 4. Pantomime, improvisation, and role playing

help students to become actively involved in what they read. Too, these creative experiences enable students to relate what they read to who they are and how they and the literature fit into their society.

4. Have students create a collage as their response to a given piece of literature. This collage may be created at home or as part of the class-room activity. Students use pictures, drawings, words and phrases, or any of these in combination. Students can paste these on large construction or poster paper so that it is suitable for sharing with the entire class. The collage should reflect the students' understanding or interpretation of the literature. Have students share and discuss their collages. Encourage interaction among members of the class as the project is shared.

5. Have students bring to class pictures which they feel reflect some important response that they have for a particular piece of literature. Pictures are very good for sharing interpretations of tone and mood of a story or poem.

6. Students frequently enjoy creating an audiovisual response to literature. They do this through the use of music, film, and slides. While this activity is perhaps best suited for end of unit projects, it can be effective when used for daily assignments.

7. Have students respond to what they have read by writing. We do urge caution when you have students write. We do not suggest writing to be used for analytical purposes unless the writers are quite experienced and have been through the writing sequence. They should be ready for the Structured Writing segment of the composing process as outlined in Chapter 5. It is our suggestion to have students simply respond to the literature. They might respond to one of the following: Did the literature make them think about something that they hadn't thought about before? Could they react to a particular character? Did the literature establish a particular mood to which they might respond? Have they had a similar experience that they could share?

8. If students are into the more structured part of the writing program, they can write more sophisticated expositions. By taking a point of view of a thesis from a work, students can develop an argumentative or informative essay.

Earlier we mentioned our concern about the teaching of terminology. Even though "how" it is taught is important, perhaps "when" it is taught is more important. As we have suggested, the personal response—the emotional level—comes first. As teachers move into the more structured analysis of the work, terminology may be important. The advantage, of course, is that it does provide handles to help in the discussion. When the terms are taught, they should be presented in such a way so that the emphasis is still on the enjoyment of reading. There are a number of terms that can be introduced from time to time: character, theme, setting, tone, mode, literal language, and figurative language. We have suggested five in the following activity.

9. Have students use the study response questions relating to plot, character, theme, setting, and style below. We caution you concerning their use: they should be used as *resource questions* that are used during discussions rather than study questions that are used in isolation.

Plot

1. What is the main conflict? Who does it involve?
2. In what way is the conflict resolved? Does the resolution flow normally from the story line, or does it seem contrived and unnatural? Explain.
3. How are the various incidents in the plot related? What is the order in which the incidents are presented? Does the order help or hinder reading? To what extent are flashback and foreshadowing used?
4. To what extent did the resolution of the conflict violate your values? Did the story end in a way that was consistent with your ideas of right and wrong?

Character

1. Who are the main characters?
2. What are the relationships among them?
3. What kind of person is each character? What are higher traits?
4. How are these traits revealed? What does the author do to help you see what kind of person the character is?
5. Who are the minor characters who have at least a supportive role in the story?
6. What are the relationships of the minor characters to the main characters?
7. How do you react to each of the characters? Why?
8. What did the characters make you think about? Explain.
9. What happens to each of the characters? What do their fates indicate about their relationships to the theme of the work?
10. Is the character presentation believable? Explain.

Theme

1. What ideas are presented in the work? Which of these are most prominent?
2. To what extent are the characters important in the development of the theme? Give examples.
3. How does the theme fit in with your experiences? Give examples of experiences that you have had that are consistent with this theme.
4. Is the theme suggested in this work consistent with your value system? Explain.

Setting

1. When, where, how and with whom does the literature begin? To what extent did this beginning affect you as you began to read this work?
2. When, where, how and with whom does the literature end? To what extent did this ending affect you as you finished the work?
3. How does the setting affect the events and the characters? How would a change in time or location affect the credibility of the story?
4. To what extent does the setting establish the mood of the story? Give examples to justify your response.

Style

1. What kinds of sentences and paragraphs does the author use in telling the story? Long or short? Simple or complex? Factual or reflective? Give examples to illustrate your answer.
2. How would you characterize the author's word choices and phrasing? Simple? Sophisticated? How do diction, phrasing, and sentence structure relate to the characters? Give examples.
3. How does the style relate to the plot?
4. Select passages that were particularly effective to you. Explain how the author's style make them that way.

WHAT LITERATURE DO WE TEACH?

The question of what literature to include in the English curriculum has been discussed for many years. Some educators feel very strongly that there is a body of knowledge—a set of literary works—in English that most students (and some would say every student) should know by the time they finish their formal education. Other educators, of course, take a different view. They contend that literature is not a body of knowledge that must be learned. They believe that literature is to provide a confrontation with life and that its function is to help students to make a personal discovery. Therefore, it would follow that not every student, necessarily, should be confronted with the works of Chaucer, Shakespeare, Milton, Dryden, Joyce, etc. Too, the major criteria that should be used in determining the choice of literature included in the curriculum are student interest and ability, as well as the appropriateness of a given work for a particular school and community. Contemporary literature, especially the adolescent novels, would most assuredly find their way into curriculums designed by teachers favoring this second approach but would probably be in conflict with attitudes expressed by those favoring the first position.

The day when every student need read the same work has gone. Because of this flexibility of choice of literature, it allows for a number of different types of literature to be read by a number of different students within the same course framework. Stephen and Susan Judy (1979) make a few suggestions when choosing literature for the curriculum. They suggest that teachers keep in mind some of the following questions:

1. Have I included literature that challenges my students' values as well as literature that reinforces them?
2. Have I made available literature that represents the ethnic backgrounds of the students in my class?
3. Have I included literature that shows peoples and life-styles new for my students?
4. Have I been attentive to the images of male and female presented in the literature I have chosen?
5. Have I been careful to balance stereotypical views of people, values, and life-styles with more precise, detailed, and authentic views?
6. Have I chosen literature that emphasizes similarities and universals as well as differences and unique qualities?
7. Have I focused on the work's literary merits as well as its social and political merits?
8. Have I been sensitive to stereotypes that might be damaging or

hurtful to students who are in the minority in the class or school
(be they Anglo, black, Oriental, male, or female)?
   9. Have I provided a richness of alternatives so that students may
      have choices in their reading?
  10. Have I provided opportunities for discussion images of people,
      their values, and their life-styles as they are presented in literature?
      (p. 133).

Young Adult Literature

Perhaps the most powerful curriculum material that can turn young
people on to reading is young adult literature. Whether it be the YA
novel, short story, poem, or drama, no other literature has made such an
impact on young adults. Authors such as Robert Cormier, Richard Peck,
Chris Crutcher, Paula Danziger, Mel Glenn and anthologists such as
Paul Janeczko, Donald Gallo, and Ellen Conford have contributed greatly
to the amount of reading done by young adults. If our goal in schools is
to make lifelong readers out of our students, these writers along with
many others not mentioned have made substantial contributions to that
end.

The major problem, as we see it, is that most of these authors are not
read in the classroom. Often young adult literature is relegated to the
book report or literature read for pleasure outside of the classroom.

Myths About Young Adult Literature

The following myths are often used as reasons for not using young
adult literature as regular fare for students to read in English classes.
   1. *Young adult literature is simplified to accommodate low reading skills
      and, therefore, the quality is not good.*
Nothing could be further from the truth. Paterson's *Jacob, Have I
Loved,* Sleator's *Intersteller Pig,* Myers' *Fallen Angels,* Cormier's *After the
First Death,* Bridgers' *Permanent Connections,* Taylor's *Roll of Thunder,
Hear My Cry,* Voight's *Dicey's Song,* and Crutcher's *Chinese Handcuffs*
have universal themes for students to work with: strong character
development; many literary techniques such as flashback, foreshadowing,
imagery, and many others; and offer students many opportunities to use
higher level critical thinking skills as they discuss or write in response to
these novels.

There are those novels that are shorter and offer less depth for study but, while they may not appeal to adults, they do appeal to their intended audience—the young adult. Danziger's *The Cat Ate My Gymsuit*, Duncan's *Killing Mr. Griffin*, Lipsyte's *The Contender*, Mazer's *When We First Met*, Hinton's *Taming the Star Runner*, and Carter's *Robo Dad* still provide opportunities for discussion, critical thinking, literary qualities appropriate for grade level and promote a great deal of literary appreciation.

2. *Young adult literature is anti-adult or anti-parent.*

Early young adult literature had more of this characteristic than the literature of today. The early literature of Paul Zindel, for example, had adult characters that were less than desirable. We have indicated below a list of contemporary young adult literature which contains positive adult role models.

Kaye's	*Real Heroes*
Bridgers'	*Keeping Christina*
Crutcher's	*Running Loose*
Peck's	*Remember the Good Times*
Mazer's	*After the Rain*
Hobbs'	*Beardance*
Rinaldi's	*In My Father's House*
Crutcher's	*Staying Fat for Sarah Byrnes*

Whether a work is anti-adult/parent is secondary to the other more positive characteristics that may be apart of the literature. Because one, two, or many YA novels have less than desirable adults is not grounds for stereotyping all young adult literature as anti-adult or anti-parent. In fact, some very fine YA novels—Cormier's *The Chocolate War*, Mazer's *Taking Terri Mueller*, Crutcher's *Chinese Handcuffs*—have adults that exert negative influences but offer powerful themes that are not unlike those found in contemporary society which, as we all know, is comprised of many negative adults. Many young people come in contact almost daily with abusive parents, negative and abusive teachers, and other not so desirable adults. As one adolescent said when asked why he was reading Chris Crutcher's *Chinese Handcuffs* in light of the very serious and sophisticated issues and themes found in the book: "I want to meet these issues in a book before I meet them in real life."

3. *YA novels are too frequently under the fire of censorship.*

It is true that young adult novels do come under the censor's ax, but this does not occur any more than with other books read in the classroom. In fact, over the years, the young adult novel, while getting full attention by the censors, certainly is not the only literature being censored. Frequently, adult books read by adolescents in schools find their way on the censor's list: Steinbeck's *Of Mice and Men* and *The Grapes of Wrath,* Huxley's *Brave New World,* Golding's *Lord of the Flies,* Vonnegut's *Slaughterhouse-Five,* Kesey's *One Flew Over the Cuckoo's Nest,* Hemingway's *The Sun Also Rises,* Fitzgerald's *The Great Gatsby,* Orwell's *1984* and *Animal Farm,* Twain's *Adventures of Huckleberry Finn,* Shakespeare's *Romeo and Juliet, Othello,* and *The Merchant of Venice,* to mention only a few. We think it safe to say that at one time or another most all books that are read in schools have been censored; therefore, we feel it unfair to suggest that young adult literature any more than any other literature be held out of the classroom due to the threat of being censored.

Creating Lifelong Readers

What it really comes down to is that teachers must resolve the question of why they have literature in the curriculum. For us, while there are many secondary reasons, the primary reason for having students read is to promote reading as a life-long endeavor. It seems to us that if we want a literate population—one that can think critically, be apart of the decision making process, be aware of relevant issues confronting society, and understand the pleasurable nature of reading—schools must educate their students with skills and understanding so that young people can become the adults that will carry on effectively the affairs of their educated community.

Reading is an important key. Choosing the right literature for the classroom enables young people to become readers who will continue to read into adulthood. Choosing the wrong literature may very well stop the reading process completely. The track record for schools is not good. Lesesne (1991) surveyed middle school students and found that "almost seventy-five percent of the middle school students reported reading less than one hour daily on a regular basis; twenty percent had read only one book for their own enjoyment in the last six months" (p. 61). O'Connor (1980) believes it isn't that students in schools can't read; it is that they don't want to read because of the lack of connection between the reader and what is read. And we know that society is comprised of many, many nonreading adults. Angelotti (1981) lays the blame at the door step of the school with its outdated literature curriculum. In sum, the works of Gary

Paulsen, Robert Cormier, Chris Crutcher, Cynthia Voight, Walter Dean Myers, Lois Duncan, Katherine Paterson, and many, many more young adult authors turn kids on to reading and keep them reading. *The Autobiography of Benjamin Franklin, Silas Marner, Great Expectations, Moby Dick, The Great Gatsby,* to mention only a few, probably will not.

Why do these works as well as most of the other literature found in the literary canon turn young people off to reading? One of the major reasons for this is that this "great" literature was written for adults, primarily educated adults, and not for young people. Writers really did not intend for young people to read their works. In addition, young adult readers struggle with the style, syntax, and vocabulary often found in the classics. In addition, not many young adults can relate to the themes and human conditions found in this literature. Therefore, students often do not read what is assigned and teachers resort to interpreting the literature for their students. As a result, students have a very negative experience in a process that should be exhilarating.

It is not that students cannot respond to literature or even make literary analyses about what they read. They can and often do it well. But they do it when they have read something that meets their emotional, experiential, cognitive, and developmental levels.

Literature Organization

How to organize literature in the English classroom offers teachers a variety of patterns: One Book, One Class; Thematically; Thematic Units; and One Book, One Student.

One Book, One Class: Perhaps the most widely used pattern of literature organization involves all students reading the same book. Problems with this arrangement include not meeting the needs and interests of each student. We know that not all students in any given class will have the same reading interests and abilities. As a result, teachers usually teach to the middle in that they choose a work that will try to satisfy the majority of students; but sometimes when this occurs, the brighter students become bored and the slower students can't seem to keep up. While we cannot list all authors whose books seem to work for this arrangement, we have listed a few. There is a danger in doing this as not all works by one author may be suitable for an entire class to read; however, with careful reading before choosing the book, teachers will be able to make appropriate choices.

The following authors have written novels that, in most situations, would be suitable for the one book, one class pattern:

Norma Fox Mazer	Robert Lipsyte	Bruce Stone
Robert Cormier	Chris Crutcher	Robb White
Lois Duncan	Peter Dickinson	William Bell
Gary Paulsen	Bruce Books	S.E. Hinton
Paul Zindel	Madeleine L'Engle	Sandy Asher
Sue Ellen Bridgers	Richard Peck	Rudolfo Anaya
Katherine Paterson	Fran Arrick	Linda Crew
Robert Newton Peck	Cynthia Voight	Will Hobbs
Lawrence Yep	Walter Dean Myers	Ouida Sebestyn
M. E. Kerr	William Sleator	Phyllis Reynolds Naylor
Mildred Taylor	Margaret Mahy	Dallin Malmgren
Lois Lowry	Scott O'Dell	Bette Greene
Sheila Gordon	Gloria Miklowitz	Robin Brancato
Lois Ruby	Cynthia Rylant	Ann Rinaldi

Thematically Arranged: The use of themes is very effective in helping students to connect literature to their lives in that most of the themes chosen are related specifically to the interests of students. The major advantage of using themes is that a variety of books can be chosen to meet varying abilities and interests. For example, at the middle level teachers may choose the friendship theme and include Sheila Gordon's *Waiting for the Rain* for the higher range of ability, Bruce Brooks' *The Moves Make the Man* for the middle range, and Robert Cormier's *Other Bells for Us to Ring* for the lower range. Through the use of groups, teachers can have students read and discuss each of these books by emphasizing the theme and how the books are similar. In addition to meeting varying needs and abilities, teachers using this arrangement are helping students to come in contact with more excellent literature. Each student reads one book but hears about two others. Below is a list of possible themes along with representative literature that fits into that theme.

Teen Pressure

Cadnum, Michael	*Breaking the Fall*
Childress, Alice	*A Hero Ain't Nothin' But a Sandwich*
Cormier, Robert	*The Chocolate War*
Cormier, Robert	*We All Fall Down*
Peck, Richard	*Princess Ashley*
Strasser, Todd	*Angel Dust Blues*

City Life/Gangs

Bonham, Frank	*Durango Street*
Hinton, S.E.	*The Outsiders*
Myers, Walter Dean	*The Mouse Rap*
Myers, Walter Dean	*Scorpions*
Santiago, Danny	*Famous All Over Town*

Decisions

Avi	*Nothing But the Truth*
Cormier, Robert	*Tunes for Bears To Dance To*
Duncan, Lois	*Killing Mr. Griffin*
Sleator, William	*The Duplicate*
Strasser, Todd	*The Accident*
Voight, Cynthia	*Izzy Willy Nilly*

Sports

Brancato, Robin	*Winning*
Brooks, Bruce	*The Moves Make the Man*
Crutcher, Chris	*Stotan*
Dygrad, Thomas	*Backfield Package*
Lipsyte, Robert	*The Brave*
Lipsyte, Robert	*The Chief*
Lipsyte, Robert	*The Contender*
Miklowitz, Gloria	*Anything to Win*
Myers, Walter Dean	*Hoops*

Ethnic Experiences

Crew, Linda	*Children of the River*
Grover, Wayne	*Ali and the Golden Eagle*
Hobbs, Will	*The Big Wander*
Myers, Walter Dean	*18 Pine Street* series
O'Dell, Scott	*Streams to the River, River to the Sea*
Paulsen, Gary	*The Crossing*
Paulsen, Gary	*Dogsong*
Paulsen, Gary	*Nightjohn*
Robinson, Margaret	*A Woman of Her Tribe*
Soto, Gary	*Pacific Crossing*
Staples, Suzanne	*Shabanu, Daughter of the Wind*
Thomas, Joyce	*Marked by Fire*
Yep, Laurence	*Dragonwings*

Thematic Units: The thematic arrangement of literature can be expanded into units which make for a very effective curriculum design. The advantage of using units allows teachers to integrate the language arts so that literature, language, writing, and oral English skills are taught in relation to one another. Another advantage, of course, is that teachers are able to broaden the use of young adult literature with the use of young adult poetry, short stories, drama, and nonfiction. We write in more detail about thematic units as a curriculum design in Chapter 9; but we do want to indicate here a few of the collections of short stories, poetry, drama, and nonfiction written with the young adult in mind which can be used quite effectively within thematic units.

Short stories

Athletic Shorts, Chris Crutcher
Baseball in April and Other Stories, Gary Soto
Connections, ed. Donald Gallo
Do You Like it Here? And Other Stories — Twenty-One Views of the High School Years, R. Benard.
8 Plus 1, Robert Cormier
A Gathering of Flowers: Stories About Being Young in America, Joyce Carol Thomas
If This Is Love, I'll Take Spaghetti, Ellen Conford
In Camera and Other Stories, Robert Westall
I Love You, I Hate You, Get Lost, Ellen Conford
Local News, Gary Soto
The People Could Fly: American Black Folktales, Virginia Hamilton
Short Circuits, ed. Donald Gallo
Sixteen, ed. Donald Gallo
Visions, ed. Donald Gallo
When the Nightingale Sings, Joyce Carol Thomas

Poetry

And Still I Rise, Maya Angelou
Back to Class, Mel Glenn
Class Dismissed! High School Poems, Mel Glenn
Class Dismissed II: More High School Poems, Mel Glenn
A Fire in My Hands, Gary Soto
In the Trail of the Wind: American Indian Poems and Ritual Orations, ed. John Beirhorst
Just Give Me A Cool Drink of Water 'fore I Die, Maya Angelou

My Friend's Got This Problem, Mr. Candler, Mel Glenn
Pocket Poems: Selected for a Journey, ed. Paul Janeczko
Poetspeak: In Their Work, About Their Work, ed. Paul Janeczko
Postcard Poems: A Collection of Poetry for Sharing, ed. Paul Janeczko
The Place My Words Are Looking For, ed. Paul Janeczko
Preposterous: Poems of Youth, ed. Paul Janeczko
Sports Pages, Arnold Adoff
A Time to Talk, Myra Cohn Livingston

Drama

Center Stage: One-Act Plays for Teenage Readers and Actors, ed. Donald Gallo
Langston, Ossie Davis
Mass Appeal, Ossie Davis
Meeting the Winter Bike Rider and Other Prize Winning Plays, ed. Wendy Lamb
The Outsiders, adapted by Christopher Sergel
A Separate Peace, adapted by Nancy Pahl Gilsenan
Theatre for Youth: Twelve Plays with Mature Themes, ed. Coleman Jennings and Gretta Berghammer
A Woman Called Truth, Sandy Asher

Nonfiction

Ain't Gonna Study War No More: The Story of America's Peace Seekers, Milton Meltzer
Beating the Odds, Stories of Unexpected Achievers, Janet Bode
Black Dance in America, James Haskins
Born to the Land: An American Portrait, Brent Ashabranner
Chapters: My Growth as a Writer, Lois Duncan
Dear America: Letters Home from Vietnam, B. Edelman
Eleanor Roosevelt, A Life of Discovery, Russell Freedman
Fighting Back: What Some People Are Doing About AIDS, Susan Kuklin
It's Our World, Too!, Phillip Hoose
Speaking Out, Teenagers Take on Race, Sex, and Identity, Susan Kuklin
Straight Talk About Death for Teenagers, Earl A. Grollman

One Book, One Student: This arrangement probably is best suited for teachers who wish to meet the individual interests and abilities of their students. Reading interests, developmental levels, and intellectual abilities are taken into consideration as teachers help students choose books to read. This arrangement is often used with outside reading culminating with a book report to be handed in or shared with the class. Some teachers use this arrangement for the regular classroom as well.

Atwell (1987) suggests that students choose their own reading. She then incorporates the literature and writing into a classroom reading/ writing workshop. Leighton (1991) describes her procedure in the classroom as "saturation reading." Each student is reading books which are incorporated into classroom discussion, writing, and projects. While this arrangement best meets the needs of individual students, it does provide more of a challenge to the teacher who must orchestrate a classroom of students all reading different books.

Young adult literature—with its conflicts, its themes, its protagonists, and its language—should be a part of the English curriculum to help young people move from the literature of the elementary grades to the more sophisticated reading of adults. In using this literature, teachers may be giving students the most rewarding gift that they can give: the desire to become lifelong readers.

BOOK REPORTS

Teachers frequently assign book reports or book projects to be completed each grading period. Our experience suggests that these book reports are often dull and boring and have very little, if any, impact on other students in the class. We make the following suggestions concerning book reports if they are to be included in your course.

Book reports should be an integral part of the English program. We believe the choice of book should be related in some way to the general study that is taking place in the class. Too, the reports themselves should be given so that other students can benefit.

What to do? After students have read the book, they do two things: write a book critique and prepare a creative project. We have provided information and examples here.

The Book Critique

Students fill out a 4- × -6 index card similar to the one shown in Figure 31. These cards are then kept by the teacher so that other students in the class and in future classes may have access to them for ideas for book choices.

Figure 31
Book Critique

Category   Title
                                            Author
                                            Reviewed by
Main characters & brief description _____
_____
_____
Time & setting of story _____
_____
Brief plot summary _____
_____
_____
_____
Main theme of story _____
_____
_____

(back of card)

Your opinion of the book _____
_____
_____
_____
_____
_____
_____
_____
_____
_____
_____
_____
_____

The Creative Projects

Oral

1. Have students create a T-shirt which displays various elements (plot, characters, setting, theme) from their book. Suggest that they wear T-shirts to class as they explain and point out the significance and relationship of its design.
2. Have students who have read the same book work together in creating a "Meet the Author" spot for a talk show. Suggest that they watch some talk shows (e.g. "Today," "Good Morning America," "The Tonight Show") for ideas on how the presentation could be set up.
3. Suggest that students select appropriate background music to enhance an oral reading of specific passages. Have them bring to class any records or tapes of musical excerpts which represent the mood or atmosphere of the book. Have students read the passages accompanied by the music.

Written

4. Have students add onto their book by doing one of the following:
   - Rewrite the introduction of the story.
   - Write an additional chapter to be attached at the end of the book.
   - Write a chapter that could have been included somewhere in the middle of the book.
5. Have students write a letter using the following suggestions:
   - Imagine that you are sending the book you've read to a friend as a present. Write a letter to your friend explaining why you think the book will make enjoyable reading.
   - Write a letter from one of the book's characters to another.
   - Then write a letter from the second character, answering the first letter.
   - Write a letter of advice to a character on how to handle his or her problems.
   - Write a letter to a character inviting him/her to dinner and explaining why you'd like to meet him/her.
   - Write a letter to your school librarian giving reasons why he/she should recommend this book to other students.
   - Pretend you are one of the judges for the Pulitzer prize for

literature. Decide whether or not you would nominate the book you've just read for such an award. Then write a letter to the author explaining why you've accepted or rejected his/her work to compete for such high honors.

6. Have students prepare a party guest list of their favorite characters in the book and follow through with one of these activities:
   a. Write a short paper explaining why you invited each of these characters.
   b. Write a one-act play about the actual party.
   c. Write a gossip column describing the actual party.

7. Suggest that students write a diary entry covering an important scene or chapter that might have been written by one of the book's main characters. If needed, have them provide enough background knowledge so that the diary is fully understood by their audience.

8. Have them take an interesting character from their book and put that character into an original short story.

9. Have students write a television commercial script advertising their book. Be sure that they include necessary stage directions as well as description of sets and dialogues.

10. Students can design a bookmark that includes a brief plot summary and recommendation for a book they may have read. Have them study blurbs from other books to gather ideas.

11. Have students write a book review on their book that would be appropriate to submit to the school newspaper. Students can study reviews from other newspapers and magazines to get ideas.

12. Have students create a crossword puzzle using characters, places, and events from their book as the entries.

Oral or Written

13. Have students explain why they would place their book in a time capsule that will be opened 100 years from now. What messages would they include to the readers of the future to explain their choices?

14. Have students put themselves in the shoes of a character in the book and respond to several of the following questions:
    • How do you feel about the way you were portrayed in this book?
    • What was your most difficult moment in the book?
    • What was going through your mind during this difficult moment?
    • If you could change any of your actions in the book, what would you do differently?

- How do you really feel about the other main characters in the book?
- Describe your strengths and weaknesses.
- Would you like the reader to know other things about you that were not covered in the book? If so, describe these characteristics.
- What are your feelings about the way the author ended the book?

15. Have students quote a favorite passage from their book and explain why it is particularly special to them. If needed, be sure that they give their audience enough background knowledge to be able to understand and appreciate the passage.

16. In an age focusing on women's rights, it would be most interesting if a female character from a book could voice her opinion. Have students choose one of the women characters from their book and give her opinion of the feminist movement.

17. If students are interested in astrology, have them choose the birth sign that best fits the major character of their book and explain their choice. Have them use specific examples from the book to support their choice.

18. Have students write a poem that they think would make a good introduction to their book. Or, they could write a series of short poems that would make good openers for each chapter. If oral, they could read these aloud and explain how they relate to the book. If written, they could include an explanation of their relationship to the book.

19. As a director casting parts for a movie or television adaptation of their book, students could tell what actors and actresses they would choose for the leading and supporting roles and why they made those choices.

20. Have students explain why they would or would not want to have one of the characters from their book as their best friend.

21. Have students create a new character for their book. Have them explain what he/she could add to the story in terms of other characters, plot, etc. At what point would they introduce their new personality? Have them rewrite a short section of the book, introducing their new character into the story. If oral, have them share this introduction with the class.

22. Have students fit one or more of the characters from their book

into any of the following roles and explain their choice(s): I could see _____ as:

A. a host of "Saturday Night Live."
B. my husband/wife.
C. Mr. "T's" rival.
D. a powerful politician.
E. Superman's best friend.

23. Have students design a large poster advertising their book to the rest of the class. They should include attention-getting headlines, blurbs, quotations, and visual materials to attract readers to the book. Also, suggest that they use appropriate propaganda techniques which would persuade others to read it. If oral, students present advertisement to class and explain why they chose the various element that they did. If written, they include a written explanation concerning the appropriateness of the advertisement for their particular book.

24. Suggest that they are planning a party with a theme based on their novel. Have them describe their ideas for invitations and decorations, as well as food and entertainment. If they're really ambitious, they might create samples of the invitations or some decorations. Have them explain what the theme is and specifically how it relates to the book.

25. Suggest that students are fixed up on a blind date with one of the characters from their book. They are thrilled when they open the door! They tell who is standing there and they explain why they are so happy. Now they imagine that they are miserable when they open the door and feel like slamming it in this person's face. Who is it? Why are they so disappointed?

26. Have students design a series of comic strips which illustrate several scenes or themes from their book. Students can reproduce dialogue from the book itself or create new, appropriate dialogue to fit the sequences. If oral, students can present comic strips to the class, relating them to the happenings in the book. If written, they can include a written explanation as to how they relate to the book.

27. Students can design a collage that reflects the mood of the book, or that in some way represents an important character from the book. They should include words with different print styles cut out from magazines or newspapers, their own drawings, different colors,

textures, and materials that convey something special about the book. If oral, they explain various aspects of the collage to the class. If written, they include a written explanation of the collage and relate several of its elements in their book.

Book Report Forms

Many times teachers are unable to incorporate these more involved book projects into their program; therefore, we have included a few less complicated Book Report Forms (See Figures 32–35). These are written so that students may give the pertinent information about the book that they read but do not have to go into a great deal of detail.

Figure 32
Book Report—Fiction

Directions: Complete the following as accurately as you can.

Title _____ Author _____

Copyright _____ Publisher _____ No. of Pages _____

1. Write a short paragraph about the author's background.

2. What is the setting (time and place) of the book?

3. Describe two main characters in the book and explain their roles in the story.

4. In most every novel there exists some type of conflict situation which usually involves the main character. Fully describe the conflict and explain how it is dealt with.

5. What is the theme in this book and how does it relate to the story?

6. Fully describe your favorite part of the book.

7. Would you recommend this book to others? Why or Why not?

Figure 33
Book Report—Non Fiction (Historical)

Directions: Complete the following as accurately as you can.

Title _____ Author _____

Copyright _____ Publisher _____ No. of Pages _____

1. How was the author qualified to write on this subject?

2. What is the setting (time and place) of the book?

3. Why was the subject important enough for a book to be written about it?

4. Fully explain the two most important things you learned about the subject.

5. Describe the conflict situation in this book and explain how it is dealt with.

6. Do you think people one hundred years from now could gain from reading about this subject? Why or Why not?

7. Would you recommend this book to others? Why or Why not?

Figure 34
Book Report—Biography/Autobiography

Directions: Complete the following as accurately as you can.

Title _____ Subject _____ Author _____

Copyright _____ Publisher _____ No. of Pages _____

1. What is the setting (time and place) of the book?

2. (Biography) What relationship exists between the subject and the author?

   (Autobiography) How does the subject describe himself/herself?

3. Describe three accomplishments of this person.

4. What obstacles did this person have to overcome to maintain his/her status in life?

5. How would you judge the technique in maintaining his/her status? (For example, was it morally sound?)

6. Do you think people one hundred years from now could gain from reading about this person? Why or Why not?

7. Would you recommend this book to others? Why or Why not?

Figure 35
Book Report—Non Fiction (Informational)

Directions: Complete the following as accurately as you can.

Title _____ Author _____

Copyright _____ Publisher _____ No. of Pages _____

1. How was the author (or editor) qualified to write on this subject?

2. Why did the subject interest you enough to read a book about it?

3. What were two new ideas you learned about this subject? Fully explain.

4. Briefly outline the steps necessary to accomplish any one task explained in the book.

5. How will you make use of the information in the book?

6. Would you recommend this book to others? Why or Why not?

YOUNG ADULT LITERATURE CITED

Adoff, Arnold. *Sports Pages.* New York: J. B. Lippincott, 1986.

Angelou, Maya. *And Still I Rise.* New York: Random House, 1978.

Angelou, Maya. *Just Give Me A Cool Drink of Wather 'fore I Die.* New York: Random House, 1971.

Ashabranner, Brent. *Born to the Land: An American Portrait.* New York: G.P. Putman's Sons, 1989.

Asher, Sandy. *Out of Here.* New York: Lodestar Books, 1993.

Asher, Sandy. *A Woman Called Truth.* Woodstock, IL: Dramatic, 1989.

Avi. *Nothing But the Truth.* New York: Orchard, 1991.

Beirhorst, John, ed. *In the Trail of the Wind: American Indian Poems and Ritual Orations.* New York: Farrar, Straus & Giroux, 1987.

Benard, R, ed. *Do You Like it Here? And Other Stories — Twenty-One Views of the High School Years.* New York: Dell, 1989.

Bode, Janet. *Beating the Odds, Stories of Unexpected Achievers.* New York: Franklin Watts, 1991.

Bonham, Frank. *Durango Street.* New York: Dell, 1965.

Brancato, Robin. *Winning.* New York: Dell, 1977.

Bridgers, Sue Ellen. *Keeping Christina.* New York: Harper Collins, 1993.

Bridgers, Sue Ellen. *Permanent Connections.* New York: Dell, 1987.

Brooks, Bruce. *The Moves Make the Man.* New York: Harper & Row, 1984.

Cadnum, Michael. *Breaking the Fall.* New York: Viking, 1992.

Carter, Alden. *RoboDad.* New York: G. P. Putnam's Sons, 1990.

Childress, Alice. *A Hero Ain't Nothin' But a Sandwich.* New York: Avon, 1973.

Conford, Ellen. *I Love You, I Hate You, Get Lost.* New York: Scholastic, 1994.

Conford, Ellen. *If This Is Love, I'll Take Spaghetti.* New York: Scholastic, 1983.

Cormier, Robert. *After the First Death.* New York: Dell, 1979.

Cormier, Robert. *The Chocolate War.* New York: Dell, 1974.

Cormier, Robert. *8 Plus 1.* New York: Pantheon, 1980.

Cormier, Robert. *Other Bells for Us to Ring.* New York: Delacorte Press, 1990.

Cormier, Robert. *Tunes for Bears To Dance To.* New York: Delacorte Press, 1992.

Cormier, Robert. *We All Fall Down.* New York: Delacorte Press, 1991.

Crew, Lina. *Children of the River.* New York: Delacorte Press, 1989.

Crutcher, Chris. *Athletic Shorts.* New York: Greenwillow Books, 1991.

Crutcher, Chris. *Chinese Handcuffs.* New York: Greenwillow Books, 1989.

Crutcher, Chris. *Running Loose.* New York: Dell, 1983.

Crutcher, Chris. *Staying Fat for Sarah Byrnes.* New York: Greenwillow Books, 1993.

Crutcher, Chris. *Stotan.* New York: Dell, 1986.

Danziger, Paula. *The Cat Ate My Gymsuit.* New York: Dell, 1974.

Davis, Ossie. *Langston.* New York: Delacorte Press, 1982.

Davis, Ossie. *Mass Appeal.* New York: Avon, 1981.

Duncan, Lois. *Chapters: My Growth as a Writer.* Boston: Little Brown, 1982.

Duncan, Lois. *Killing Mr. Griffin.* New York: Dell, 1978.

Dygrad, Thomas. *Backfield Package.* New York: William Morrow, 1992.

Edelman, B, ed. *Dear America: Letters Home from Vietnam.* New York: W. W. Norton, 1985.

Freedman, Russell. *Eleanor Roosevelt, A Life of Discovery.* New York: Clarion Books, 1993.

Gallo, Donald, ed. *Center Stage: One-Act Plays for Teenage Readers and Actors.* New York: Harper & Row, 1990.

Gallo, Donald, ed. *Connections.* New York: Dell, 1989.

Gallo, Donald, ed. *Short Circuits.* New York: Delacorte Press, 1992.

Gallo, Donald, ed. *Sixteen.* New York: Dell, 1984.

Gallo, Donald, ed. *Visions.* New York: Dell, 1987.

Gilsenan, Nancy Pahl. *A Separate Peace* (Play). Woodstock, IL: Dramatic, 1990.

Glenn, Mel. *Back to Class.* New York: Clarion, 1987.

Glenn, Mel. *Class Dismissed! High School Poems.* New York: Clarion, 1982.

Glenn, Mel. *Class Dismissed II: More High School Poems.* New York: Clarion, 1986.

Glenn, Mel. *My Friend's Got This Problem Mr. Candler.* New York: Clarion, 1991.

Gordon, Sheila. *Waiting for the Rain.* New York: Dell, 1987.

Grollman, Earl A. *Straight Talk About Death for Teenagers.* Boston: Beacon Press, 1993.

Grover, Wayne. *Ali and the Golden Eagle.* New York: Greenwillow Books, 1993.

Hamilton, Virginia. *The People Could Fly: American Black Folktales.* New York: Alfred A. Knopf, 1987.

Haskins, James. *Black Dance in America.* New York: Harper Collins, 1990.

Hinton, S.E. *The Outsiders.* New York: Dell, 1967.

Hinton, S.E. *Taming the Star Runner.* New York: Dell, 1988.

Hobbs, Will. *Beardance.* New York: Atheneum, 1993.

Hobbs, Will. *The Big Wander.* New York: Atheneum, 1992.

Hoose, Phillip. *It's Our World, Too!* Boston: Little Brown, 1993.

Janeczko, Paul, ed. *Pocket Poems: Selected for a Journey.* New York: Bradbury, 1985.

Janeczko, Paul, ed. *Poetspeak: In Their Work, About Their Work.* New York: Bradbury, 1983.

Janeczko, Paul, ed. *Postcard Poems: A Collection of Poetry for Sharing.* New York: Bradbury, 1979.

Janeczko, Paul, ed. *The Place My Words Are Looking For.* New York: Bradbury, 1990.

Janeczko, Paul, ed. *Preposterous: Poems of Youth.* New York: Orchard, 1991.

Jennings, Coleman and Bretta Berghammer, eds. *Theatre for Youth: Twelve Plays with Mature Themes.* New Orleans: Anchorage Press, 1991.

Kaye, Marilyn. *Real Heroes.* San Diego: Harcourt Brace Jovanovich, 1993.

Kuklin, Susan. *Fighting Back: What Some People Are Doing About AIDS.* New York: G. P. Putman's Sons, 1989.

Kuklin, Susan. *Speaking Out, Teenagers Take on Race, Sex, and Identity.* New York: G. P. Putman's Sons, 1993.

Lamb, Wendy. *Meeting the Winter Bike Rider and Other Prize Winning Plays.* New York: Dell, 1986.

Lipsyte, Robert. *The Brave.* New York: Harper Collins, 1991.

Lipsyte, Robert. *The Chief.* New York: Harper Collins, 1993.

Lipsyte, Robert. *The Contender.* New York: Dell, 1967.

Livingston, Myra Cohn, ed. *A Time to Talk, Poems of Friendship.* New York: Macmillan, 1992.

Mazer, Norma Fox. *After the Rain.* New York: Avon, 1987.

Mazer, Norma Fox. *Taking Terri Mueller.* New York: Avon, 1981.

Mazer, Norma Fox. *When We First Met.* New York: Scholastic, 1982.

Meltzer, Milton. *Ain't Gonna Study War No More: The Story of America's Peace Seekers.* New York: Harper & Row, 1985.

Miklowitz, Gloria. *Anything to Win.* New York: Dell, 1990.

Myers, Walter Dean. *18 Pine Street* (series). New York: Bantam, 1992.

Myers, Walter Dean. *Fallen Angels.* New York: Scholastic, 1988.

Myers, Walter Dean. *Hoops.* New York: Dell, 1981.

Myers, Walter Dean. *The Mouse Rap.* New York: Harper Collins, 1990.

Myers, Walter Dean. *Scorpions.* New York: Harper & Row, 1988.

O'Dell, Scott. *Streams to the River, River to the Sea.* New York: Ballantine, 1986.

Paterson, Katherine. *Jacob, Have I Loved.* New York: Avon, 1980.

Paulsen, Gary. *The Crossing.* New York: Orchard, 1987.

Paulsen, Gary. *Dogsong.* New York: Bradbury Press, 1985.

Paulsen, Gary. *Nightjohn.* New York: Bantam Doubleday Dell, 1993.

Peck, Richard. *Princess Ashley.* New York: Dell, 1987.

Peck, Richard. *Remember the Good Times.* New York: Dell, 1985.

Rinaldi, Anne. *In My Father's House.* New York: Scholastic, 1993.

Robinson, Margaret. *A Woman of Her Tribe.* New York: Charles Scribner's Sons, 1990.

Santiago, Danny. *Famous All Over Town.* New York: Simon & Schuster, 1983.

Sergel, Christopher. *The Outsiders* (Play). Woodstock, IL: Dramatic, 1990.

Sleator, William. *The Duplicate.* New York: Dell, 1989.

Sleator, William. *Intersteller Pig.* New York: Dutton, 1984.

Soto, Gary. *Baseball in April and Other Stories.* New York: Harcourt Brace Jovanovich, 1990.

Soto, Gary. *A Fire in My Hands.* New York: Scholastic, 1990.

Soto, Gary. *Pacific Crossing.* New York: Harcourt Brace Jovanovich, 1992.

Soto, Gary. *Local News.* San Diego: Harcourt Brace Jovanovich, 1993.

Staples, Suzanne. *Shabanu, Daughter of the Wind.* New York: Alfred A. Knopf, 1989.

Strasser, Todd. *The Accident.* New York: Dell, 1988.

Strasser, Todd. *Angel Dust Blues.* New York: Dell, 1979.

Taylor, Mildred. *Roll of Thunder, Hear My Cry.* New York: Bantam, 1976.

Thomas, Joyce Carol, ed. *A Gathering of Flowers: Stories About Being Young in America.* New York: Harper & Row, 1990.

Thomas, Joyce Carol. *Marked by Fire.* New York: Avon, 1982.

Thomas, Joyce Carol. *When the Nightingale Sings.* New York: Harper Collins, 1992.

Voight, Cynthia. *Dicey's Song.* New York: Ballantine Books, 1982.

Voight, Cynthia. *Izzy Willy Nilly.* New York: Atheneum, 1986.

Westall, Robert. *In Camera and Other Stores.* New York: Scholastic, 1992.

Yep, Laurence. *Dragonwings.* New York: Harper & Row, 1975.

FOR ADDITIONAL READING

Angelotti, Michael. "Uses of the Young Adult Literature in the Eighties." *English in Texas,* 13, 32–34, 1981.

Applebee, Arthur. *Literature in the Secondary School.* Urbana, IL: NCTE, 1993.

Atwell, Nancy. *In the Middle. Writing, Reading, and Learning with Adolescents.* Portsmouth, NH: Boynton/Cook, 1987.

Beech, Richard. *Reader-Response Theories.* Urbana, IL: NCTE, 1993.

Beech, Richard and Marshall, James. *Teaching Literature in the Secondary School.* San Diego: Harcourt Brace Jovanovich, 1991.

Bushman, John H. and Bushman, Kay Parks. *Using Young Adult Literature in the English Classroom.* New York: Macmillan, 1993.

Dixon, John. *Growth Through English.* Urbana, IL: NCTE, 1967.

Gallo, Donald. *Authors' Insights.* Portsmouth, NH: Boynton/Cook, 1992.

Gallo, Donald. *Speaking for Ourselves.* Urbana, IL: NCTE, 1990.

Gallo, Donald. *Speaking for Ourselves, Too.* Urbana, IL: NCTE, 1993.

Judy (Tchudi), Stephen; and Judy, Susan. *The English Teacher's Handbook.* Cambridge, Mass.: Winthrop, 1979.

Karolides, Nicholas. *Reader Response in the Classroom.* New York: Longman, 1992.

Kaywell, Joan F., ed. *Adolescent Literature as a Complement to the Classics.* Norwood, MA: Christopher Gordon Publishers, 1993.

Leighton, Dolly. "Saturating Students with Reading: A Classroom Lab Approach." *English Journal,* 80, 81–85, 1991.

Lesesne, Terri. "Developing Lifetime Readers: Suggestions from Fifty Years of Research." *English Journal,* 80, 61–64, 1991.

Monseau, Virginia R. and Salvner, Gary M. *Reading Their World.* Portsmouth, NH: Boynton/Cook, 1992.

Nilsen, Allene Pace. "Big Business, Young Adult Literature and the Boston Pops." *English Journal,* 82 (2), 70–75, 1993.

Nilsen, Alleen Pace; and Donelson, Kenneth L. *Literature for Today's Young Adults,* 4th Ed. New York: Harper Collins, 1993.

O'Connor, M. E. *A Study of the Reading Preferences of High School Students.* Arlington, VA: ERIC Document Reproduction Service. (ED 185524).

Pope, Carol. "Our Time Has Come: English for the Twenty-First Century." *English Journal,* 82 (1), 37–41, 1993.

Probst, Robert E. *Response and Analysis: Teaching Literature in Junior and Senior High School.* Portsmouth, NH: Boynton/Cook, 1988.

Rosenblatt, Louise M. *Literature As Exploration.* New York: Noble and Noble, 1968.

Spencer, Patricia. "YA Novels in the AP Classroom: Crutcher Meets Camus." *English Journal,* 79 (7), 47–48, 1989.

Webb, Anne. *Your Reading.* Urbana, IL: NCTE, 1993.

Wurth, Shirley. *Books for You.* Urbana, IL: NCTE, 1992.

Chapter 7

READING IN THE ENGLISH CLASSROOM*

Reading is the major activity of learning in the middle or secondary school classroom. While lectures, demonstrations, discussions, and laboratory activities are an integral part of instruction in such settings, textbooks and other reading materials remain the major source of information in content areas.

In relationship to this reliance on the printed page is the additional reality of the wide differences among students' reading abilities. Selected reading materials must be assessed in relationship to these abilities and a thought given to whether they will help or hinder the students' ability to learn the desired content or subject-related skills. An acceptance by the content teacher of the need to provide appropriate reading instruction in the study of their content materials will increase learning in the content area and should be a goal for all content teachers (Roe, Stoodt, & Burns, 1983).

RATIONALE

An awareness of the need to teach reading in secondary content-area classrooms has become increasingly more accepted. Assumptions about students abilities to read content material without such instruction have been misleading and have limited the learning of content by students in subject areas. It was thought that after students knew "how to read," that was all the reading instruction they needed. Little thought was given to how readers must change in their reading skills as they learn to apply them at different levels of sophistication—from the embryonic beginnings of developmental reading to the advanced forms of reading required in content areas. No longer is it taken for granted that students necessarily transfer what was learned in a reading class to what skills are needed

*The authors are indebted to Doctor Margaret Anderson, Department of Curriculum and Instruction, University of Kansas, for the preparation of this chapter.

to learn in a content-area class. Student success in reading classes does not insure similar success in other subjects.

Chall (1983) states that reading development actually occurs in six stages and that changes occur as the reader moves from one stage to another. Her stage theory suggests that reading is not always the same thing at each level and that each stage of development has its own tasks and crises. Her stages of reading development cover the full continuum from primitive beginnings to advanced ability to read abstract and multilevel materials:

Stage 0   Prereading
Stage 1   Initial Reading, or Decoding
Stage 2   Confirmation, Fluency, Ungluing from Print
Stage 3   Reading for Learning the New
Stage 4   Multiple Viewpoints
Stage 5   Construction and Reconstruction—A World View

Such a developmental theory hypothesizes that each stage builds on skills acquired in the preceding one and that each stage is subsumed by the following one. This makes it essential that students be provided the appropriate instruction at each successive level of education so that they modify and apply their developed reading skills to meet the level of sophistication required by the new materials they are expected to read.

Gradually, it has come to be understood that perhaps the most appropriate place to provide reading skills needed to read specific types of subject material is in the specific subject where such materials are required. The reading instruction needed by students as they study content is determined by the specific content to be studied. Packer and Rubin (1966) state that content determines process and that implicit in the content of what you want to be read are the skills needed to achieve that task. How material is presented, what concepts are developed, and what information is conveyed establish how the material should be read. As students read the material for the content area, they also can be taught the skills of reading needed to accomplish that task. Reading skills and subject content are taught simultaneously as students learn how to apply skills learned previously, or newly acquired skills, to more sophisticated materials.

Each content area has its own unique cluster of needed reading skills and represents reading demands that are built on both general reading skills and specialized applications of these skills in relation to the content material. This requires that content-area teachers be involved in a reading program that extends the skills learned in elementary settings and guides students' reading of their required printed materials. McDonald (1961), Crane (1967), Karlin (1978) and Roe, Stoodt, and Burns (1983) summarize general areas where content-area teachers should provide reading instruction for students: vocabulary and concept development (common vocabulary, specialized usage of common vocabulary, technical vocabulary of content area, figurative language, content in shorthand such as abbreviations, symbols, acronyms, formulas, and equations); comprehension (literal, interpretive, applied, critical thinking, and creative thinking); and study skills (location, selection, organization, and retention of information); reading and interpreting graphic aids, rates of reading (varied rates to adjust to purpose, difficulty, and type of content).

Each of these areas is important within each content area, but the application of each skill varies from subject to subject. The specific configuration of skills demanded by each subject must be determined by each content teacher as he/she determines what unique ways these skills must be applied in relationship to the particular materials to be used.

READING IN THE ENGLISH CLASSROOM

The English curriculum presents a challenge, as it contains the most varied content of all content subjects. Since it focuses on communication skills between writer and reader, it is involved primarily with the use and appreciation of the English language. The study of English requires readers to understand grammar, composition, and many varieties of literature—novels, short stories, poetry, essays, plays, biographies, autobiographies, and journalistic materials.

This diversity in English makes it necessary that the English teacher develop awareness and sensitivity to the configuration of skills demanded by each of the areas within English as well as to the relationship between areas.

Materials related to the rules and conventions of writing tend to be explanatory or precriptive in nature. Writing exercises present models for examination, practice, and then application to original work. The reading demands of such material demand that the student understand the model presented by interpreting the specimen with understanding, analyze what is meant from this interpretation, and then demonstrate comprehension through application. There is an emphasis on technique and the development of abstract reading skills.

It may be that the focus of study goes beyond grammar in the more traditional sense and looks at the nature of language from a more philosophical point of view. Such a study may include the study of linguistics or the communication literature that takes the student beyond the simple "reading" of a word. The reader may be called on to recognize the impact words have within different cultures and how this varies across time and societies. Such awareness of the nature of language provides the student with psychological insight into language and its uses within such civilizations. The study of literature as usually taught in English classes often provides an extension of the kind of reading experienced in earlier grades where the emphasis was on narrative-type materials. Through such material the student extends personal experience by exploring the experience of others and gaining new awareness of human experiences not previously experienced or understood.

The reader of a novel may be required to experience the perceptions of a main character, to visualize a foreign country where the story takes place, or to sense the emotion building as the conflict between characters deepens.

The language of the literature type may be complex or organized in ways unknown to the reader. Sentences may be longer, more complex, and use vocabulary in unknown ways. The writer makes cognitive demands on the reader as well as involving the reader emotionally in the material.

This variety of materials used in English classrooms may seem confusing and complex, but the transformation or adaptation of skills learned in one area can be achieved through the relationships among the English areas. Learning to write is related to the reflective thinking focused on in the study of literature, and because both writing and literature study language and communication, it is related as well to the study of the nature of language.

Functional Teaching of Reading in English

If it is accepted that reading instruction is a part of the curriculum in English, how can that best be achieved by the content specialist? It is often erroneously assumed that the English teacher knows more about the teaching of reading than other content-area specialists. But English teachers are not trained in reading instruction. They have been trained to teach the ideas and concept of their content area just as other content specialists have. The fundamental difference between the reading specialist and the content specialist is in the focus of their instruction. The reading specialist decided on a skill to be taught and uses material to teach that skill. The content specialist is concerned with content acquisition and selects material for that purpose. But it is through the teaching of the content ideas that the related skills of reading can also be addressed.

Herber (1978) suggests that reading in the content area be taught "functionally" using the basic and supplementary materials of the content area. The functional teaching of reading is achieved (1) when the reading skills chosen for instruction are those required to understand material assigned to read, (2) when these reading skills are taught simultaneously with the reading of course materials, and (3) when materials have been chosen because of content rather than reading skill instruction. In other words, the teacher provides instruction in only those reading skills needed to understand what is assigned to read and only as students read these materials.

PROCEDURES FOR FUNCTIONAL INSTRUCTION OF READING SKILLS

The English teacher determines the content objectives of a unit or lesson. These objectives reflect the information, concepts, or generalizations the teacher has determined are needed for understanding of a content area. These are *content* decisions and reading issues are not a concern at this level.

After content objectives are determined, the teacher selects the materials to be used as information vehicles to teach the content selected for instruction. Materials are selected in relationship to the content objectives selected.

Once the materials are selected, the teacher must analyze the material to assess what skills of reading are demanded by the material. Since it is the goal of the content specialist to teach content well, this assessment of what is needed to gain comprehension is crucial. There is no scope or sequence chart of what skills are required in functional reading. The content specialist must recognize what skills are needed and when, in relationship to the course text or other readings. The teacher must determine what modifications or transformations of existing skills are needed or whether new skill development is demanded by the material.

Needed reading instruction will be required in the areas summarized earlier in this chapter:

1. vocabulary and concept development
2. comprehension
3. study skills

This section of the chapter focuses on the reading issues in these areas and their relationship to English content.

Vocabulary and Concept Development

Vocabulary and concept development are integral parts of English instruction, as they are critical in the manipulation of ideas. Words, concepts, and content are all interrelated and facilitate thinking and intellectual organization.

Vocabulary words are the labels used to communicate ideas and concepts. Such labels make the world conceptually manageable and understandable. Within content areas words are the labels needed to learn from content materials. Without such word understanding, the reader has no schemata for concepts within the content area.

Words provide the reader with material needed to build a schema about objects and ideas. This process of conceptualizing creates a mental filing system that enables the reader to categorize and organize relationships between objects and experiences as they are acquired and refined. This process creates an ever-expanding schemata for the reader that can be applied to gain conceptual understandings and modified as new concepts are acquired. English teachers have an important role in this process of concept acquisition, and they are most aware of what vocabulary and concept formation is important in their content area.

Words chosen for vocabulary instruction fall into five categories. The first category, common vocabulary, consists of words that have generalized meanings and appear in general reading materials as well as English materials. Words such as *gloom* and *prejudice* fit in this group. The second category, specialized usage of common vocabulary, is comprised of words that have generalized and specialized definitions. In general usage, the word *period* has one meaning and it also has a technical meaning in English context. Technical vocabulary specific to the content area is a third category of vocabulary concern. These words have a concept specific to English and are often the most difficult for the reader.

Hyperbole and *precis* are examples of such technical words. Figurative language, the fourth category, uses words to express a concept that differs from its literal or standard construction. We speak of breaking the ice, bring frozen with fear, a rose between two thòrns, or reading between the lines. Such figures of speech are departures from the literal form and fall into following three categories (DeChant, 1973):

1. Figures of resemblance
   allegory
   onomatopoeia
   personification
   metaphor
   simile
   metronomy
2. Figures of contrast or satire
   antithesis
   epigram
   irony
   apostrophe
3. Others
   hyperbole
   euphemism
   synecdoche

The last category is content vocabulary expressed in shorthand. The use of abbreviations such as *viz.* and *e.g.* are examples of such shorthand. Symbols and acronyms are further examples of this vocabulary group.

Assessing which vocabulary is essential to the understanding of material to be read is important in identifying which words should receive instructional focus. Time constraints make it essential that the teacher focus on those words which are essential to comprehension of the material.

Vocabulary instruction can occur at various times during the content work, and the timing of this instruction is determined by the demands placed on the words. Such instruction can be part of readiness before the reading of the material or be integrated with the actual reading of the material. Follow-up vocabulary instruction after reading the selection is another alternative. Such vocabulary instruction is worth the time utilized, as it improves the learning of content (Stoodt & Ballo, 1979).

Methodology

Research related to words and concept acquisition reveals four major approaches for the instruction of vocabulary (Roe, Stoodt, & Burns, 1983).

1. Word meanings can be achieved through concept development methodologies such as experiences, association strategies, attribute analysis, example/non-example activities, categorization activities, concept relationship activities, and application of words.

    Experience — Real (direct) and vicarious (films, speakers, field trips, etc.) experiences should be utilized to provide experience with new concepts. Concept development occurs when there is an interfacing of experience and thought. It should be remembered that as reading experiences distance from experiences, they become increasingly more abstract (Dale, 1969). Verbal and visual symbols are the most abstract and require experience to make them more meaningful.

    Association — Association strategies make use of word meanings already known by students to provide connections to unknown words with similar meanings. Association activities include cross-word puzzles, matching exercise, analogies, and in-depth word studies.

    Attribute analysis — word meanings can be achieved through attribute strategies requiring students to analyze ideas and concepts on how they are alike or different.

    Example/Non-example — Once attributes are understood, students can identify examples or non-examples of the desired concept. Students choose between concept examples and non-examples and explain how they categorized their choices.

    Categorization — Categorization requires the student to sort concepts into categories using common characteristics as determiners. Gillet and Temple (1978) identify two types of "sorting" activities: open ended and closed ended. In a closed-ended sort, the common property to be used as category determiner is identified for the student (e.g. Sort the list of titles into the following categories: novel, short story, essay, play). In an open-ended sort, the student must identify what exemplar was used (e.g. Draw a line through the word that doesn't belong: pronoun, hyperbole, verb, adverb).

Structured overview — A structural overview is a graphic device that diagrams the relationship between concepts. It is based on the theory of Ausubel (1978) that students need an orderly arrangement of concepts to learn new concepts. A structured overview is usually organized in the following way:

Main Concept

Related Concept   Related Concept

Subordinate Concepts   Subordinate Concepts

Application — Application activities are helpful in assessing whether students have developed the understanding of a word. Such assessment can be achieved by asking the student to define words in various ways:

1. demonstrate the word's meaning by using it in a sentence
2. provide a synonym or antonym for the word
3. categorize the word
4. use the word in comparison to another word
5. illustrate the word by drawing or finding a picture of the word.

2. Word meanings can be understood by using clues present in the word's contextual setting. Contextual analysis required the reader to analyze words in relationship to their semantic and/or syntactic environment. The reader must search for clues and generate meaning possibilities. They must recognize and use aids present in the context that provide word understanding.

   The success of the use of context as a methodology in gaining word meaning is related to factors already existing in the reader. The reader must be capable of reasoning ability, already possess a store of word meanings, have some knowledge of the topic, and have the ability to read and understand most of the other words in the material.

3. Word meanings can be gained by using word structures by synthesizing the relationship between root words and affixs. This strategy encourages the student to analyze the morphemes of words. The reader must be able to combine meanings of prefixes, root words, and suffixes to obtain the meaning of new words. Compound words are also an aspect of structural analysis.

4. Word meanings can be developed through encouraging students

in the use of the dictionary and thesaurus. There are situations in which students should use a dictionary for a precise word meaning or a thesaurus to develop an understanding of related synonyms. These are useful references and provide the student independence in developing vocabulary and concept development.

Vocabulary development is a part of the principle of functional instruction of reading in the English classroom. The language of a subject is its vocabulary and is required to communicate the ideas essential to learning the content. Vocabulary and content cannot be separated, so it must be taught simultaneously.

Comprehension

Comprehension of written materials is the essence of reading and critical to the learning of content ideas. The ability to comprehend the variety of materials used in the English area is necessary if understanding is to occur and the student is to develop into both a mature reader and writer of English materials.

The mature reader of English materials must be able to use personal schema, semantic and syntactical knowledge, and thinking skills to comprehend materials at differing levels of difficulty and which encompass different reading demands. This process requires that the student must be able to integrate previous knowledge with new information presented in course materials. The level of difficulty of this task for the student is dependent upon the comprehension task set by the teacher whether it requires a literal, interpretive, applied, critical, or creative thinking response.

Comprehension of material specific to English content may be helped or hindered by the reader's knowledge or lack of knowledge about written language or the topic focused upon for study. The active, involved reader must utilize language, knowledge, prediction, and familiarity of text structure to build the connections needed to bring comprehension of the material.

The instructional components of skills needed for reader comprehension can be taught by the English teacher in a "functional" manner simultaneously with content. The English specialist should address the following four components of comprehension instruction:

1. active reading
2. schema development (context/textual)

3. prediction
4. levels of reasoning

These four areas of comprehension development have been synthesized from the reading research on comprehension and represent functional reading tasks for the English specialist (Burns & Roe, 1983).

Active Reading

Active readers are interested and motivated as they explore new areas of information. This active student participation leads to better comprehension of material and a firmer grasp on the content. Active participation leads to greater involvement in learning and opens the way for new schema development.

The English teacher can take advantage of such reading strategies as exploration of controversial issues, prereading questions, problem-solving strategies, and hypothesis proposing to engage the student in exploration of content materials. Such activities require the student reader to make a commitment to a personal point of view and create an interest in reading to confirm or reject this personal investment. Activities like these are timed for use prior to the reading of content materials and are intended to stimulate the reader into active, rather than passive, involvement.

Schemata

Schemata is developed from the experience that each individual has encountered. It is developed and refined over time and represents a personal abstraction of reality. It is constantly changing as new experiences and awareness modify the existing structures. When a reader is relatively familiar with a topic under study, it is easier for that student to understand material about the topic and less threatening to explore more difficult related material. Unfamiliar topics create a more difficult reading task for the student and require more teacher intervention in schemata development.

Content Schemata. Content schemata are critical to the comprehension of content materials. Such schemata provides the reader with a context or frame of reference from which information can be organized, understood, and remembered. Students who lack experience in specific areas are hindered in their attempts to read about, understand, and apply topics related to such an area. The reader possessing some schemata about Elizabethan England has a much greater understanding of the literature of that time than the student lacking such schemata.

Due to the often, new aspects of content materials, the English content specialist must intervene and assist students in their development of schemata needed for the topics to be studied or the literature to be explored. Sometimes this is only a question of providing opportunities for the reader to recognize knowledge already understood and its relationship to the new concepts presented. Other times it requires teacher-planned direct or indirect experiences to build or complete schemata needed for the further study of an area.

Textual Schema. Textual schema refers to the reader's knowledge of a specific structure of writing that allows them to predict, follow, and organize material as they read. This ability allows the reader to discriminate between how a research article should be read and how a newspaper, magazine, or narrative story should be read.

The English specialist can assist students in their development of textual schemata needed to read the variety of materials found in the English area. English materials related to the technical or expository aspects of English are structured by sentences, paragraphs, main ideas, details, and the organization of passages. Plot, theme, setting, and character development provide the organizing structure of literature materials.

Readers need instruction in comprehension of the individual sentences in a selection as well as help in discovering the inter-sentential relationships of an entire paragraph. English teachers can help students analyze these relationships between and among sentences in a paragraph and facilitate paragraph understanding and comprehension.

The increased understanding of sentences and paragraphs results not only in greater comprehension of the written material but also enables the student to distinguish between well-developed paragraphs and those which are poorly constructed. This functional instruction provides awareness for the reader of good or poor models of writing. As the reader becomes a writer of original material, this instruction will have provided a schemata for writing.

The main ideas and important details of content-area materials are those which are important and critical to the understanding of topics under study. These ideas and details provide the key structure of organization in the material to be read. Teachers can emphasize these important concepts by providing instruction in how to locate key ideas and important detail in textbooks, novels, essays, magazines, or other material used in the course.

Expository materials such as textbooks in grammar or composition are organized in recognizable ways. By assisting students in gaining awareness of the organizational patterns used in such materials, their development of textual schemata will be refined, enhanced, and will provide student recognition of an author's organizational pattern. This awareness increases content comprehension and provides the student with writing forms useful in his/her own writing development.

Organizational patterns most used in content materials are chronological or sequential order, compare and contrast, cause and effect, definition or explanation, and enumeration or listing. By instructing students in how to analyze materials in relationship to organizational patterns used, the student can observe how the author used a predominate pattern or a combination of pattern forms. Not only is comprehension and organization awareness developed but, simultaneously, models of writing are provided the student, as well.

Recognition of organizational patterns also provides the student with understanding of how sentences are placed in paragraphs and how paragraphs are organized into larger passages that create an entire selection. This understanding leads to development of textual schemata that provides skills to the student necessary for the organization of new information with previous knowledge. This instruction greatly facilitates like understanding and retention of content ideas.

Due to the nature of reading instruction in the early grades, students are more accustomed to the textual schemata of literature: plot, theme, setting, and character development. This familiarity with the written forms of stories, novels, plays, and similar materials provides a foundation upon which to develop a greater understanding of literature. The existing schemata can be greatly enhanced and refined by providing students opportunities to explore each of these library elements more thoroughly.

Plot development can be greatly refined by aiding students in understanding that plot is more than the order in which things happened in a story. It is important they recognize that the sequence chosen by the author was selected as the best way of telling the story and that the conflict, tension, and action found in the literature were not accident choices. The author selected a particular narrative order, conflict type, and pattern of action to arouse and hold the reader's interest. There may be variations or combinations of plot structures within a story and these provide the reader with awareness that diversity within a story is acceptable.

Theme in literature provides the unifying idea that cements a story together. It is the main idea of a piece of literature and provides a comment on human nature, the human condition, or society as a whole. It provides the thread that turns a simple narrative into a piece of literature. The primary theme may be explicitly or implicitly stated with multiple supporting or secondary themes. Reader recognition of theme allows the student to enlarge understanding of literature and contributes to student growth and discovery.

The enactment of the plot and the character depiction occurs in a time and place. Understanding of story settings provides the reader with an awareness of the details and mood of a particular time and how that provides an integral or only a backdrop atmosphere for the characters and conflict present in this story. Plot, characters, and setting are interdependent and influence and reflect each other. The developing reader should gain awareness of the role of setting in clarifying the conflict, playing the role of an antagonist, illuminating aspects of the character, establishing the needed mood, or providing symbolism for the story. This sense of place and time allows the reader to accept the story and writer's view of society, human nature, or the human condition.

Character development in a story is the use of an author's use of person, animal, or object to act out the events and episodes of the story. The reader of literature can discover how the author reveals a character's nature by looking for revelations made by characters through actions, speech, appearances, reactions of others, or by the author's comments. Characters unify the action of the story and reveal the intent of the author. Such reader awareness is critical to the understanding and appreciation of literature.

Prediction

The ability to predict when reading content materials allows the reader to develop hypothesis about what is coming in the selection and creates interest in reading further for confirmation or rejection of these hypothesis. This interest, to confirm or reject, provides the reader with the motivation needed to explore an author's meaning, search for important ideas, or develop a mind set for further study. Utilization of a student's prior knowledge allows the reader to form hypothesis and create the conduits necessary to connect old and new knowledge.

Ausubel's (1978) concept of advance organizers is helpful in facilitating development of a conceptual framework that connects existing schemata with author ideas. The English specialist can easily create advance organizers for material to be read by writing short reading passages to precede the longer selection.

The use of purposing questions is another technique useful to student prediction of coming material. Such questions are closely related to the content objectives selected by the teacher and provide structure for the student in organizing content during the reading. By providing students with two or three purposing questions for a selection, the reader gains a sense of what important ideas are to be looked for and discovered in the material.

The development of prediction guides as suggested by Herber (1978) is another technique useful in helping students form a hypothesis. Such guides are useful in stimulating interest in a topic, facilitating the formulation of a hypothesis, and creating a vehicle for discussion of concepts as students defend or reject their predictions.

Levels of Reasoning

Levels of reasoning suggests the development of thinking skills at various levels. The development of such skills is critical to reading comprehension. Thinking at different levels about content read enables the student to look beyond the literal meaning of words to the ideas behind those words.

Paramount to this development of thinking or reasoning is the teacher's use of questioning strategies or statement guides that force the readers beyond the minimal level of comprehension to refocused thinking, exploration of ideas different from their own, and the attempting of ways of thinking not experienced before. In an environment that encourages such development of thinking ability, divergency in answers will be tolerated, encouraged, and supported with acceptance and needed time for thinking.

Levels of reasoning can be divided into the following five levels: literal, interpretive, applied, critical, and creative. Selection of questions or discussion strategies for a given lesson can be aided by teacher use of the following questions:

1. What are the important concepts or ideas found in this selection?

2. What ideas or concepts do I want students to get from reading this selection?
3. What thinking skills do my students already have?
4. What thinking skills do I want to develop in these students?
5. What is the best way to develop these thinking skills?

Answers to these questions guide the teacher in the development of questions or discussion guides for topics under study.

Literal Thinking. This level of reading or thinking is a basic level and is related to ideas explicitly stated in the selected material. It includes the recognition of main ideas, details, and the comprehension of meanings of words, sentences, and paragraphs. These are basic factual questions or statements that are answered or stated in the content material itself.

Interpretive Thinking. This level includes many types of thinking. It is founded on the ability to do literal thinking but requires the reader to find relationships between facts, generalizations, and other elements of the content. The reader must be able to read between the lines and to make cognitive leaps to arrive at understanding implicit in the selection. This level of thinking demands that the reader use some personal knowledge in combination with the message presented by the author. Such questions or statements do not have direct answers in the reading material, but there must be support for an opinion or answer within the printed material.

Applied Thinking. The applied level of thinking is a process of reading where use is made of what was already known in combination with what was first learned. The student develops ideas that contain both schemas but extends beyond them. Evidence comes from both sources, student and author, and are equally respected.

Critical Thinking. Critical thinking requires the reader to make judgments about the quality, value, or validity of material read. In order to make informed evaluations, the reader must utilize experience, research, and expert opinions in the related field. Students need instruction on how to be logical and objective when evaluating content or data supporting an author's ideas. Wolf, Huck, and King (1967) categorize the critical reading skills into the three groups of semantics, logic, and authenticity. Semantic evaluative abilities include an understanding of words as persuaders and the denotative and connotative meanings that words carry. Logic skills provide the reader with the ability to understand and assess the reliability of an author's argument, recognition of propaganda techniques, and discrimination of fact from opinion. Authenticity skills provide the reader with techniques useful in determining if correct information is given by the author or if the author is a credible source of information about a topic.

Creative Thinking. Creative thinking encourages the reader to explore novel ways of viewing a selection and to put together in a different form things already known. This may be in the form of a product or the development of a unique creative process.

Encouraging students to attempt new levels of thinking is essential to the development of abstract reasoning ability and mature comprehension skills. Without the development of such skills as students read materials, we are left with an emphasis on memorization and passivity rather than creative analysis and higher-level thinking. The use of comprehension strategies in the English classroom develops students with skills needed to become independent in their reading and reasoning of English content.

Study Skills

The development of study skills is one of the most important instructional areas in the content areas. These skills are the key to effective study and permit student independence. The capacities to use textbooks as sources of information, establish effective study habits, and develop efficient library skills are important components of education. These skills provide the student with tools needed to be an independent reader and learner.

Study Methods

Study reading is a requirement of any content area. Its purpose is to build student organization of subject knowledge and to facilitate reader thinking.

Many methods of approaching study reading have been recommended. Perhaps the best known and most used technique is the SQ3R method (Robinson, 1961). The steps in this method are *S*urvey, *Q*uestion, *R*ead, *R*ecite, *R*eview. Spache (1977) suggests a method known as PRST: *P*review, *R*ead, *S*ummarize, *T*est. A method suggested specifically for prose, poetry, and drama is Pauk's (1963) EVOKER procedures: *E*xplore, *V*ocabulary, *O*ral reading, *K*ey ideas, *E*valuation, and *R*ecapitulation.

The REAP (Ernst & Manzo, 1976) method (*R*ead, *E*ncode, *A*nnotate, and *P*onder) and Edward's (1973) Panorama technique (*P*urpose, *A*dapting rate to material *N*eed to pose questions, *O*verview, *R*ead and relate, *A*nnotate, *M*emorize, *A*ssess) are general techniques useful for study reading. All of these methods are designed to help the reader establish a purpose or mindset for reading material, create questions related to that purpose, and to either summarize or reach conclusions about the material with these questions and purpose in mind.

Study reading requires a plan to provide a context or structure for exploring new material and "fix" it in the reader's mind. Study methods structure how a reader approaches a selection and aids in the retention of material and reorganization of reader schemata. Development of an effective study method can help the reader overcome deficiencies in their information-processing systems and help them discover ways of utilizing these systems more effectively.

Teachers cannot assume students know or practice good study methods. They need instruction in the methods and guidance in applying them to material used in the course. Students need opportunities for guided practice with teacher feedback before being expected to use them independently.

ORGANIZATIONAL SKILLS

Organizational skills are needed, as students have a need to structure ideas encountered in content material reading. Such skills of organization are outlining material, summarizing material, and note taking.

Outlining

Outlining is a technique useful in making a record of information read that clearly illustrates the main idea of a selection and the related supporting details. The ability to outline is reliant upon student understanding of main ideas, details, and the ability to recognize them. Without the ability to locate main ideas and details, the student will be unable to outline effectively.

Outline formats differ, and some are more appropriate with specific materials or for particular purposes. Free-form outlines or arrays provide a graphic view of material using lines and arrows to indicate relationships (Hansell, 1978). More structural forms of outlines are sentence or topic outlines.

English teachers should model how to extract main ideas and supporting details from a selection and present them in a specific outline format. Guided practice is essential as formats are explained and modeled. As students mature in their ability to outline, more and more independence can be afforded them in outline tasks.

Summarizing

When a reader can put ideas into his/her own words, learning has become internalized and integrated into the student's mind. Summaries represent the form content has in a reader's mind and represents the reader's processing of materials.

The reader must comprehend the author's material in order to summarize the ideas. Relationships between main ideas and essential supporting details must be recognized and recorded in a summary of a selection. Essential details and ideas must not be omitted, and unessential material must not be included.

Practice in summarizing materials is best provided in a functional way as students' study course materials and have a functional use for such instruction.

Note Taking

Good note-taking strategies are a good study technique and assist meaning as a reader explores materials and attempts to put them into his/her own words. Well-constructed notes make rereading of material unnecessary, aids retention of ideas, and facilitates thinking of content ideas.

Note taking demands that a student must be able to extract essential meaning from a selection in such a way that reconstruction of what was read or heard can be accomplished at a later time. The better constructed the notes are, the more assistance they are to the student at the time of application. Students need instruction in how to structure notes in well-organized, condensed ways, how to read and interpret them, and how to use them appropriately.

Students should be encouraged to utilize the form of note taking that is most helpful to them. They may find an outline form (array, sentence, or topic) or a summary of read materials more helpful or appropriate. Opportunities should be afforded students to learn, practice, and apply a variety of note-taking forms in the English classroom.

Location Skills

Location skills are important if students are to utilize effectively all resources available to them for study. The ability to locate information within books and libraries is critical and will be remembered long after specific facts have been forgotten. Having skills needed to find information provides the foundation needed for self-directed and independent learning.

TEXTBOOKS AND REFERENCE BOOKS

Students need instruction in how to use their textbooks effectively by recognizing the purpose, value, and potential of the book. Instruction should be provided that helps the student use the following components:

1. Cover
2. Title page
3. Author
4. Copyright page
5. Preface
6. Table of contents
7. Glossary
8. Index
9. Appendix
10. Footnote
11. Bibliography

Students need guided practice in previewing each section of the book and developing awareness of what information is found in each section and how it might be used.

Reference books such as encyclopedias, dictionaries, almanacs, and atlases are often used by students having little instruction in how to use such materials. Students may have little concept of how such books can effectively be used. Readers need instruction on how these materials are organized and how to use guide words; cross-references; pronunciation keys; map legends, scales, and directions; and volume selection.

It should be remembered as well that these special reference books are usually written on high readability levels. This fact may make these materials too difficult for many students unable to read at such high readability levels.

Libraries

Library facilities provide a wealth of resources for students, and instruction in how to use this wealth is essential. Library skill is essential to becoming a good student and an informed adult. These skills go beyond the school experience and provide students with freedom to be lifetime learners.

Libraries share many common characteristics, but each one has its own individual nature, as well. Instruction in library skills should be given in the facilities to be used by the student. Content specialists and librarians together can give students an awareness of general library knowledge and specific resources useful in the study of course topics. Instruction is needed in the use of the following library resources:

1. circulation and reference desks
2. audiovisual facilities
3. card catalog, computerized catalog, or other data bases
4. periodical and citation indexes
5. specialized sources relevant to English area
6. microfilm and microfiche
7. special collections

The content teacher can develop projects that require the students to utilize library resources. By teacher manipulation of the requirements of such projects, students can gain awareness of many library areas.

Without an understanding of how to make use of resources available in library settings, the library is little more than shelves of books. Through repeated experiences as needs arise in the classroom, library skills will be learned and reinforced when the student uses available resources for a variety of purposes.

Graphic Aids

Textbook authors often choose to include a number of graphic aids to increase understanding of concepts. Maps, graphs, charts, diagrams, tables, and pictures often convey an idea better than written discourse. Skill in reading such graphic aid is critical to understanding the information contained in such materials. Students must have the capacity to read materials written at a factual level, be able to make inferences, and be able to generalize or draw conclusions from the condensed information found in graphic aids.

Each type of graphic aid has its own nature, and the functional instruction of how to gain understanding from such a form of information can occur as it is found in the reading material. As the conventions of each aid are understood, the student will be less likely to disregard the information provided within the aid and may even utilize these graphics in personal writing.

RATE OF READING

Mature readers are flexible in their ability to adjust the rate of reading to fit material and reading purpose. They recognize that all materials are not read the same way or rate and that adjustments are made in relation to the following factors:

1. Reader related
      background experience (schema)
      reading ability
      reader attitude
      reader interest
      purpose for reading
2. Material related
      type—size/style
      page format
      illustrations
      organization
      author writing style
      ideas—complexity/abstractness

These factors differ in combinations as each reader approaches different reading tasks. The flexible reader recognizes what adjustments are needed and responds by adjusting reading rate while maintaining an acceptable level of comprehension. The rate of reading is always parallel to comprehension and is never faster than the reader can comprehend. Whether the speed of reading is skimming, scanning, study speed, or extremely slow to savor a section of poetry, it is always done with awareness of comprehension.

Students need assistance in determining when a rate is suitable with course materials. Teachers can facilitate student understanding of rate flexibility by providing instruction as materials are studied.

READING AND WRITING IN THE CONTENT AREAS

Reading and writing are naturally related and should be functionally brought together in the English classroom. As students read and learn about a content topic, they are also in a position to use that material as a model for writing.

The value of integrating the teaching of reading and writing has gained support and is supported by research. Effective writers are better readers and this results in greater comprehension and learning of a particular content area. As students gain understanding of vocabulary, concepts, levels of comprehension, and awareness of organization style and conventions, this knowledge can be extended to teach writing, as well.

A rich variety of reading/writing activities develops and enriches the students' schemata of content, genres, and writing conventions. Reading and writing skills are an integral part of content instruction and should be taught functionally when appropriate.

FOR ADDITIONAL READING

Ausubel, D. *Educational Psychology: A Cognitive View.* New York: Holt, Rinehart, and Winston, 1978.

Chall, J. *Stages of Reading Development.* New York: McGraw-Hill, 1983.

Crane, A. "Action and Reactions to Reading in the Public and Parochial Secondary Schools." *The Training School Bulletin,* Aug., 62–65, 1967.

Dale, E. *Audiovisual Methods in Teaching.* New York: Dryden Press, 1969.

DeChant, E. *Reading Improvement in the Secondary School.* New Jersey: Prentice-Hall, 1973.

Canet, M., & Manzo, A. "*REAP*—A Strategy for Improving Reading/Writing Study Skills." *Journal of Reading,* 19, 647–652, 1976.

Edwards, P. "Panorama: A Study Technique." *Journal of Reading,* 17, 132–135, 1973.

Gillet, J., & Temple, C. "Developing Word Knowledge: A Cognitive View." *Reading World,* 18, 132–140, 1978.

Hansell, T.S. "Stepping Up To Outlining." *Journal of Reading,* 72, 248–252.

Herber, H. L. *Teaching Reading in Content Areas.* New Jersey: Prentice-Hall, 1978.

Karlin, R. *Teaching Reading in High School: Improving Reading in Content Areas.* Indianapolis: Bobbs-Merrill, 1978.

McDonald, A.S. What research says about poor readers in high school and college. *Journal of Developmental Reading,* Sp., 184–96, 1961.

Packer, J.C., & Rubin, L.J. *Process as Content.* Chicago: Rand McNally, 1966.

Pauk, W. "On Scholarship: Advice to High School Students." *The Reading Teacher,* 17, 73–78, 1963.

Robinson, P.F. *Effective Study.* New York: Harper & Row, 1961.

Roe, B.D., Stoodt, B.D., & Burns, P.C. *Secondary School Reading Instruction: The Content Areas.* Boston: Houghton-Mifflin Company, 1983.

Stoodt, B.D., & Balbo, E. "Integrating Study Skills Instruction With Content in a Secondary Classroom." *Reading World,* (18), 247–252, 1979.

Spache, G. *Reading in the Elementary School.* Boston, Allyn and Bacon, 1977.

Wolf, W., Huck, C.S., and King, M.L. *The Critical Reading Ability of Elementary Children.* Columbus, OH: Ohio State University Research Foundation, 1967.

Chapter 8

TEACHING THE ENGLISH LANGUAGE

The language component of the English curriculum is important and should be made an integral part of the program of study. When we think of language study, our first thoughts conjure up naming parts of speech, parsing sentences, and diagramming; but there is so much more. A rich and worthwhile study can be exciting as students explore the nature of language, its structure, and usage items pertinent to standard English, as well as other varieties of English. Students can explore language heritage, geographical and social dialects, semantics, and the "silent language," as well. It seems to us that when students explore these areas, they are more aware of the language that they speak, and by knowing of the linguistic choices available to them, they may participate to a greater degree in the community in which they learn, play, and make a living.

It is in this broader sense that we suggest various activities in the teaching of the English language. As in the other chapters, we have included sample activities as well as descriptions of activities that you can prepare for yourself.

STRUCTURE

Arguments about the usefulness of grammar study in isolation and its relationship to writing have been going on for years. All of the research dating back to Hoyt's study in 1906 clearly indicates that the teaching of grammar in isolation has no relationship to an increase in writing ability. Hoyt concludes: "(1) about the same relationship exists between grammar and composition, and grammar and interpretation as exists between any two totally different subjects such as grammar and geography; (2) grammar is of little avail in strengthening one's power to use language" (Meckel, 1963, p. 975). A series of studies followed Hoyt's and has shown that throughout the time period from 1906 to the present, grammar in isolation has no effect on writing ability. Boraas (1917), Hatfield (1935), and many studies reported in *Encyclopedia of Educational Research* (1950), *Research in Written Composition* (Braddock et al., 1963), and *Research on Written Composition: New Directions for Teaching* (Hillocks, 1986) all confirm that instruction in formal grammar has no effect on the quality of student's writing. A more contemporary research piece (Warner, 1993) reaffirms these general conclusions.

If the research is not strong enough — although it should be — perhaps the fact that classroom experience in teaching grammar should stop it from continuing. With all the grammar teaching that goes on in grades 2 through 12, one would think that writing should improve, if, indeed, it had the effect that those who teach it believe it has. Not so. The 1986 report of the National Assessment of Writing (Applebee et al., 1986) confirms what most of us already know: "Most students, majority and minority alike, are unable to write adequately except in response to the simplest of tasks" (p. 9).

And to make matters worse, the teaching of grammar in isolation turns kids off to English, a subject that could provide a great deal of enjoyment. If all students experience is the labeling of parts, the placing of parts on a tree diagram, and the understanding that their language choices are wrong, they never will enjoy the fun and excitement that can come from a study of linguistics. There can be so much excitement with writing, literature, and general language study, but students may never get to these important areas if they are continually faced with the drab, dull, boring grammar exercises, especially since we know from many sources that grammar teaching does no good.

All of these reasons, plus their own experiences, ought to persuade teachers to consider very carefully the time spent and the results attained in teaching formal English grammar as an aid to writing.

We think it important to know the difference between teaching grammar and hoping for some transfer to writing, *and* teaching writing and using structural strategies that help students make their writing more effective through the revision process. The former is grammar-oriented and has, in our opinion, little, if any, positive impact on students' writing ability. The latter emphasizes writing and uses discussion of structural variations, usage items, and general language conventions to help each individual student evaluate his/her writing behavior.

Activities

1. A most useful activity for helping students learn the structure of their language and the effectiveness of this structure is sentence combining. This activity is most relevant for students who are using short, choppy sentences in their writing. Have students compare and contrast their new sentences with each others' so that they may see that many ideas may be communicated effectively in many different ways. Be sure to relate the sentence-combining process to the writing process. This activity should not be done in isolation but in relation to the students' writing.

Have students combine the following group of sentences into one sentence. Be sure the finished product includes all the information from the base sentence.

1. Linda played the dirge.
2. Linda played the dirge on the organ.
3. The dirge was in a key.
4. The key was minor.
5. The dirge was sad.
6. The dirge was mournful.
7. The organ was electric.
8. The organ was in the church.

After students have combined the previous group of sentences into one and shared the possible final sentences, have them combine the following groups of base sentences into one sentence. When the activity is completed, students should have created ten sentences from the 56 base sentences.

Base Sentences

1. I went into the classroom.
2. It was decorated.
3. It was bright.
4. It had bulletin boards.
5. The bulletin boards displayed letters.
6. The letters were made of construction paper.
7. The letters were red.
8. The bulletin board displayed pictures.
9. The pictures were of teenagers.
10. There was a desk.

11. The desk belonged to the teacher.
12. The desk was grey.
13. The desk was metal.
14. The desk was in the front of the room.
15. There were several student desks.
16. The desks were in groups of four.
17. The groups were set throughout the room.
18. The desks were flat-topped.
19. The desks were wooden.
20. There was a blackboard.
21. The blackboard was behind the desk.
22. The desk was the teacher's.
23. The blackboard had announcements.
24. The announcements were regarding orientation.
25. The announcements were written in chalk.
26. The chalk was multicolored.
27. There were windows.
28. The windows were covered with venetian blinds.
29. The blinds were white.
30. The windows were in the back of the room.
31. I looked out the windows.
32. I could see the courtyard.
33. I could see several trees.
34. The trees were dogwood.
35. I could see a bench.
36. A boy was sitting on the bench.
37. A girl was sitting on the bench.
38. The bell rang.
39. The bell was a warning.
40. The warning was for students.
41. Class would begin in five minutes.
42. I heard footsteps.
43. The footsteps were scurrying.
44. The footsteps were in the hall.
45. The students entered through the door.
46. The students entered hurriedly.
47. The students are pushing.
48. The students are shoving.
49. The students headed for their seats.

50. The bell rang.
51. It is the final bell.
52. The teacher entered the room.
53. The teacher was new.
54. The teacher was eager.
55. The school year had begun.
56. The school year was new.

The following group of base sentences may be combined using key words to combine the major elements. Again, have students share their products.

Base Sentences

that   1. Mr. Mitchell made an announcement.
     2. Band practice would be cancelled.
because 3. Mother's cleaning was diligent.
     4. The house always looked immaculate.
who   5. Carol enjoys playing practical jokes.
     6. Carol is in charge of the April Fools' Day celebration.
that   7. The game was played on Friday.
     8. The game was for the championship.
     9. We raised money for the field trip to go to the museum.
by   10. We sold candy.
    11. The choir sang a hymn.
    12. The hymn was special.
as   13. The hymn was a praise.
    14. The offering was being collected.
    15. The ushers collected the offering.
    16. George was the team's only hope.
    17. The hope was for victory.
although 18. George knew this.
    19. George remained calm.
    20. George was standing at the free throw line.
    21. The bus was delayed.
because 22. The bus carried the football team.
    23. The game began an hour late.
    24. The seniors dedicated their gift.
    25. The gift was annual.

whom   26. The gift was dedicated to Mrs. Patrick.
        27. The gift was dedicated at the assembly.
        28. The seniors respect the teacher.

Figure 36
Homonym Crossword Puzzle

Directions: Complete the following crossword puzzle by using the appropriate homonyms.

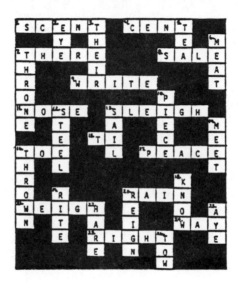

ACROSS

1. Perfume's smell
4. Penny (Homonym of #1A)
7. The book is over _____.
   (Homonym of #3D)
8. Clothes are cheaper when they're
   on _____.
9. & 25. She needed to ___9___
   (correspond) her mother ___25___
11. Used to smell with
13. Used to ride on snow
15. Seventh note on musical scale
16. A foot part
17. Opposite of war
20. Precipitation
21. Use a scale to do this
24. "Watch me and I'll show you the
   _____ to do it."

DOWN

2. Used to see with
3. _____ car is being repaired.
5. A beverage (Homonym of #15A)
6. Food from animals
7. What kings and queens sit on
10. A part of the whole
12. Hard metal
13. Piece of canvas that makes a
   boat move in the wind
14. To join
16. "Have you ever _____ a football?"
   (Homonym of #7D)
18. "Do you _____ the answer?"
19. Religious ceremony (Homonym of #9A)
20. To rule
22. Rabbit
23. Synonym of "yes".
26. To pull (homonym of #16A)

2. After completing the sentence-combining activity above, students can reverse the process with the following procedure. This, again, enables the students to be aware how sentences are put together to make effective and ineffective discourse. Take any rather complex sentence from a piece of literature and have students dismantle it into its component parts. Then, have them put the sentence back together again in a number of effective ways. Any complex sentence will work. The following is a suggestion from Irwin Shaw's "The Eighty-Yard Run."

> He smiled a little to himself as he ran, holding the ball lightly in front of him with his two hands, his knees pumping high, his hips twisting in the almost girlish run of a back in a broken field.

As a follow-up activity, have students look through their writing folders and choose a piece of writing for revision emphasizing this sentence-combining technique.

3. A creative way to help students with homonyms and, thus, to alleviate some of the spelling problems that are often found with homonyms is to use the Homonym Crossword Puzzle (See Fig. 36). Duplicate this puzzle without the homonyms and give to students.

4. The misuse of commas frequently hinders the inexperienced writer. The Comma Activity Sheet (See Fig. 37) is a creative approach to help students to think through how important the comma is for effective communication.

Figure 37
Comma Activity Sheet

Directions: The following exercise indicates the importance of the simple comma in effective communication. Respond to the following questions by circling the appropriate letter.

1. Which person is inviting the most guests?
   a. Doris is inviting Mary Jane, Sue, Ellen, and Billy Joe.
   b. Nancy is inviting Mary, Jane, Billy, Joe and Sue Ellen.
2. Who's buying the most groceries?
   a. At the store Norman bought cream, cheese, ice, milk, chicken soup, and and ginger snaps.
   b. At the store Jerry bought ice, milk, chicken, soup, ginger, snaps, and cream cheese.
3. In which case does the doctor have a broken leg?
   a. Dr. Brown, my husband, broke his leg while skiing.
   b. Dr. Brown, my husband broke his leg while skiing.
4. In which case does the woman live outside the United States?
   a. Florence moved to New Mexico.

Figure 37 (**continued**)

b. Gladys moved to New, Mexico.

5. Which girl has more than one brother?
   a. Roberta's brother who lives in Colorado is an airplane pilot.
   b. Rita's brother, who lives in Colorado, is an airplane pilot.

6. In which case would the soap irritate the skin?
   a. The harsh smelling soap lay by the lavoratory.
   b. The harsh, smelling soap lay by the lavoratory.

7. In which case will all ninth graders be excluded from school?
   a. Freshmen who skipped school will be expelled.
   b. Freshmen, who skipped school, will be expelled.

8. In which case is an explanation called for?
   a. Why, did you get a ticket?
   b. Why did you get a ticket?

9. Which of the following commands suggests poor table manners?
   a. Eat your salad and roll in your dish.
   b. Eat your salad, and roll in your dish.

10. In which case does the employer need further applications?
    a. "No, one fit the qualifications for the position," the employer replied.
    b. "No one fit the qualifications for the position," the employer replied.

5. The worksheets (See Figs. 38–40) emphasize working with ambiguous sentences, agreement, and capitalization. All three of these areas frequently offer the inexperienced writer problems.

Figure 38
Ambiguous Sentence Activity Sheet

Directions: Rewrite the following sentences so that the meanings are clear and make sense.

1. Jan told her mother she needed a new winter coat.

2. Turning the corner, an accident occurred.

3. Upon seeing the red light, the car was brought to a halt.

4. Take the glasses from the cupboards and clean them.

5. At the circus we saw the clown juggling balloons and the fat lady.

6. Having the TV on for over an hour, my parents made me turn it off to do my homework.

7. To become an expert gymnast, hours of practice must be scheduled every week.

8. As Emily handed her completed test to Mrs. Patrick, she smiled.

9. Being in a glass jar, I could see how many cookies were left.

10. Being without electricity for 24 hours, I was afraid the food in the refrigerator would spoil.

Figure 38 (**Continued**)

11. Roger and Doug played Monopoly until he had to go home.

12. Seeing the fire, it was obvious that the shops were in danger.

13. When the boys put the electric train on the track, it broke.

14. Trying to raise money for the club, the bake sale was set up for Saturday.

15. Having won the game, the victory party was a success.

Figure 39
Agreement Activity Sheet

Part I Directions: Choose the appropriate form of the verb in the parentheses and write it in the blank at the left.

_____ 1. Between the rows of trumpet players (march, marches) the drum major.

_____ 2. One of the three football players who collided (was, were) hurt.

_____ 3. The varsity team (is, are) to receive the first place trophy.

_____ 4. Bad news (was, were) found all over the front page.

_____ 5. The United States (is, are) over two hundred years old.

_____ 6. Twenty acres of farmland (was, were) ready for harvest.

_____ 7. Neither Heidi nor Becky (has, have) enough money for the movie.

_____ 8. There (is, are) too many outfielders on the field.

_____ 9. Susie Hinton's *The Outsiders* (is, are) very popular among young readers.

_____ 10. Each of the rock stars (play, plays) before a sell-out crowd.

_____ 11. Social Studies (take, takes) up more of my homework time than any other subject.

_____ 12. Fifty gallons of water (run, runs) through the fountain in the park.

_____ 13. Either Tom or his parents (attend, attends) every club meeting.

_____ 14. Three-fourths of the class (participate, participates) in extracurricular activities.

_____ 15. Trisha says she (don't, doesn't) like to get up early in the morning.

Part II Directions: Choose the appropriate form of each pronoun in parentheses and write it in the blank at the left.

_____ 1. Could you and (they, them) help decorate for the party after school?

_____ 2. The coach gave Bob and (I, me) some extra help on free throws.

_____ 3. None of the students has (his, their) drivers license yet.

_____ 4. (We, Us) boys will sit together at the game.

Figure 39 (**continued**)

_____ 5. Did you sell as many tickets as (he, him)?

_____ 6. Jack and (I, me, myself) went for a walk along the lake front.

_____ 7. Neither Elaine nor Shawna has (her, their) locker combination memorized.

_____ 8. The teacher called a meeting for (we, us) girls on the cheerleading squad.

_____ 9. Brad can run faster than (he, him).

_____10. Everyone polished (his, their) skateboard for the contest.

_____11. Some of the teachers have (his, their) students do outside reading for class.

_____12. Either (they, them) or the Adams must arrange for renting the clubhouse for the party.

_____13. Last summer (she, her) and Linda were tennis partners.

_____14. Awards for best performances went to Lauren and (I, me).

_____15. The typists for the paper were Beth and (he, him).

Figure 40
Capitalization Activity Sheet

Directions: Put an X through the small letter that you believe needs to be capitalized and put the capital letter above it.

1. We traveled on interstate 70 through kansas on our way to colorado.

2. The president spent several days in the soviet union discussing the salt treaty.

3. The north and the south fought bitterly during the civil war.

4. Are you attending the university of illinois or a university in the east?

5. The baileys live twenty miles east of the state line.

6. Our club meets every tuesday night in the summer.

7. The archeologist dated the fossil to be around 600 b.c.

8. On friday we had substitutes for english and math.

9. At the store mother bought twenty cans of campbells soup and five bottles of heinz ketchup.

10. We found an old new york newspaper in the rumbleseat of the model t ford.

11. Her husband is a second-year medical student at john hopkins university.

12. My aunt owns a boutique in the san francisco bay area.

13. The united nations was formed shortly after world war II.

Figure 40 (continued)

14. My mother and father are members of the first baptist church on manchester boulevard.

15. During the american revolution, general george washington took control of the troups in july of 1775 after the april battle of lexington.

USAGE

The concept of "right vs. wrong" in language is vitally important to young people. Students should investigate language usage from its early beginnings through the "authoritarian" influence of the eighteenth century, and through the "usage docturine" advocated by the linguists of the nineteenth and twentieth centuries. How does this "myth of absolute correctness" fit in with how usage is handled in schools and how young people, as well as adults, speak and write?

What constitutes "good" and "bad" English? Many linguists and language educators recommend that teachers accept as good English language what is appropriate to the purpose of the speaker, true to the language as it is, and comfortable to the speaker and listener. They see such language as the product of custom neither cramped by rule nor freed from all restraint. It is never fixed but changes with organic life of the language.

It is our belief that the curriculum should be relevant to the students' needs, (i.e. it should give students the opportunity to practice their language), which is used for different purposes, for different listeners/ readers, and for different occasions.

Activities

6. There are three usage activities (See Figs. 41–43). These activities allow the students to make choices concerning usage items in relation to given situations, to make decisions about the appropriate form of a few troublesome verbs, and to offer alternative verbs to the overused verb "to get." Be sure to discuss the basis for the choices as well as the choices themselves.

Figure 41
Usage-Situation

Directions: Ten different situations are briefly described below. After each description you will find an idea expressed in various ways. Choose the most appropriate response for each situation by circling the letter of the response.

Table 41 (**continued**)

1. A boy who has just torn the leg on his good pants is talking to his friends.
   A. My mother will show a great deal of anger upon learning of my torn pants.
   B. My mother will be upset with me.
   C. My Mom's gonna kill me!

2. Knowing that her parents are expecting a long-distance call, ten-year old Sara is answering the phone:
   A. Who's there?
   B. Dustin residence; Sara speaking.
   C. Hello.

3. Your mother asks you to leave the room so she can speak privately to your father.
   A. Would you please leave the room for a few minutes.
   B. I beg you to absent yourself from our presence.
   C. Get out of here.

4. Your teenage brother asks you to leave his room so he can talk privately to his friend.
   A. Would you please leave the room for a few minutes.
   B. I beg you to absent yourself from our presence.
   C. Get out of here.

5. A lost three year old is speaking to a store clerk.
   A. I seemed to have wandered away from my mother.
   B. I can't find my mother.
   C. Where's my mommy?

6. A fourteen year old speaking to a store clerk.
   A. Ain't you got no jellybeans?
   B. I would like to purchase some jellybeans.
   C. Do you have any jellybeans?

7. You have knocked at the door of your best friend's house and someone asks "Who is it?"
   A. It's me.
   B. It is I.
   C. Who do you think it is?

8. You have answered the door; it is your father's boss.
   A. Good evening sir. Please come in!
   B. Hi! C'mon in!
   C. Oh! It's you! So you want my Dad?

9. You are telling your teacher that your softball team won its game.
   A. Our team was victorious!
   B. We beat those creeps!
   C. We won our game.

Figure 41 (**continued**)

10. Your best friend is telling you that he doesn't want to take his little brother
brother to the movies Saturday afternoon.
   A. I ain't going to take him! No way!
   B. There's no way I'm taking him.
   C. He is a nuisance, I shall not take him!

Figure 42
Usage—Troublesome Verbs

Directions: In the blank at the left, write and spell correctly the appropriate form
of the verb in parentheses.

_____ 1. Ted (bring) three of his visiting cousins to the party.

_____ 2. Debby has (lie) down in the nurses office every day this week.

_____ 3. Our home football team was (beat) only twice last season.

_____ 4. When the skier fell from the lift, he (break) his leg.

_____ 5. We nearly (freeze) while walking to school in the snow.

_____ 6. At the inauguration, the President was (swear) in by the Chief Justice
of the Supreme Court.

_____ 7. I was so embarrassed when I (wear) blue jeans to the party. Everyone
else was dressed up.

_____ 8. Have you (began) studying for next week's math exam?

_____ 9. Lori (bring) so much coffee that it kept her awake all night.

_____ 10. I'm sure that I (lay) the keys next to the telephone, but they're not
there now.

_____ 11. Ron had never (swim) on the relay team until this year.

_____ 12. Even though it was her eighteenth birthday, Judy (blow) out all the
candles with no problem.

_____ 13. The entire chocolate cake was (eat) in one day.

_____ 14. Last night the dog (lie) faithfully on the porch.

_____ 15. Gas prices have (rise) tremendously over the past few years.

_____ 16. When Rick (set) the table, he forgot they were expecting company.

_____ 17. *The Mona Lisa* has (hang) in the Louvre for years.

Figure 42 (**continued**)

_____ 17. *The Mona Lisa* has (hang) in the Louvre for years.

_____ 18. Sharon (raise) the windows to let in some fresh air.

_____ 19. Pam (sneak) into the house very carefully so her parent's wouldn't wake up.

_____ 20. Yesterday Jason (lie) on the lawn for an hour while he observed the the clouds.

Figure 43
Usage — Verb Variety

Directions: The following story about Steve includes many uses of the verb "got." Choose a more appropriate verb and place it in the space provided.

Steve _____ (got up) at six-thirty. He _____ (got) his breakfast and then _____ (got off) to junior college 20 minutes late. Steve _____ (got) a reprimand from his instructor for being late. He _____ (got to) brooding about it. As a result of his tardy, Steve _____ (got) behind in his work. He tried to _____ (get) some help from his friends, but he could not _____ (get) any. Soon, he _____ (got) ready to go to lunch. Since Steve couldn't afford to _____ (get) the regular school lunch, he just _____ (got) a salad. It was cold in the cafeteria and he _____ (got back) to his next class feeling lousy.

Steve thought about his job. He wished he could _____ (get) another after school job. He really couldn't _____ (get along) on his present pay. Steve just simply wanted to _____ (get) more money. Too, he really _____ (got) no satisfaction from working at this job. He hoped to _____ (get away from) the drudgery of it. He tried to _____ (get up) enough courage to quit.

He knew, however, he had _____ (to get) more education. So, he _____ (got back) to his studies. He wasn't able _____ (to get) anything from them. He couldn't _____ (get) his mind on them. He _____ (got) discouraged. His girlfriend _____ (got) him to buy a lottery ticket. He _____ (got) a big prize. On his way home from getting the prize, he _____ (got) run over. And, thus, we _____ (get) to end this sad story.

7. After a discussion of the levels of usage—formal, informal, and non-standard—involve the students in an informal dramatic situation in which they demonstrate the appropriateness of language choices. Prepare slips of paper which contain two categories: a level of usage and a situation. Students are then given the slips and they act out the situation using the appropriate language. You may wish to have the slips contain inappropriate usage with a particular situation to highlight the rightness and wrongness of language for that situation. For example, the usage may be formal, but the situation may be a party with friends, or the usage

may be non-standard, but the situation is an interview for a job. After the dramatizations, discuss the situations and the language choices.

8. Have students create a slang dictionary. Instead of the regular notebook form, have students use a collage format. Students should explore newspapers, magazines, radio, and television for one week and record each slang term that they find. They then place the slang term along with the literal and connotative definition on the collage. Place the collages around the room and share. Discuss with students the role of slang in the language, how it comes into the language, and how long it usually remains. Some of the slang terms of the twenties, fifties and sixties are interesting to include in the discussion.

9. Frequently, phrases come into the language and are used repeatedly. A number of these are listed below. Have students substitute original expressions for those listed.

Sadder but wiser.	Don't cry over spilled milk.
Pure as the driven snow.	Fit as a fiddle.
By and large.	Honest as the day is long.
Get into the act.	That's the way the ball bounces.
Run at the mouth.	Smooth as silk.
Hard as a rock.	Sharp as a tack.
Get your drift.	Play second fiddle.

Ask students to create a list of their own by using their common expressions. Then, again, ask them to make substitutions.

10. To help students practice the use of a variety of usage decisions, have students write an account of a car accident in which they are the driver. Tell them to describe the same accident to each of the following people:

- The insurance agent
- A best friend
- Parents

Discuss the writing and usage decisions made. Explain how the particular audience has affected the word choice, tone, and use of details.

LANGUAGE HERITAGE

A study of the history of the English language enables students to realize that their language is not static—that it has changed over the years and will continue to change. This concept of linguistic change is extremely important as students and teachers try to understand and to accept the varieties of social and geographical dialects found among students.

It is important to note the importance of English. It is spoken in all six continents today and also has a strong effect in many regions in which it is not the principal language spoken. Important, too, is the past from which this English language came. English belongs to the Indo-European family of languages; so, it is therefore related to most other languages spoken in Europe and western Asia. Modern English is analytic, mostly un-inflected, although its history dates back to a highly inflected, artificial form. In addition to this simplicity of inflections, English has two other basic characteristics: flexibility of function and openness of vocabulary.

The beginnings of English date back to 450 A.D. in what we now call England. Its origins started with the language of three tribes: Anglos, Saxons, and Jutes. The language survived and grew through many influences: invasions from the Danes, influences from the Scandinavians, the invasion of the Normans (usually referred to as the Middle English Period), and a number of other influences through the Early Modern English Period to the changes that are still occurring today.

Why study language history? The most important reason is to show student's that our language has changed and that it will continue to change. If we understand that language is changing and that many varieties are acceptable, perhaps we also will be more tolerant of how people speak differently. Students can see that different language habits are not inferior. In addition, historical study shows how words change in meaning and usage. Students are often quite surprised of the double negatives of Chaucer and of the acceptance of "ain't" in the works of Shakespeare.

We believe that there is great value in teaching the history of the English language. We think it should be presented in very practical ways, largely through the use of student activities and investigations. We have developed the following activities to help you present this very interesting and exciting study to students.

Activities

11. Have students (in pairs or in groups) prepare a visual representation of the chronological development of the English language using a river and its tributaries to depict language change. The river itself is English; the tributaries are the influences on the language. Students should consider the placement and size of the tributaries so that they are consistent with the time and degree of influence of the change on the language. An alternative activity: Have groups choose various segments of language development to illustrate pictorially on large pieces of butcher paper. When finished, segments can be joined together for a continuous mural.

12. Select words of interesting origins and give each student one or two words to research the etymology. After the research is done, students write the information in a brief creative story.

Example: **bonfire.** In the Middle Ages plagues often wiped out half the population of a city at once. There was no time for proper burials, and even in those days it was realized that disease spread from the sick and dying to the well. So bodies were piled in heaps and burned. When the flame died out, only the bones were left. These funeral pyres were called **bone-fires.** Think of that the next time you toast marshmallows over a **bonfire**!

The following is a list of possible words with interesting origins:

yuletide	taxicab
flamingo	tantalize
chivalry	stigma
hippopotamus	sinister
spider	salary
thug	rehearse
pretext	remorse
precocious	pencil
parasite	pavilion
orchestra	melancholy
gymnasium	lace
escape	gossip
derrick	bonanza
boycott	pedigree

13. Throughout history there have been certain words, phrases, or chants—most of them having to do with superstitions—that have put fear into many a heart. Have students look into the origins of some of these "midnight" words. The following is a partial list: ghoul, genie, vampire, goblin, werewolf, banshee, incubus, succubus, nightmare, voodoo, witch, witch hazel, warlock. Have students make a collage for each word, giving a visual drawing and an etymological background showing in what country and from what language(s) the word originated. A discussion of the backgrounds and beginnings of words and how they come into the language should follow.

14. Have students investigate the differences in Old English, Middle English, and Modern English. The most effective way for this activity to work is to couple language study with the study of literature. Use *Beowulf*, Chaucer's *Canterbury Tales* (Prologue), and any modern English work. Most English anthologies have these works in translation but will include a portion in the original language. To complement the study include a recording of segments of the language periods so that students may hear the differences. Some background on the history of the language should be furnished before this activity gets underway.

15. As a follow-up to the previous activity, have students read the Old English, Middle English, and Modern English versions of the Lord's Prayer. Discuss the three versions. Have students note the alphabet letters and words no longer used. Discuss the concept of linguistic change.

The Lord's Prayer (Matthew 6: 9–13)

Old English
> Fæder ure þu þe eart on heofonum, siþin nama gehalgod.
> Tobecume þin rice. Gewurþe ðin willa onðeor an swa swa on heofonum.
> Urne gedæghwamlican hlaf syle us to dæg.
> And forgyf us urne gyltas, swa swa we forgyfað urum gyltendum.
> And ne gelædðu us on costnunge, ac alys us of yfele.
> Soþlice.

Middle English
> Fader oure þat art in hevene, i-halwed beeþi name.
> I-eume þi kingreiche, y-worthe þi wylle also is in hevene so be on erthe.
> Oure iche-dayes-bred gif us to-day.

And forgif us oure gultes, also we forgifeth oure gultare.
And ne led ows nowth into fondingge, auh ales ows of harme. So be hit.

Early Modern English

Our father which art in heaven, hallowed be thy name.
Thy kingdom come. Thy will be done in earth, as it is in heaven.
Give us this day our daily bread.
And forgive us our debts, as we forgive our debtors.
And lead us not into temptation, but deliver us from evil:
For thine is the kingdom, and the power, and the glory, for ever.
Amen.

16. This activity helps students to see that words change in meaning from one generation or one century to another, that these changes become more specialized or generalized in application, and that the meaning becomes elevated or degraded. For this activity have students use *The Oxford English Dictionary* or material from this dictionary that you provide the students. Have students work in pairs to research the way words have changed meanings through ages of language use. They would determine if the words have become more specialized or generalized and whether the meaning has been elevated or degraded.

Examples: **nice:** In 1560 it meant foolish or stupid. Now the meaning has been elevated to mean pleasing or kind.

meat: Originally it referred to any kind of food from an animal.

butcher: It has a general meaning now to refer to slaughtering and cutting up animals for food. When it was first used, butcher referred only to one who killed goats.

lewd: It originally meant "ignorant." Now the meaning has undergone the process of degradation to mean "carnal," "lecherous," or "indecent."

The following words are suggested for exploration: boor, chest, knight, knave, girl, marshal, pastor, gig, wench, villian, cupboard, liquor.

17. Have students use the coat of arms shown in Figure 44 to record the research they find on their last names. Have students secure the following information: country their name comes from, meaning of the name, what the name is in other countries, two famous people who have the same name, and alternate spelling of the name. In section six have

students place a picture or symbol which represents their name. Display and share the name coat of arms.

DIALECTS

Regional Dialects

In our pluralistic society, a wide variety of languages and dialects are spoken daily. Even though each person has a dialect—an idiolect—the dialect concept is widely misunderstood. Many people believe that the dialect is a corruption of the standard language rather than a valid variation. It is important, then, for students to become aware of and appreciate the variety of dialects as valid forms of language use.

Generally, there are three dialect regions in the U.S.: northern, southern, and midland; however, because of improved communications, these boundaries are not as clearly defined as they used to be. Too, within each region, there are many dialect pockets. For example, within the northern area there exist dialects of northeastern New England, southeastern New England, southwestern New England, New York City, the Hudson Valley, western Vermont, and upstate New York.

The differences among the dialect areas usually occur in three areas: vocabulary, phonology (sound), and syntax. The following gives a brief example of each:

	Northern	*Southern*	*Midland*
Vocabulary	string beans	snap beans	green beans
Phonology	greasy (grisi)	greasy (grizi)	greasy (grizi)
Syntax	sick to his stomach	sick at his stomach	sick in his stomach
	catch a cold	take a cold	take cold

There are many reasons for these dialect differences. The settlers from England brought with them a variety of dialects from various parts of the mother country. These dialects became the basis for the dialect areas that we presently have in the United States. In addition, we mustn't forget the important impact that the native American made on these dialects. The Indian influence is heard almost daily, as we speak the American language.

The western migration of the colonists contributed to the differences, as well. The language changed as people moved from one area to another.

Figure 44
Coat of Arms—History of Names

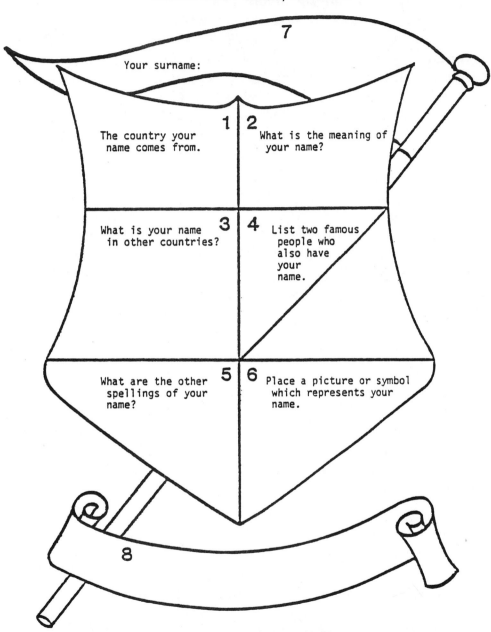

The differences among the dialect areas usually occur in three areas: vo
cabulary, phonology (sound), and syntax. The following gives a brief ex
ample of each:

Another very important factor is the immigration during the nineteenth century of people from many different lands.

Physical geography influences the nature of the language, too. Mountains, rivers, deserts, and marshes often block the spread of different words and expressions. This influence does not have such an effect now but played an important role in the early establishment of the various dialects. A good example is the Connecticut River, which serves as the natural boundary between Vermont and New Hampshire. This river also serves as the major dividing point between the eastern New England and the Vermont, upstate New York dialect areas.

The study of geographical dialects arouses a great deal of enthusiasm in the students as they have opportunity to investigate their own dialects. Students begin to notice how their dialects are different from their neighbor's, and soon they begin to see how their dialects are different from those of others in their school, community, state, and nation. We believe, too, that as students begin to learn more about each other's language differences, they begin to learn more about each person's uniqueness. As a result, there may be more tolerance toward the differences found in people. An important concept to teach is that language difference is not language inferiority.

Activities

18. We have included below a list of words and phrases that are frequently expressed in varied ways in different dialect sections of the country. Have students go through the list indicating just what they do say! Discuss the regional varieties.

1. *Apple and Pastry Dessert Baked in a Deep Dish:* apple cobbler, apply dowdy, apple pan dowdy, apple slump, deep-dish apple pie, pot pie, bird's nest, deep apple pie.
2. *Cornmeal Bread Baked in Large Cakes:* corn bread, Johnny cake, corn pone, pone, spoon bread, butter bread, hoe cake, corn dodger, corn duffy, cracklin bread.
3. *Corn Served on the Cob:* sweet corn, sugar corn, mutton corn, green corn, roasting corn, corn on the cob.
4. *Round Confection with Hole in the Center:* doughnuts, crullers, fried cakes, fat-cakes, raised doughnuts, nig doughnuts, nut cakes.

5. *Round Flat Cakes, Fried on a Griddle:* pancakes, griddlecakes, batter cakes, hot cakes, flennel cakes, flapjacks, slapjacks.
6. *Stone of a Peach:* stone, pit, seed, kernal.
7. *Food Eaten Between Regular Meals:* a bite, snack, a piece, piece meal, lunch.
8. *Green Leafy Cover of an Ear of Corn:* cap, husk, shuck.
9. *Piece of Furniture with Drawers:* chest of drawers, bureau, chifferobe, chiffonier.
10. *Center of County Government:* county seat, county capital, shire town, county site, parish seat.
11. *Devices at Edge of Roof to Carry off Rain:* eaves houghs, eaves, gutters, spouts, canals, water troughs.
12. *Water Device Over Sink:* faucet, tap, sicket, spigot, hydrant.
13. *Pan for Frying:* frying pan, fry pan, spider, skillet.
14. *Paper Container for Carrying Groceries:* sack, bag, poke, toot.
15. *Seesaw:* seesaw, teeter-totter, teetering board, teeter horse, see-horse.
16. *Room Where Guests are Entertained.* sitting room, parlor, front room, living room, best room.
17. *Long Chair:* sofa, couch, divan, davenport.
18. *The Sun Appears At:* sunrise, sunup, dawn.
19. *The Sun Disappears At:* sunset, sundown, dusk.
20. *It's _____ from here:* kitty-cornered, catter-cornered, catty-cornered, catty-wampus, zig-zag, caper-cornered, bias ways.

19. As a follow up to the previous activity, have students use the Dialect Survey Sheet (See Fig. 45) to survey dialect differences in their community. Stress the importance of selecting a wide variety of people from different ages, occupations, and socioeconomic backgrounds, as well as from different regions; discuss with students the results. Include in your discussion information about social dialects. It is important to discuss the results even though there may be little variation in some communities; students should explore why this difference does not exist.

20. Students frequently enjoy "firsthand data" in their dialect study. Have them record a passage and send it to another school in another community in a different dialect area. This is not as difficult as it may seem. Simply choose a community from a map and send a letter of inquiry about the project to the English teacher of that community's junior or senior high school. Exchange the recorded passages and discuss them.

Figure 45
Dialect Survey

Directions: Survey people of various geographical regions (who much to your surprise can be found in your own school and community) to see what they call the objects below. Record their responses, along with the biographical information requested.

Participant's Name

Age				
Birthplace				
Other Residences				
Pan for frying				
Corn served on the cob				
Open vessel for carrying water				
Carbonated beverage comes in bottle or can				
Insect that glows at night				
Cottage cheese				
Bone from a chicken breast				
Carriage for carrying a baby				
Large porch with roof				
Short heavy rain				
Worthless dog				
Water device over sink				

21. There are many authors who use dialects in their writings. Have students read some of the following authors and investigate their use of dialects:

Langston Hughes
James Weldon Johnson
Robert Newton Peck
Mildred Taylor
Willa Cather

Walter Dean Myers
Ring Lardner
Damon Runyon
J.D. Salinger
John Steinbeck

| Ole Rolvaag | Sue Ellen Bridgers |
| Mark Twain | Jessamyn West |

22. Have students write and record versions of a familiar story such as "Goldilocks" or "Cinderella" as it would be told by someone living in the various dialect regions. In addition, have students emphasize social dialects by retelling the story as it would be told in Black English, in typical teenage talk, or by someone who speaks a prestigious, formal social dialect.

Social Dialects

In addition to the geographical dialects, students of all language varieties ought to be aware of the social dialects, especially of those that are predominant in their community. There are many varieties of nonstandard English. Taylor (1985) cites eight: Appalachian English, Athabascan English (Alaska), black English vernacular, general American nonstandard English, Keaukaha English (Hawaii), New York City nonstandard English, Southern American nonstandard English, and Spanish-influenced English (p. 10). For our purposes in this chapter, we have included a description of the black English vernacular (BEV) since it has more of a national appeal. Two important points seem to be in order: what is BEV and what relationship does it have to the English classroom?

It is generally accepted that the black English Vernacular is significantly different from the standard dialect in that it does have a system; and, therefore, it is a dialect with observable characteristics. Linguistic research indicates five systematic differences exist between BEV and standard English:

Copula Deletion:	They mine.
Negative Concord:	He don't know nothing.
Invariant Be:	I be here.
Dummy It:	It's a student at the door.
Negative Inversion:	Didn't nobody see it.

Geneva Smitherman makes a strong and pointed comment about the relationship of BEV to the educational system:

> Ain nothin in a long time lit up the English teaching profession like the current hassle over black English. One finds beaucoup sociolinguistic research studies and language projects for the "disadvantaged" on the scene in nearly every sizable black community in the country. An educators from K–Grad. School bees debating whether: (1) blacks should learn and use only standard

white English, (2) blacks should command both dialects, i.e., be bi-dialectal, (3) blacks should be allowed (?????) to use standard black English. The appropriate choice having everything to do with American political reality, which is usually ignored, and nothing to do with the educational process, which is usually claimed. I say without qualification that we cannot talk about the black idiom part from black culture and the black experience. Nor can we specify educational goals for blacks apart from consideration about the structure of (white) American society. An we black folks is not gon take all that weight, for no one has empirically demonstrated that linguistic/stylistic features of black English impede educational process in communication skills, or any other area of cognitive learning (Smitherman, 1977).

When referring to the educational implications of BEV, these three points emphasized by Smitherman are discussed. But most educators, although there are exceptions, would come down on the side of Smitherman's second point: teachers should help speakers of BEV be bi-dialectal; i.e., speakers should be able to speak and write effectively in both dialects to satisfy the purpose of the speaker/writer as well as the audience for whom the communication is intended and the occasion on which the communication is given. If this is followed, it seems that young people would not be asked to "give up" their own dialect but add to it by knowing and using the standard dialect when necessary. In doing this, it seems that students would be given more chances of success in a world which seems to be dominated by users of standard English.

SEMANTICS

Students should be encouraged to observe how language is being used around them and to what extent it has an effect on them. They should listen carefully to radio and television advertisements, political speeches— persuasive and informative speeches of any kind—and the use of language around school by their peers, teachers, and administrators. Students should read critically, too. Articles, ads, news items in the school and local newspapers should be included in classroom discussions.

Language is an important part of the students' lives. It is imperative that they are able to control it and not let it control them. Therefore, students need to be conscious of the meaning of words in the context in which they are found. For example, what is the senator trying to say? Or, How can I tell him/her more clearly? Or, What kind of doublespeak is that?

Teachers need to help students to be aware of labeling and certainly careful of absolutes when used in language. In addition, students should be allowed to discover relevance of the study of language. Just why do words mean what they mean? What relationship does semantics have to the culture in which we live?

23. To help students in understanding the differences between denotation and connotation, have them use the words listed below. Students should find their denotations by looking them up in the dictionary, and they should list as many connotations for the words that they can.

Words	Denotative Meaning	Connotative Meaning
red		
black		
cat		
apple		
strike		
politician		
chicken		
ghetto		
clown		
cool		
baby		
student		

24. Using the euphemisms worksheet (see Figure 46), have students indicate euphemisms for the words listed. Help students understand the euphemism concept; explore with them that in most cases the use of the euphemism is done in a positive way. No harm is done. No deception or misinformation is suggested. It softens the message without altering it. There are, however, softened words and expressions that have an altogether different intent—the intent to deceive. This is called Doublespeak, the

> language which pretends to communicate but really does not. It is language which makes the bad seem good, something negative appear positive, and something unpleasant appear attractive, or at least tolerable. It is language which avoids or shifts responsibility, language which is at variance with its real meaning. It is language which conceals or prevents thought. Doublespeak is language which does not extend thought but limits it (Lutz, 1987, p. 10).

To help fight this misuse and abuse of language, the National Council of Teachers of English established the Committee on Public Doublespeak. In 1975, the Committee established the George Orwell Award to recognize each year the author or authors of a work which has made an outstanding contribution to the critical analysis of public discourse. The year earlier, the Committee established the Doublespeak Award to that person or group who has misused and/or abused the language. The Committee recognizes through this award the public display of language what has as its purpose to deceive those who receive it.

Politicians, government agencies, education, business, advertising provide ample sources of doublespeak. A few examples follow:

initiate operations improvement	firing of workers
proactive downsizing	firing of workers
poorly buffered precipitation	acid rain
sales credits	bribes and kickbacks
relocation centers	concentration camps
technical collection sources	wiretaps
pedestrian facilities	sidewalks
age-controlled environment	a bar
rough-and-tumble neighborhood	slum or ghetto
impacted with ground prematurely	unexpected crash
transportation counselor	car salesperson
wage-based premium	a tax
investment	spending

25. Using the Doublespeak Activity Sheet (See Fig. 47) have students play with the doublespeak possibilities in preparing a menu. While not as serious as those doublespeak items listed above, menu items listed in a particular way do try to take plain food items and offer descriptions that sound as if they were delicacies.

26. Sexism prevails throughout our society. Many feel that this affects our relationships with each other to the extent that communication breaks down. Explore with students the extent to which sexism is found in television. Have students observe TV programs and record the following information:

1. Name of program
2. Number of major female characters
3. Roles and occupations of major female characters
4. Number of females in listing of credits
5. Number of major male characters
6. Roles and occupations of major male characters
7. Number of males in listing of credits

Discuss with students their attitudes toward sexism.

27. As a follow up to the previous activity, have students use a print ad and rewrite it or take a television commercial and act it out differently so that they are free from stereotypical attitudes. Discuss if the alternatives are as effective in making the product desirable.

Figure 46
Euphemisms

In the course of time, some words acquire a connotation that many people find unpleasant. When this happens, people use a euphemistic term instead. (A euphemism is a better-sounding word or phrase used in place of one that seems too harsh or direct.) Thus "death" becomes "passing away" and a "janitor" becomes a "custodial engineer."

Directions: Write euphemisms for the following words and phrases.

1. spy	2. grease monkey
3. old people	4. garbage
5. stool pigeon	6. wierd
7. snobbish	8. touchy
9. undertaker	10. crippled
11. false teeth	12. a lie
13. toilet	14. fired
15. slum	16. conceited
17. stubborn	18. insane asylum
19. prison	20. fat
21. skinny	22. graveyard
23. poor	24. dog catcher
25. sick	

Directions: Give new examples of euphemistic expressions not previously mentioned which have the following purposes:

1. Gives a more prestigious title for a job or occupation.

2. Spares the feelings of another.

3. Attempts to cover up the truth.

28. Have students bring children's pictures and storybooks to the classroom. Have them go through the books looking for stereotypical examples of masculine and feminine roles and characters. Especially look for the following:

1. words used to describe females
2. words used to describe males
3. jobs of women

Figure 47
Doublespeak Activity Sheet

Directions: People frequently select particular words to mislead or deceive the listener or reader. This often happens in advertising, politics and government, and education. Too, it can and often does happen in relation to food, especially in the naming of food items on a menu. In the appropriate column, choose a doublespeak term that best names each item of food that is normally found in a full-course dinner. Then, give the actual food content in the last column. For example, you might have a "San Francisco Supreme" as a meat dish, but in reality, what you have is a giant hamburger patty topped with cheese and served with sourdough bread wedges.

Item in Dinner	*Doublespeak Term*	*Actual Food*
appetizer		
soup		
salad		
meat dish		
potato		
vegetable		
dessert		
beverage		

4. jobs of men
5. sex of major verses minor characters

Discuss the possible effect, if any, of these books on young children.

29. As a follow up to the previous activity, have students in small groups create a children's literature book in which males and females are portrayed in a non-sexist manner.

30. List several nouns, particularly applying to job descriptions, on paper. Have each student indicate whether they think of these nouns in terms of male, female, or both. Tally results for students and follow up with a discussion. After talking about the results, discuss the effects of stereotypical behavior and attitudes on individuals and why it is important to discard them. The following is a partial list:

newscaster	senator	president
movie star	writer	teacher
cook	police officer	lawyer
principal	major	engineer
chemist	dentist	pilot

babysitter	pharmacist	musician
professor	artist	dancer
nurse	telephone operator	firefighter
carpenter	plumber	salesperson
athlete	interior decorator	mechanic
secretary	hairdresser	architect
photographer	computer analyst	receptionist

31. To help students have a clear understanding of propaganda and its uses, have students complete a Propaganda and Persuasive Techniques worksheet as shown in Figure 48. A full discussion of their findings should occur.

Jeffrey Schrank (1974) has created another language manipulative

Figure 48
Propaganda and Persuasive Techniques

Directions: After a class discussion of the propaganda and persuasive techniques listed below, choose 10 of the 15 to illustrate. For each of your 10 choices give 1) a brief explanation of the example which illustrates the technique and 2) the source (magazine/newspaper/TV title and date).

Technique	*Source*	*Explanation*
Glittering Generalities		
Name Calling		
Testimonial		
Bandwagon		
Transfer		
Concern for the Public Good		
It's New		
Card Stacking		
Statistics		
An Expert Says		
Plain Folks		
Snob Appeal		
Romantic Appeal		
Eye Appeal		
Youth Appeal		

system that is used primarily for analysis of advertising in newspapers and magazines and on television and radio. His schema involves analyzing the following 10 basic advertising techniques:

1. The Weasel Claim—a word or phrase is included to negate the claim.
2. The Unfinished Claim—offers a comparison but doesn't finish it.
3. The "We're Different and Unique" Claim—a supposed difference would lead to superiority.
4. The "Water is Wet" Claim—something is true of that product but is true of all products in that category.
5. The "So What" Claim—something is true of a product but has no advantage.
6. The Vague Claim—claim not clear—colorful but meaningless words.
7. The Testimonial—celebrity or authority speaks for the product.
8. The Scientific or Statistical Claim—scientific terms, scientific proof, statistics are offered.
9. The "Compliment the Consumer" Claim—offers flattery to the consumer.
10. The Rhetorical Question—a response supporting the product is requested.

32. Instruct students as a class to generate a list of products or ideas that could "sell" through advertising. Have them choose one. Divide the class into two groups. One group will "sell" its product/idea by using straightforward, factual information; the other group will use the Schrank list of advertising techniques listed above to "sell" its product/idea.

33. Have students analyze the rhetoric of a political campaign. This may come from a variety of elections: class, school, community, county, state, or national. Have students share their examples from the various political speeches or reports of statements made by those running for office. Have students examine not only the content of what is said but also the particular language used in making the statement.

34. This activity may be used in a number of areas: connotation and denotation, sexism, and doublespeak. Have students complete the following sentences (you may wish to add more). After the responses are made, students should reflect on the words or phrases that they used. Were their responses closer to a denotative or connotative definition? Was there sexism in their responses? Is the completion clearly expressed? The following is a list of possible sentence starters:

1. Truck drivers are _____
2. Blondes are _____
3. Southerners are _____
4. Athletes are _____
5. Republicans are _____
6. Communists are _____
7. Little brothers and sisters are _____
8. School teachers are _____
9. Lawyers are _____
10. Women's libbers are _____

THE SILENT LANGUAGE

Have you ever said "yes" with your voice but communicated "no" with your tone of voice and facial expression? If you haven't, you are truly an exceptional person. We all communicate in many different ways: verbally and nonverbally. It is our job as English teachers to help students know the impact we make with our nonverbal communication, as well as the words we use.

There are many common ways to communicate nonverbally: facial expressions, tone of voice, eye contact, and gestures. Our curriculum should include materials and activities that help students to learn the impact they have on other people when they use these nonverbal communicators. There are other ways we communicate nonverbally that are not so common: distance between people, relationships with furniture and other objects, and time. For example, many people feel that of most concern is their personal space. Personal space has been likened to a bubble or sphere that serves to protect the individual from intrusion by others. In the American culture, usually three to five feet is the comfortable range for this personal distance; in other cultures, the space is much less.

The following activities will help you to explore with your students the use and misuse of nonverbal communication.

Activities

35. Help students to understand the concept of communicating with nonverbal cues by encouraging them to make an "un-word" dictionary. Students should list in their dictionary all the ways that they and others

communicate nonverbally. The list should include, but not be limited to, the following: gestures, facial expressions, eye contact, body movements, space, time, signs, symbols, etc.

36. Encourage students to think how space talks. Have them think of the many ways that space communicates an idea, an attitude, or a feeling. To get them started, have them consider the following: Do they sit in the same seat in the class voluntarily? The same seat on a bus each time they ride it? Do they have their own chair at home? Does each parent? Does each family member have his/her own space in the home? Compare and contrast their findings with other cultures.

37. Have students bring to class a comic strip of their choice. Have them analyze the strip from the point of view of the nonverbal clues that are evident. As a follow up, have students create their own comic strip communicating a particular message with no words, just nonverbal clues.

38. Play the game of charades with your students. The game consists of one member of the group communicating a message nonverbally to the group. Refresh the memory of the students on the key signals, such as the sign for book, movie, song, first word, it sounds like, etc. Structure the activity so that it meets the strengths and weaknesses of your class setting. Emphasis should be given to the analysis of the nonverbal language that is used.

39. Encourage students to think how time talks. Have them think of the many ways that time communicates an idea, attitude, or a feeling. To get them started, have them consider the following: Are some students late for your class? What does this say about their attitude about the class? When is it appropriate to arrive for a dinner engagement? How important is the time element in dating? Compare and contrast their feelings with other cultures.

FOR ADDITIONAL READING

Andrews, Larry. *Language Exploration and Awareness.* New York: Longman, 1993.

Applebee, Arthur, Judith A. Langer, and Ina V.S. Mullis. *The Writing Report Card.* National Assessment of Educational Progress, 1986.

Arnheim, Rudolf. "Learning by Looking and Thinking." *Educational Horizons,* 71, 2, (Winter, 1993), pp. 94–98.

Boraas, J. *Formal English Grammar and the Practical Mastery of English.* Unpublished doctoral dissertation, University of Minnesota, 1917.

Braddock, Richard, R. Loyd-Jones, and L. Schoer. *Research in Written Composition.* Urbana, IL: NCTE, 1963.

Bushman, John H. *Teaching the English Language.* Springfield, IL: Charles C Thomas, 1988.

Encyclopedia of Educational Research. New York: MacMillan, 1950.

Fehlman, Richard. "Making Meanings Visible: Critically Reading TV." *English Journal,* 81, 7 (1992), pp. 19–24.

Hall, Edward. *The Silent Language.* Garden City, NY: Doubleday, 1959.

Hatfield, Wilbur. *An Experience Curriculum in English: A Report of the Curriculum Commission.* New York: Appleton-Century, 1935.

Hayakawa, S.I. *Language in Thought and Action.* New York: Harcourt, Brace, 1964.

Hillocks, George. *Research on Written Composition.* Urbana, IL: NCTE, 1986.

Hook, J.N. *History of the English Language.* New York: Ronald Press, 1975.

Hoyt, F.S. "The Place of Grammar in the Elementary Curriculum," *Teachers College Record,* 7, (1906), 1–34.

Lederer, Richard. "Good Usage and Good Taste." *Writer's Digest,* 71 (June) pp. 40–43.

Lutz, William. "Notes Toward a Description of Doublespeak (Revised)." *Quarterly Review of Doublespeak,* 13, 2 (January, 1987), pp. 10–12.

Meckel, H. "Research on Teaching Composition and Literature." In *Handbook of Research on Teaching. A Project of the American Educational Research Association.* Ed. N.L. Gage, Chicago: Rand McNally, (1963), 966–1006.

Pooley, Robert C. *The Teaching of English Usage.* Urbana, IL: NCTE, 1974.

Quarterly Review of Doublespeak. Urbana, IL: NCTE (offers articles on doublespeak as well as current examples. Winners of the Orwell and Doublespeak Awards are also published here.

Sanborn, Jean. "Grammar: Good Wine Before Its Time," *English Journal,* (March, 1986), 72–80.

Schrank, Jeffrey. "The Language of Advertising Claims." *Media and Methods* (March, 1974), pp. 44–49.

Smitherman, Geneva. *Talkin and Testifin': The Language of Black America.* New York: Houghton Mifflin, 1977.

Strong, William. *Creative Approaches to Sentence Combining.* Urbana, IL: NCTE, 1986.

Taylor, Orlando. "Standard English as a Second Dialect?" *English Today.* ET2 (April, 1985), 9–12.

Warner, Ann. "If the Shoe No Longer Fits, Wear It Anyway?" *English Journal,* 82, 5, (September, 1993), 76–80.

Wilhelmi, Kail. "Mini-Lessons on Language." *English Journal,* 82, 1 (January, 1993), 75–77.

Chapter 9

TEACHING THINKING SKILLS

Thinking skills have been a part of the school program for many, many years. The most common way to convey this study has been through workbooks. Students plowed through workbook after workbook doing exercises which purported to help them think critically. Of course, this approach failed as do most all programs which emphasize teaching skills in isolation. Vocabulary, spelling, and grammar are other areas that are often taught in isolation, and while there may be some success in the short run—long enough for the students to pass the test on Friday or at the end of the unit—there is very little, if any, longterm success; so it is with thinking. When people find themselves having to think through a problem, they do not stop to consider what was taught to them in isolation about thinking in order to solve that particular problem.

It isn't surprising, then, to read of the continued interest in teaching thinking skills in the curriculum. A part of most, if not all, of the current national reports criticizing schools and public education is the edict that educators have not been successful in helping students to think. Publications such as *A Nation at Risk* (1983) and *High School* (1983) along with many others are continually calling for a reassessment of curricula, particularly the English curriculum, and are suggesting that while school programs may continue to provide curriculum materials and teaching strategies to help students with basic education, this basic education must respond to the need for teaching young people to think. To that point, educators in general speak of the need for schools to return to the basics but suggest that the basics of the contemporary students should emphasize thinking skills, such as the ability to analyze and synthesize, to infer accurately, to have in mind problem-solving strategies, to evaluate, to predict, and to be able to communicate effectively. However, we don't do these processes, i.e., we don't think, in isolation. We don't think about thinking except in the sense of reflection, i.e., we may think about the thinking we have done. Even in this way, we evaluate our thinking in terms of the content we thought about. In this way we take the opportunity to reflect on how our own minds have worked. We analyze the process of thinking. So, usually, we think about something—a content. Whether it be about our girl or boy friend, a good book, a concept, or what we had for breakfast, we do think about something. We think using language and therein lies the connection with English.

For many years thinking skills have been attempted at various levels and in various subject-matter classes—(somehow, math people seem to think they have the edge on teaching problem solving). The fact that these skills have been taught in isolation and spread around the curriculum for application has led to their failure. One current approach is that thinking should be taught, of course, when students confront any subject matter but that emphasis be given to these specific thinking skills in the English classroom primarily due to this language connection. The major thrust is to teach students these processes as they encounter literature, language, and oral and written composition. Through these components of the English curriculum students are asked to experience activities which have them relate, connect, predict, recall, comprehend, apply, associate, analyze, synthesize, evaluate and solve problems.

We accept the premise that when students read and write, they are, indeed, engaged in the thinking processes. It would follow, it seems to us, that the inclusion of practice in and some theory about thinking while students read, write, listen and speak will nurture growth in both areas: English skills and thinking skills.

As we indicated in Chapter 10, the integration of the English skills is most important and this importance continues when working specifically with thinking skills. There must be a relationship—a reality—of the skills in thinking and the subject matter thought. Robert Sternberg (1985) seems to indicate a similar view when he states, "Solving inconsequential problems does little to teach students to solve the consequential problems of life" (p. 198). As we have indicated throughout this book, relevance is so important in teaching English. What students listen to, write, read, speak (and now we add think) about must be relevant and meaningful to the lives of these students. Therefore, we do not have a list of activities to consider when teaching thinking skills. What we do have is gentle reminders of how the activities in this book do provide the structure for teaching thinking along with the various language arts of the English curriculum. What follows, then, is a reflection on what we have previously written in terms of teaching thinking skills.

WRITING

It would seem that writing is, indeed, the essence of thinking. Many writers have commented that they really don't know what they *think* about until they begin to *write* about it. Perhaps one of our major failings in the traditional English program has been related to this thinking and writing relationship. Because teachers have not included much writing in the classroom, we wonder to what extent that has had an effect on the thinking or lack of thinking by our students. Certainly we are not suggesting that thinking does not take place, but we are suggesting that writing is a very important avenue for thinking; therefore, we would want as much writing as possible to be in evidence not only in English but also in all content areas. Critical thinking about math, social studies, and science, as well as other subject-area concepts, will most probably be enhanced through writing.

The writing sequence as described in Chapter 4 strengthens thinking skills. Prewriting, writing, and rewriting engage students in processes in which they relate, connect, predict, associate, analyze, synthesize and evaluate. By using the writing sequence, students sharpen their ability to think.

For example, very important in the thinking process is the ability to relate, connect, or in some way associate one idea or concept to another idea or concept. To know how one idea is related to another or to a series of ideas demands this thinking ability. Prewriting, perhaps better than any other process, involves students with these thinking processes. In a brainstorming session, for example, students may generate as many as 50 or so ideas on a given topic. But the job is not done. Students must make decisions as to the appropriateness of each idea generated. Can this idea be used? How is it connected or associated to the topic under consideration? What sequence might these ideas follow? All these questions that students might consider (a thinking skill in itself) are asked either internally or externally before much writing takes place. Most of the external questioning or discussion occurs with a partner or with students in a group before writing; the internal questioning will most frequently take place with the writer himself/herself as the writing occurs.

Another major component of the writing process is revision. Frequently omitted or at least diminished in importance in the traditional writing programs, revision is now a most important factor in helping students to achieve success as they move toward a written product.

Thinking skills play an important role in this revision process. Students must analyze, synthesize, and evaluate among other skills when they "resee" or "review" their writing. Again, they are asked to make judgments concerning the right word or the right phrase; they evaluate the sequence of ideas. In general, they think critically about what they have written: they take their own writing apart and put it back together again. By having students involved in these processes, teachers are helping students to sharpen both their writing and thinking skills.

LITERATURE

The questions at the end of the story so many times serve as the vehicle for thinking as students "study" literature. While some of the questions may come from the higher-order range of Bloom's (1956) taxonomy many, however, do not. Even if the questions were of that nature, they are so limiting in what they have students do. A second type of "non-thinking" response to literature is the study packet in which is found a chronological order of questions that students answer as they read a work. We suggest that this model is "non-thinking" because the questions are frequently found at the lower range of Bloom's taxonomy, and they are sequenced so that students may do very little reading since they skim to find the answer to the question rather than emersing themselves into the literature.

In both of these models, the response that is requested does not seem to be consistent with the response suggested by Rosenblatt (1968), Purves (1968), and Probst (1988), and the approach does not meet the expectations described in Chapter 6 of this book. The major weakness, it seems to us, is that this is a very limited approach to the study of literature, especially since most of the thinking that takes place is generated by someone else and students are given little opportunity to make their response by starting off in a direction of their choice. The response and, therefore, the thinking is teacher or book centered rather than student centered.

If we are to answer some of the critics who complain that students pass through our schools without developing the ability to think creatively and critically, we must structure our lessons so that students have the opportunity to apply what they know, to analyze material read and heard, to synthesize material of varying points of view, to evaluate information from standards that they create, as well as from standards created and accepted by others, and to solve meaningful problems that will offer some benefit for them in a particular way but also for others in a more general way.

We believe that the study of literature offers students this chance. We have suggested in Chapter 6 that students should make a personal response to what they read. We have also suggested many activities that teachers can use to structure lessons so that students can make this personal response and can use important thinking skills. For example, in the second activity in Chapter 6, we ask teachers to have students respond to Value Sheets. A Value Sheet consists of thought-provoking statements duplicated on a sheet of paper, accompanied by a series of questions. These Value Sheets serve the thinking process in many ways: they offer students the opportunity to make connections, to clarify, to predict, to analyze, to synthesize and to evaluate. We go on to suggest the use of a moral dilemma as part of their Value Sheet. On their sheets, students suggest how they think a character would solve a problem. In addition, to increase their own problem-solving expertise, students solve the problem themselves. To emphasize other thinking skills such as perceiving, comparing, contrasting, and categorizing, we suggest that students decide in what ways they and the character are similar or different.

One very important medium for making a personal response is the collage. Some see this as simply a cut-and-paste activity which serves only to entertain students. We disagree. The collage, if done well, calls on many higher-order thinking skills. Certainly perceiving, selecting, arranging, associating, evaluating, and synthesizing are thinking skills which are called into play when creating an effective collage.

Literature serves the development and reinforcement of thinking skills very well. Because students have so many options in how they can make their responses to what they have read, they, indeed, draw upon a wide range of levels of thinking.

LANGUAGE

Critical thinking is essential for an effective language study. Many people use a variety of media to misuse and abuse the English language, and young people are often the target of that language deception. Whether it be through blue jeans, music, make-up, or automobiles, the pressures to buy or to use confronts young people on a daily basis.

Young people are not the only recipients of this language abuse. Adults, as well, are frequently barraged with language that people have used to deceive the reader or listener. People in government, politics, business, and education, to mention only a few areas, go through the motions of communicating but in reality serve the communication process very little. The communication seems to say one thing but may say something else or nothing at all. For example, during the Vietnam Conflict, there were many statements made by people in various agencies which carried little, if any, direct meaning. One such statement suggested that a group of soldiers was going to go on a "reconnaissance mission with extreme prejudice." Most people reading that casually or even with a little attention would not likely realize that the writers of that statement were indicating that the soldiers were going on a bombing mission to destroy property and people.

We in education do not refrain from the use of this type of language — the language to obfuscate. Many times educators use language terms and expression which are vague, unclear, or empty. Terms used to describe student behavior, student learning, and general classroom activities such as individualized learning, open-ended learning, academically enriched, viable feedback, allocated resources, optimal advantage, and visual aspects coordinator are potentially dangerous from the standpoint of interfering with clear and concise communication which carries a substantial message to the general public.

With this misuse and abuse of language found throughout all segments of society, it is imperative to equip students with the thinking strategies that cut through this double speak to the "real" meaning, or at least the intent of the speaker or writer. Many activities in Chapter 8 help teachers to direct their students to evaluate language choices and to analyze the written and oral expressions for exact meaning. The study of connotation, denotation, euphemisms, double-speak expressions, usage choices, and propaganda devices sharpen students' abilities to think. While most thinking skills will be applied, it seems to us that comprehension, analysis, synthesis, and evaluation will be emphasized. To not involve students in these activities or similar activities seems irresponsible in light of the persuasive language that students confront and will continue to confront daily.

ORAL EXPRESSION

Earlier in this chapter we wrote of the criticisms that have been levied at education in general and English programs in particular. Many of the suggestions offered as remedies for the alleged educational problems frequently included the idea of "returning to the basics." Now, as we have noted, not many critics tell us exactly what the basics are, but when they do discuss this question, noteworthy is the lack of any mention of orality. This seems very odd to us since the oral tradition is one of the most basic communicative devices known to humankind. If we are to "return" to the basics, shouldn't we consider the medium used by Socrates and Aristotle? To communicate orally comes out of a tradition long substantiated for its importance, and while some forms of communication vary in their importance from time to time, orality is just as important today as it has been through the ages.

Chapters 3 and 4 make a strong case for using oral activities in the English class, whether these activities be in the form of speeches, discussions, conversations, interviews, role plays, or improvisations. Included in the chapters, too, are specific activities which involve students in this orality.

Now, how can thinking be enhanced through the oral approach? Because of the *interactive* nature of most of the oral activities that are found in the English class, teachers have the opportunity to strengthen many thinking skills through this oral participation. The dialogue that occurs in a conversation, the free verbal exchange that frequents a discussion, and the extemporaneous talk that characterizes creative drama allows students to think quickly, creatively, and critically.

Problem solving involves many related thinking skills and is extremely important in the lives of students as well as adults. While problem solving may be found as an activity in writing, literature (we mentioned an activity with Value Sheets in the "Literature" section), or language, we have chosen to discuss the skill in more detail in the oral composition section, simply because we believe the skill or combination of skills is used so frequently when people talk with other people in structured or even unstructured settings. The interesting and important point to consider is that while the oral approach is used in a problem-solving situation, it is, indeed, frequently used in combination with written composition and literature. Again, the integration of the language arts is still taking place.

First and foremost, in any study of problem solving, students need to recognize that a problem exists, that it can be solved, and that there is an approach that seems appropriate to use to solve the problem. Stanford and Stanford (1985) suggest three kinds of problems to be solved: scientific problems, interpersonal problems, and inner problems. A general discussion with students characterizing and differentiating these kinds of problems will help students as they begin sharpening their problem-solving skills.

The oral activities suggested here and in Chapters 3 and 4 offer the means for students to try out their problem-solving techniques. Problems suggested by the teacher or read about in the literature can be explored through discussion, role playing or improvisation. Certainly, some problems lend themselves to the logically sequenced scientific model, while others are not so clearly solved. Students quickly realize the role that interpersonal relationships and emotions play in solving problems. A thorough discussion of these elements and their significance in solving problems is imperative.

Problem solving is an important skill for students to attain. General content of the classroom as well as incidents in the school and community can provide material for practice with this thinking skill. The important consideration, it seems to us, is for students to solve problems that are relevant and meaningful to them. If this is not done, students may see little value in doing the activities and, therefore, carry little of the skill into their future.

FOR ADDITIONAL READING

Bloom, Benjamin. *Taxonomy of Educational Objective: Cognitive Domain.* New York: David McKay, 1956.

Boyer, Earnest L. *High School.* New York: Harper & Row, 1983.

Flower, Linda et.al. *Making Thinking Visible.* Urbana, IL: NCTE, 1994.

Kirby, Dan and Kuykendall, Carol. *Mind Matters: Teaching for Thinking.* Portsmouth, NH: Boynton/Cook, 1991.

Muldoon, Phyllis. "Challenging Students to Think: Shaping Questions, Building Community." *English Journal* (April, 1990) pp. 34–40.

National Commission on Excellence in Education. *A Nation at Risk: The Imperative for Educational Reform.* Washington, D.C.: U.S. Government Printing Office, 1983.

Nystrand, Martin et.al. "Using Small Groups for Response to and Thinking about Literature." *English Journal,* 82, 1 (January, 1993), pp. 14–22.

Probst, Robert. *Response and Analysis: Teaching Literature in Junior and Senior High School.* Portsmouth, NH: Boynton/Cook, 1988.

Purves, Alan C. *The Elements of Writing about a Literary Work: A Study of Response to Literature.* Urbana, IL: NCTE, 1968.

Rosenblatt, Louise M. *Literature as Exploration.* New York: Noble and Noble, 1968.

Smith, Douglas. "Taking Language Arts to the Community." *Educational Leadership.* 47, 6, (March, 1990), pp. 74–75.

Stanford, Barbara Dodds; and Stanford, Gene. *Thinking Through Language, Book II.* Urbana, IL: NCTE, 1985.

Sternberg, Robert. "Teaching Critical Thinking, Part 1: Are We Making Critical Mistakes?" *Kappan* 67, 3 (November 1985), 194–198.

Von Orch, Roger. *A Whack on the Side of the Head.* New York: Warner Books, 1983.

Chapter 10

THE ENGLISH CURRICULUM

Just as styles of fashions have taken on many changes over the course of several years, so, too, have trends in teaching methods come and gone with the swing of the pendulum. Today, if we were to examine the approaches used in various English classrooms, we would probably find a great number of teachers using the tripod (or triad) and the thematic approaches—two curriculum designs which have little in common.

THE TRIPOD/TRIAD DESIGN

The tripod/triad method separates and isolates the English curriculum into three district components: language (including grammar), composition, and literature. Many teachers using such an approach are apt to divide their school year into somewhat equal sections which focus individually on the three areas, or, at the least, they sequence their lesson plans, alternating from literature to grammar to compositions, with little cohesion among the three.

While this tripod/triad method may set up an in-depth approach to studying the various elements of the language (such as grammar, dialects, semantics, etc.), it makes little sense to leave it at that when the main purpose is to teach students to communicate effectively. As a result, the language elements should immediately be put into use in speaking and composition activities rather than waiting until a later time set aside for composition or speech alone. At the same time, it would seem more meaningful if the various language elements were pulled from pieces of literature or media articles rather than using dummy sentences from a grammar text.

In addition, separating composition from the other language arts skill areas causes a problem of what to write about. When topics are assigned in isolation, it is often difficult for students to relate to them; therefore, the topic becomes a barrier to skill improvement. On the other hand, when teachers allow students a wide-open choice of choosing any topic they wish, much time is often wasted in dreaming up a topic. Also, changing the topic for each writing assignment seemingly sets up a rather choppy program with little or no continuity experienced.

By focusing on the literature element alone, within this tripod/triad approach, it can be noted that many teachers treat its presentation through chronological or genre approaches. The chronological method is probably one of the oldest teaching designs; however, we feel that the oldest design definitely should not connote that it is a good design. First of all, it is seldom that adolescents show a great deal of interest in the early literature writings, as they usually consist of very difficult reading, plus the content is often irrelevant to today's youth. Also, despite the good intentions of the teacher, due to the structure of the program, the course may turn into a literary history, emphasizing historical trends and movements rather than focusing on literary skills appropriate to today's society.

With the genre approach, the teacher focuses, in depth, on the different types of literature: poetry, drama, short story, novel, nonfiction, etc. Although the individual selections used may be selected to fit the interests of the students, this method still has its drawbacks. First, students are likely to tire of any particular genre if a great deal of concentrated time is spent on it. Secondly, the student becomes so involved with differentiating the technical aspects of the various genre types that what the author has to say is overlooked. As a result, the students cannot respond to it in a meaningful way.

Due to its isolated presentations of content material, we strongly suggest that the tripod/triad method is not the best approach for establishing an opportunity in which students can pursue appropriate content material and improve their needed communication skills. Although the tripod/triad method is based on the assumption that the concentration of grammar skills enhance the composition part of the program, there is no research to support that this enhancement exists. We see the tripod/triad method as one in which skills are isolated and, thus, presented in a meaningless way.

THE THEMATIC UNIT DESIGN

In contrast, we feel that skills should be integrated to provide for more of a real-life, meaningful situation for today's students. The approach which speaks to this integration of skills is the thematic unit—a language arts design incorporating language, speech, writing, literature, and media around a central theme or concept (e.g. identity, decisions, future, love, death, etc.). Unlike a unit approach in a social studies class, the English unit's theme is of secondary importance to the language arts skills themselves. The theme merely provides a purpose to use the skills. However, the unit theme does allow for teachers to deal with the problems which frustrates today's youth and does provide students with opportunities to obtain values and solutions to real-life problems which should not be ignored by the schools.

The integration, rather than isolation, of skills in this method reduces artificial fragmentation and, instead, enables students to realize that relationships do exist among the different things they encounter in their lives. As a result, they may be better able to apply skills learned in English to their other school subjects. This meshing of skills into one unit also allows a student's command in one area to help reinforce that of another.

Another tremendous advantage to the thematic approach is that it allows for a great deal of flexibility to meet the needs and interests of the students. It provides an opportunity to use a wide range of activities: large and small group work, individual study, and creative drama. It also is conducive to the use of a wide variety of literature so that students don't all have to read the same work. This is especially practical in classes containing mainstreamed students, as the variety in both activities and materials allows for students to work at their own levels and on individually needed skill-building areas.

Finally, the thematic approach instills order into the teacher's planning, as it forces them to determine unit objectives in advance. Then, based on the intended objectives, the teacher examines and chooses appropriate materials as well as sequences meaningful activities. This process enables the teacher to evaluate continually whether or not the materials and activities do indeed serve as a means to accomplish the predetermined objectives.

Because the thematic approach encourages process-oriented skill-building through the integration of language arts skills and because interesting materials and topics can be discussed to accomplish language arts objectives, teachers will find that students consider the English class much more meaningful and, thus, respond more enthusiastically to it.

The following thematic units, created by Maria Connors, Ottawa, Kansas (middle school model) and Connie Harmon, Shawnee Mission,

Kansas (high school model), include several language arts activities centered around the themes of "relationships" and "teen pressures." These units are to act as guides to promote successful acquisitions of language arts skills; and, therefore, substitution of different objectives or activities may be needed to fulfill the needs and interests of the students. In many cases, thorough suggestions for dealing with individual skill achievement within the unit have not been covered, as emphasis has been placed on the activities themselves. We strongly suggest, however, that continual referral be made to the previous chapters in this resource book which discuss techniques for dealing with the various language arts skills. As a result, the incorporation of these techniques into the thematic units should result in a well-rounded program.

Theme Title: "Relationships" Middle School Model

Unit Description

Students will examine the concept of "relationships" by exploring the various factors which aid in its development as well as the problems surrounding maintaining a good solid relationship. They will then examine their own relationships and try to form some conclusions as to the factors which influenced them. This examination will be done through exposure to various genres of literature as well by class discussions, small group sharing, and writing experiences.

Unit Objectives

The following are general objectives for this unit. Additional specific objectives may need to be written to meet the needs and abilities of the individual students.

Thematic Objectives. The student will

gain an understanding of how various factors help to attain relationships

become aware of how values are formed and how they aid in keeping strong relationships

explore the influences that work against sustaining strong relationships.

Language Arts Objectives. The student will

understand how brainstorming can aid in exploring issues.

identify the characteristics found in journal writing.

identify and use the components of effective discussions in large and small groups.

identify techniques which enable the expression of personal responses.
understand the process of critical thinking.

demonstrate an increased proficiency in oral and written composition.

demonstrate an understanding of literature which is varied in form but related in theme

Materials

Novels

The Forbidden City, William Bell (excerpts)
The Island, Gary Paulsen (excerpts)
The Moves Make the Man, Bruce Brooks (selected students)
Waiting for the Rain, Sheila Gordon (selected students)
When the Phone Rang, Harry Mazer (selected students)

Short Stories

"The Chief's Daughters," anonymous.
"In the Heat," Robert Cormier

Poems

From *Where the Sidewalk Ends,* Shel Silverstein
  "Two Boxes"
  "For Sale"
  "Love"
From *A Light in the Attic,* Shel Silverstein
  "Rock 'N' Roll Band"
  "The Little Boy and the Old Man"
  "Nobody"
  "Friendship"
From *Class Dismissed,* Mel Glenn
  "Ellen Winters"
  "Marie Yeageman"
  "Dominique Blanco"
  "Song Vu Chin"

Activities (a representative selection; teachers will want to create others)

As an introduction, read the "Prologue" of *Forbidden City* by William Bell. Ask students to think of a time when they didn't fit in. Students do not have to respond orally, just to think about this time in their lives.

They are to think of a time that they found out some information concerning relationships with others that made them grow up a little faster than they wanted. After some discussion, have students respond about their experience in their journal.

Read selected poems by Shel Silverstein and Mel Glenn to students. These poems revolve around the topic of relationships. Talk about the variety of forms of the poetry and make the comparison to the variety of people that exist in their world. After the discussion of poetry forms, have students create a "name" poem. Students write their name vertically down the paper and then write something that describes them next to each of the letters of their name. An example follows:

> *A*nything to satisfy the
> *N*utty craving for a
> *N*ice big
> *E*ven scoop of ice cream

To explore the relationships with others, read three passages (pps. 100–101; 123; and 143) from the novel *The Island,* modeling the writing convention of the journal. Each passage deals with different emotions or situations a young adult might experience like the effects of blaming, daydreaming, and relationships to adults. Ask students to write about someone or write a reaction to someone or something in their journal.

Continue the discussion of relationships after reading additional poems of Silverstein and Glenn (see materials list). Then, make a list of pertinent relationships that adolescents deal with. From this list, have students choose one and freewrite about the topic. After the freewriting, have students create a Found Poem by having them remove unnecessary words from the freewriting until they have created a poem from the words that remain.

Give book talks on the three novels (*The Moves Make the Man, Waiting for the Rain, When the Phone Rang*) that will be read in groups in this unit. Ask students to make a choice of the book that they want to read. The three books are of varying difficulty so students should be given their choice if that book meets their ability. Ample time should be given students to read their book before an activity takes place. Some in-class reading time can be given.

Discuss with students how relationships with others can change a person's life. Talk about how childhood experiences can affect one's life. Relate this discussion to the three books that are being read. This is one good way to see how much reading has taken place. Bring this discussion to a close with a reading from Fulghum's *All I Really Need to Know I Learned in Kindergarten.*

To keep interest in the books being read, have students periodically do short activities that relate to their particular books. For example, have students create a biopoem on one of the characters in their respective books. The biopoem is as follows:

Line 1   First name
Line 2   Four traits that describe character
Line 3   Relative (brother, sister, friend, etc.) of _____
Line 4   Lover of _____ (list three things or people
Line 5   Who feels _____ (three items)
Line 6   Who needs _____ (three items)
Line 7   Who fears _____ (three items)
Line 8   Who gives _____ (three items)
Line 9   Who would like to see _____ (three items)
Line 10 Resident of _____
Line 11 Last name _____

When students have completed their books, have them update their poems. See an example of a finished poem in next unit.

Using the biopoem, students create a character sketch. They work together as a group to generate ideas for the sketch. Each student writes the sketch individually but takes it through the process by involving group members at each stage.

Have students in the group which is reading *When the Phone Rang* discuss briefly the passage about Billy's shame of forgetting for just a brief span of time the death of his parents (broken relationship). This leads to the reading of Cormier's "In the Heat." After reading, discuss the short story. Some of the areas to consider include:

What effect does the story being told from the father's point of view have on the reader?
Can you relate better by realizing the parent was young once too — experiencing the same things as the son?
Even though the story is about death, is it completely sad?

Ask students to follow this discussion with a short journal entry about a childhood memory that they can recollect.

Before this activity begins, collect several pictures of different people in different relationships. Show these pictures to your students and ask them to respond to these questions:

What kinds of people are these characters?
What kind of occupation do they enjoy?
What did these people do before this picture was taken? After?
What emotion are these people experiencing?

After discussion of these questions and others, have students choose two or three of these characters and place them in a creative story. After thinking about characters, have students create a setting and a conflict. Students can work with partners or in groups as they move through the process of creating this short story. After revising and editing, the final product is turned in for evaluation.

To end the unit, have students write an expository paper, a narrative, or a poem incorporating in some way the factors that they think are important in establishing various kinds of relationships. They can draw from specific examples in their lives to support their selections, as well as refer to themes from the various literature read and topics discussed.

Theme Title "Teen Pressures"
High School Model

Unit Description

Students will explore a variety of pressures with which they are faced through each day. These pressures and stresses range from making good grades to juggling school and work loads to family problems to struggling to find one's place in the world. By reading about pressures that other people have and to see how these pressures are handled, students may become better equipped to handle their own stress. Students will work with a variety of literature—novels, short stories, poetry, nonfiction, and film; large and small groups; and oral and written composition.

Unit Objectives

Thematic Objectives. The student will
become aware of how pressures come about and how to deal with them.
examine issues related to teen pressures from many perspectives and use this information to make informed, objective choices.
relate literature read to the theme of teen pressures.

Language Arts Objectives. The student will
    understand how brainstorming can be an aide to exploring issues.
    identify the characteristics found in journal writing.
    demonstrate effective discussion skills in large and small groups.
    demonstrate strategies found in making personal responses to
        literature.
    identify literary elements in literature.
    acquire an understanding of audience as it relates to writing.
    demonstrate interviewing techniques.
    demonstrate the techniques of delivering an informational report.
    understand and demonstrate correct letter-writing form.
    identify figurative language as it is used in literature.
    demonstrate the components of an essay of opinion.
    understand the power of language and show how language shapes
        opinions.
    demonstrate the writing process—prewriting, writing, and revising.

Materials

Novels
    Breaking the Fall, Michael Cadnum (selected students)
    Motown and Didi, Walter Dean Myers (selected students)
    Princess Ashley, Richard Peck (selected students)
    We All Fall Down, Robert Cormier (selected students)
    Mote, Chap Reaver, excerpts.

Short Stories
    "On the Bridge," Todd Strasser
    "Initiation," Sylvia Plath
    "T.L.A.," Jan McFann

Poetry
    "I Hear the River Call My Name," Sheryl L. Nelms
    "Preface to a Twenty Volume Suicide Note," Leroi Jones
    "Marcy Mannes," Mel Glenn
    "Juan Pedro Carrera," Mel Glenn
    "Robert Ashford," Mel Glenn

Nonfiction
    Don't Be S.A.D., Susan Newman

Film
   Can't Buy Me Love, Touchstone Films

Activities

(a representative selection; teachers will want to create others).

Have students begin the unit by brainstorming different types of pressure that they face each day. Discuss with students how these pressures have changed their lives, how they handled the pressures, and to what extent were others affected by the pressures.

After reading Strasser's "On the Bridge," have students make a personal written response to the short story. Then in discussion, have them consider, but not be limited to, the following ideas:

Can you relate to the pressure Seth feels to be like Adam?
Have you ever felt betrayed by a friend like Adam betrays Seth?
How would you have dealt with the pressure to conform? How would
   that change the ending?

Have students read Chapter 1 of *Don't Be S.A.D.* Place students in four groups and have them discuss different pieces of advice they could give the person described in the book. Also have students discuss how a pamphlet on teen pressures would be different if made for students by students or for administrators by students.

Begin by having students brainstorm pressures involved in making decisions. Then have students read "T.L.A." aloud but stop the reading before Holly decides whether or not to jump. Have students write the ending of the story. Read students responses. Finish reading the short story and compare the various endings with the author's ending.

Do book talks on the four books for this unit. Have students rank the books from first choice to last choice. Assign books to students making sure that books are appropriate for ability level of students. Students should have novels read in a week.

Read "Initiation" in class and have students respond. Discuss the following areas plus others that are important to you:

How did Milicent change throughout the story?
Compare Milicent's situation to examples generated by the class.
If Herb had told Milicent he would take her out as soon as she joined
   the sorority, how would her decision have been affected?

Have students freewrite in their journals about the sources of stress in their lives and what they can do to change the situation. Talk about well-known people (school, community, nation) who are under stress because of their occupations. Ask students to identify questions that would be important to ask those people about stress and pressures. Discuss the interview process (making the appointment, questions to ask and not to ask, and follow up). After sufficient preparation for interviewing, have students select a member of the community to interview about the pressures and stresses they deal with on the job. Students should present their findings in an informational oral presentation.

Ask students to jot down questions that they have about the novels that they are reading. What problems do they have at this point in the novel study? Put students in their novel groups to discuss these questions.

Have students in their respective novel groups discuss the novels. Students may use the following questions but also add more as they discuss.

What is your response to what you have read?

To what extent did this novel evoke any feelings/emotions in you?

What happened in the literature? Discuss the plot.

What was your favorite scene in the novel? What effect did that have on the plot and on the characters?

Are you like any of the characters in the book? Explain.

If you could change anything about the novel, what would it be? Why?

Have students do the following writing activities based on the novels that they have read.

Breaking the Fall: Assume the persona of Stanley filling out an application for a baseball scholarship. Answer the question, "Who was the most influential person in your life during your teen age years?"

Motown and Didi: Write a letter to the University of Wisconsin Scholarship Committee explaining why Didi is qualified and why she wants to attend school there.

Princess Ashley: Write a letter to the editor similar to Pod's letter that addresses a school or social issue:

designated smoking areas
drinking and driving
violence in schools
selling liquor to minors

We All Fall Down: Write letters of advice to characters about how you think they can get their lives back on track.

Have students as a group activity write a biopoem on a character in their novel (see biopoem form in previous unit). An example is given here from the novel *Princess Ashley.*

Ashley
Wealthy, independent, beautiful, popular
Friend of Chelsea
Lover of herself, power, manipulation
Who feels lonely, in control, desperate
Who needs money, power, vulnerable people
Who fears rejection, loneliness, Chelsea
Who gives nothing of herself, power to those around her, love to no
    one
Who would like to see Craig change, people need her, Chelsea move
    away
Resident of Crestwood
Packard.

Discuss with students the nature of dialects, both geographical and social. How did regionalisms develop? To what extent does the United States still have dialect areas? Prepare materials to discuss with students social dialects. Read a portion of Chap Reaver's novel *Mote* (p. 175). Discuss with students the pressure that some may feel (perhaps all young adults in some way or another) to speak in a certain way and how different dialects evoke different feelings and opinions. You could have students create I Search papers on the dialect question.

As a follow up to the previous activity, have students in the respective groups do the following:

Breaking the Fall: Write Stanley's or Jared's account of a break-in and his confession to that crime. Tell this account to police, a friend at school, and the occupants of the house. Discuss differences in speech in each scenario.

Motown and Didi: Create or rewrite a conversation between Motown and Didi, in which you transform Didi's dialect into BEV and Motown's into Standard English. Discuss the differences.

Princess Ashley: Choose or create a dialogue between Chelsea and Ashley, but transform the language into "valley girl" dialect. Discuss differences in meaning and authority of the speaker.

We All Fall Down: Rewrite the description of the trashing using other imagery and figurative language. Based on this description, describe the clean-up process.

Have students do the following oral activities, again within their respective groups. Before activities begin, groups should give a brief overview of their novels to the entire class.

Breaking the Fall: Write a eulogy to be given by Stanley for Jared at the funeral. Role play the funeral scene and give eulogies within the small group, then for the entire class.

Motown and Didi: Organize a mock trial for Touchy. Address the charges of drugs and Anthony's death. Role play the court scene in small groups, then for the entire class.

Princess Ashley: Role play Crestwood High's ten year reunion. Draw conclusions about the futures of the characters. Consider occupations, financial status, marital status and families, and locations. Present to class.

We All Fall Down: Role play extended conversations in small group, then to the entire class:

Karen and therapist when Karen remembers night of trashing.
Jane and Harry when they meet and Jane doesn't know that the boy is
  Harry.
Buddy and Mr. Jerome when he finds out Buddy was a trasher.

As a culminating activity, have a general large group discussion on the various novels. Even though four books were read, they can be discussed by the entire class because they have similar themes. Have students respond to the following, giving examples from their particular books:

Treatment of the theme of teen pressure by the author. How is it
  handled?
Discuss plot. How does the author create the plot and move the action
  along in the work?
Author's craft. What specific writing techniques do the authors use?
  Are they similar or different from book to book?
How realistically does each author present the problems faced by
  young people?
How are adults presented in the books?
Character development. Are characters round or flat? Are they presented
  realistically; are they believable?

Chapter 11

CELEBRATE THE SPECIAL DAYS

Celebrating the special days in the language-arts classroom is a way to capitalize on the student's interests which may already be attuned to events of the day. These days could then serve as motivators to further explore problems and skills in the language-arts area.

Because many of the days mentioned are not solely related to the field of English, the creation of language-arts activities in connection with them can help to show how relationships do exist among the various subjects in the school curriculum. Also, these activities provide both teacher and students with a break from the normal classroom routine. At the same time, however, many of the activities can be meshed with activities of pre-existing unit plans while they also add the interest of celebrating the special day.

September 4, 1985:

In New York City, the first self-service restaurant opened. It was named the Exchange Buffet and became the forerunner of today's cafeteria.

Activity: Have the students explore the element of doublespeak in restaurant menus. For example, a menu item might be named The Earl's Favorite which turns out to be a classy name for a simple ham and cheese sandwich on rye with a side order of potato salad. After students have presented their various findings to the class, a discussion may follow on the effect of doublespeak on the consumer.

Activity: Have students make their own menus for a restaurant that they would establish. In doing so, encourage them to play with doublespeak in naming their entrees. Display the menus through the room.

September 9, 1926:

NBC was first organized to produce national network radio broadcasts from New York City.

Activity: Take a class poll to find out how many hours per day or week each student usually spends listening to the radio. Follow this with a discussion of the importance of the radio as a medium. Include the following considerations: What satisfactions and needs do we receive from listening to the radio? How were these needs and satisfactions met before radio was invented? How has the radio changed since the invention of television?

Activity: Take your class on a field trip to a local radio station.

Activity: Have your class create and put on a radio program. Include music, newscasts, weather reports, advertising, items of special interests, etc. Tape their completed broadcast for playback. Share tapes of each class with your other English classes.

September 11, 1862:

Birthday of O. Henry (William Sydney Porter)

Activity: Read one of O. Henry's short stories such as "Ransom of Red Chief," "The Last Leaf," "After Twenty Years," or "Mammon and the Archer."

Activity: Discuss the element of surprise endings. Have the students write their own short stories using this element. Share writings.

Activity: Let students select their own pen names for some further writing assignments. Discuss their reasons for choosing the names that they did. Also, discuss why many authors write under pen names.

September 11, 1875:

"Professor Tigwissel's Burglar Alarm," the first newspaper cartoon strip, was published in the *New York Daily Graphic.*

Activity: Have different groups of students follow selected cartoon strips for several days. Then, have them design the next week's series of the cartoons and share them with the class. Have them cut out the real cartoon strips during the next week to bring to the class and compare with their groups.

Activity: Have the students act out one of their favorite cartoon characters while the rest of the class tries to guess which character they are portraying.

Activity: In coordination with your school's newspaper sponsor, run a contest for your students to create original cartoon strips for publication in the school newspaper. On a more serious line, have students investigate the procedures required for publication in your town's newspaper. Perhaps, a noted cartoonist could speak to your class on the craft as a career.

Activity: Hold a class discussion on the characteristics of the longlasting cartoon characters such as Snoopy, Charlie Brown, Dick Tracy, Brenda Starr, Little Orphan Annie, etc. What traits do each of these characters possess which attribute to their great popularity? Then have the students write a short paper on "My Favorite Cartoon Character is _____ Because. . . . "

September 15:

Old People's Day in Japan
Activity: Have students write a letter to their oldest living relative. In the letter they could relate something they did in the last week that was particularly fun (e.g. an update on the family's activities, an account of their summer vacation, etc).

Activity: Have the students write about their hopes and expectations for themselves when they reach senior citizen age. Where will they live? What will they have accomplished? How will they spend their retirement years. Share writing.

September 21, 1866:

Birthday of H.G. Wells
Activity: Read one of his science fiction stories such as *The Time Machine* or *War of the Worlds.* Play the record *War of the Worlds* and discuss the similarities and differences of the two ways the story was presented. Which method did the students like better? Why?

Activity: Have the students share what their favorite science fiction stories are. Discuss why science fiction stories are so appealing.

September 22:

The First Day of Autumn
Activity: Bring a sack of fall leaves to school and give a leaf to each student. Tell the students they are to jot down descriptive words which they can apply to their leaves in relation to the five senses. Ask them questions to stimulate this play with descriptive words: What does your leaf look like? What are its colors? How would you describe its shape? What physical characteristics does it have that might set it off from other leaves? What does it feel like? What is its texture? What does it sound like when you move it a little? What does it smell like? What are some tastes associated with fall leaves? Students may volunteer to put some of their descriptive words on the board under the different senses headings. Then, have the students write a personal history of their leaves displaying

their uniquenesses. In their writings they could include where they were born, history of schooling, family life, hobbies, honors, occupation, medical history, etc. Share writing with class members.

Activity: On the board, have students brainstorm "Fall." For about five minutes, have students call out any word that comes to their minds regarding the subject. At the end of that time, have them all write about an experience that they once had in the fall. Share writing with the class.

September 26:

Good Neighbor Day

Activity: Have the students write a letter of appreciation to one of their neighbors.

Activity: Have students write abstractions for "A Good Neighbor is. . . . " Share these with the class.

Activity: Have students write a short essay indicating the elements of being a good neighbor. These could be based on their own personal experiences.

October 10, 1835:

Birthday of Camille Saint-Saens, French Pianist and Composer.

Activity: Play the recording of "Carnival of Animals" to the class. While listening to it, the students should write to the music in "stream-of-consciousness" style. After the writings have been shared aloud, have students discuss the various differences and similarities of their interpretations of the music.

October 16, 1758:

Birthday of Noah Webster

Activity: Bring to the room several different types of dictionaries and have students explore the different types available. Prefaces should also be read to determine the philosophy behind which they were structured. Then have students determine which types are best for finding information concerning the following: (1) historical background of words, (2) simplistic and understandable definitions, (3) example sentences in which the words are used, and (4) definitions for slang terms.

Activity: Have students compile their own dictionary of teenage slang. Divide class into various groups dealing with identifying pronunciation keys and syllabication, parts of speech, historical background, definitions, and example sentences using the word. Having completed entries mimeographed to provide copies for each student.

October 25, 1854:

It was on this day that the famous Charge of the Light Brigade occurred.

Activity: Read the poem, by Alfred Lloyd Tennyson, named after this famous event. Investigate how Tennyson was able to record this event in poem form. What truly vivid passages exist in the poem which enable the reader to clearly picture this event?

Activity: Take another historical event and record its details by an "I-was-there" poem. Have students share these aloud after providing adequate background information concerning the event.

October 27, 1914:

Birthday of Dylan Thomas

Activity: Read "My Love Affair with Words" which explains how Thomas was first motivated to make writing his career. Have students write a short essay on an occurrence or situation which motivated them to pursue a goal in their lives.

Activity: After reading "My Love Affairs with Words," have students list what they consider to be ten beautiful-sounding and ten ugly-sounding words in the English language. Have students share lists and then compare them with those in *The Book of Lists*.

October 31:

Halloween

Activity: Since Halloween is a time for wearing masks, discuss the different "masks" each of us wear. Why do we feel the need to put on masks rather than be ourselves all the time? Do some activities to establish trust among the class members so that these "masks" can be avoided in the future (refer to Chapter 2).

Activity: Have students write descriptive paragraphs describing a mask that they would like to wear for Halloween. Read these descriptions aloud to determine how effective they were. Could the students clearly picture the masks being described? What suggestions would they offer each other to improve the quality of description?

Activity: Read short stories representing the mood of Halloween. Selections from Edgar Allen Poe would be most appropriate.

Activity: Have students write their own scary stories to share aloud for the class. Discuss the element of suspense in the stories.

November 1, 1928:

National Author's Day

Activity: Have each student select an author on which to become an expert. The students should investigate the lives of the authors as well as read several selections written by them. At the end of their studies, students should present the results of the class by presenting pictures of them, relating important aspects of their lives, and reading one of their contributions to literature. This activity could be expanded into an "open-house" concept where projects are put on display for other students, teachers, and parents.

Activity: Explore the career of writing. Have students investigate the details of the career of writing and report findings to the class. Perhaps a local author could be invited to the class to explain the career from a first-hand point of view.

November 4:

Mischief Night in England (based on the 1605 Gunpowder Plot to blow up Parliament)

Activity: Investigate the background to this special day as well as explore the activities that typically occur to celebrate it. Have students write detailed accounts of a mischievious plan in which they were a part. Papers should be shared with the class.

Activity: Read accounts of mischievious characters in literature such as Huck Finn and Tom Sawyer. Discuss the degree of seriousness behind their pranks. Discuss the consequences of such pranks in today's society.

November 6, 1869:

The first formal intercollegiate football game was played between Princeton and Rutgers.

Activity: Set up a classroom panel or debate in which members discuss the pros and cons of competitive sports in our schools and society.

Activity: Have students make lists of terms which are unique to football. Discuss the connotations evident in the meanings of the words. For those words which have a predominantly violent or negative connotation, have students suggest alternative terms to describe the same situations. Are the alternatives as effective? Why or why not?

Activity: Explore sports headlines in newspapers and discuss the various words used to indicate results of games. Have students suggest alternative words that could be used in headlines. Discuss their effectiveness.

November 30, 1835:

Birthday of Mark Twain

Activity: Have students investigate why Samuel Clemens chose "Mark Twain" as his pen name. (This may be done by reading "A Pilot's Needs," a short story taken from *Life on the Mississippi.*) Discuss why authors, in general, may have chosen pen names for themselves. Then encourage students to choose pen names for themselves and explain the chosen names to the class. These pen names may be used on future writing assignments.

Activity: Read excerpts from several of Twain's works and have students discuss why his writing has gained and remained popular. If Twain were alive today, could he still write books which would be appealing to today's society? Why or why not?

Activity: Have students describe the characteristics that a modern day Huck Finn might possess. Is there any modern-day character or real-life person who would fit this role?

December 5, 1901:

Birthday of Walt Disney

Activity: Although full-length Disney cartoons were big box-office sellers, much criticism has labeled them as possessing a great deal of violence. Have students study the cartoons or stories and form panels or debate teams to discuss the justification of such criticism.

Activity: Through pantomime have students take turns acting out their favorite Disney characters as the others try to guess their identities.

Activity: Have students try their hands at cartooning. First invite a cartoonist to the class to speak on the career of cartooning. Then have students, perhaps in groups, create their own cartoon strips. Really adventuresome students could make a cartoon film.

December 10, 1830:

Birthday of Emily Dickenson

Activity: Many women's rights groups argue that it has been extremely difficult for a female author to gain recognition for her talents. Yet,

Emily Dickenson is considered one of the greatest poets of her time. Have students read several of her poems and discuss the unique characteristics which may have attributed to her greatness.

December 10:

Human Rights Day (In celebration of the Universal Declaration of Human Rights adopted in 1948 by the United Nations)

Activity: Have students read the actual document adopted by the United Nations and discuss the formal language used in it. Have students explore other documents for this same purpose. In groups, students might then rewrite the document in less formal language and discuss the effectiveness of both versions.

Activity: Have students write plays or short stories depicting societies in which few, if any, human rights are granted by the government. Share these with the class.

December ?:

Underdog Day (Always celebrated on the third Friday in December) This is a special day which salutes all the underdogs and unsung heroes— "the number two" people who contribute so much to "number one" people.

Activity: Present an Underdog Award. Have students select their favorite underdog for nomination and present reasons for the selection. Then list all the nominations on a ballot and have the class vote on the "Number One Underdog."

Activity: Have students write a short story in which their favorite underdog is the main character. They may choose to include the "Number One Hero" in the story or leave him/her out. Share writings with the class. This would be a good activity with which to discuss point of view.

December 21, 1913:

The *New York World* printed the first published crossword puzzle.

Activity: Bring sample crossword puzzles from various magazines and newspapers and have students determine their various levels of difficulty.

Activity: Obtain a crossword puzzle poster and post it on a wall of the classroom. Invite students to fill in its squares in their spare time.

Activity: Have students construct a crossword puzzle of their own in which the major clues are based on a recent book they have read. Present copies of the puzzles to others who have read the book.

January 1:

New Year's Day

Activity: Although students are usually not in school on this day, upon their return have them write several resolutions and then rank them as to their importance. Students might also keep track of their resolutions in a journal. If the resolutions are broken, they might write down an account of how and why they were broken.

Activity: Because this day marks the start of a new calendar year, the element of time might be discussed. Have students discuss the importance of time in our society. How important is it to be aware of the hour, day, month, year, etc.? How are we individually affected by the time element? Then have students envision a society in which there were no forms of time—no clocks, calendars, sundials, etc. Have students write short stories, poems, dramas, or descriptive paragraphs which deal with such a society. Share writings with the class.

January 2, 1920:

Birthday of Isaac Asimov

Activity: Discuss the current popularity of science fiction among today's readers. How does it differ from other literature types? How is it similar? What are its unique characteristics?

Activity: Have each student read a science fiction short story or novel and write about the author's predictions for the future. Orally or in writing, have students discuss if they consider the predictions to be realistic or not.

January 6, 1412:

Birthday of Joan of Arc (She was greatly criticized by the clothes she wore, judged a witch, and burned at the stake.)

Activity: Read "Clothes Make the Man" by Henri Duvernois. Discuss how the wearing of different types of clothes might affect a person's behavior and self-image.

Activity: Discuss how we are likely to judge people based on the types of clothes they wear. Show pictures of people wearing different types of clothes and discuss what character types might be represented. Then discuss if these judgments can be trusted to be true.

January 7, 1887:

The character of Sherlock Holmes was first introduced into modern literature.

Activity: Have students read various short stories by Arthur Conan Doyle and discuss why they would have the great appeal that they do. Discuss the mystery as a literary work and list other mystery stories for the students to read.

Activity: Have students create their own Sherlock Holmes mysteries but use the setting of the current year. How would his character have to change to be an effective detective in today's society? Share writings with the class.

January 8, 1935:

Birthday of Elvis Presley

Activity: Elvis is entitled the "King of Rock and Roll." Examine the lyrics of several of his songs for effective uses of language and determine to what extent they play a part in this success.

January 12, 1737:

Birthday of John Hancock

Activity: Since Hancock is well known for his famous signature on the *Declaration of Independence,* have students experiment with their own signatures. They could come up with several different signatures which might display various styles of appropriateness for different situations. For a follow up, design a classroom document of some type and have students, in their most elegant signatures, sign their names to it.

February 7, 1478:

Birthday of Sir Thomas More

Activity: Sir Thomas More was a man who would not back down from his values to appease the King of England. For a trust-building activity, have students list values of their own that they consider so important that they would never back down from them. Have students share these with the class.

Activity: Have students take parts and read, or act out, *A Man for All Seasons.* After each scene have students make a diary entry as it might have been made by More.

February 7, 1812:

Birthday of Charles Dickens

Activity: Charles Dickens was noted for exposing the injustices of life in his works. In fact, much credit goes to him in successfully establishing Child Labor Laws in England. Have students write short stories or plays which expose what they feel to be an injustice in our society.

Activity: Dickens wrote some of his works at regular serials in newspapers in England. Have students write stories in serial form which would be appropriate for publication in the school newspaper.

Activity: Many of Dicken's stories are autobiographical. Have students create short stories based on their own real-life happenings. Share these stories with the class.

February 10, 1868:

Birthday of William Allen White

Activity: Explore the career of journalism by having guest speakers or groups of students investigate the different jobs in the field. Students could then form informational panels and make displays for the journalism careers.

Activity: Have students bring copies of various nursery rhymes to class as well as copies of newspapers. After exploring the newspaper articles and discussing their styles, have students rewrite the nursery rhymes as news articles.

February 14:

Valentine's Day

Activity: Brainstorm Valentine's Day on the chalkboard. Then have students write greetings for Valentine's cards. They may even decorate the cards and send them to special friends. A contest could be held to have each class choose the greeting with the most effective use of language, the funniest greeting, the most romantic greeting, etc.

Activity: This would be a good day to begin a thematic unit on *love*. Have students explore the various types of love in the world and the many different ways *love* is used in our language. Dictionaries might also be used to examine the different definitions attached to the word.

March 3:

National Anthem Day

Activity: See how many students actually know the words to our national anthem. Ask them to write down the words on paper. Follow this by a discussion as to the importance of knowing about the various symbols of our country.

Activity: Read and study the verses as a poem. Discuss the effective uses of language present which might have caused this song to be chosen as our national anthem.

Activity: Create a short unit on patriotic poetry and songs as forms of literature. Discuss, especially, the element of symbolism as it applied to these works. Encourage your students to write their own poems displaying their patriotic feelings.

March 6, 1806:

Birthday of Elizabeth Barrett Browning

Activity: Have students read some of the many beautiful love poems written by both Elizabeth Barrett Browning and her husband Robert Browning. Discuss the effective uses of language along with the various poetic techniques used. Then have students create their own love poems and share them with the class.

March 21, 1750:

Birthday of Johann Sebastian Bach

Activity: Play recordings of Bach's compositions as students write to them in "stream-of-consciousness" style. Share writings with the class.

Activity: Have students write letters to Bach describing today's popular music to him and explaining why he would/would not like it as well as the music in his time.

March 26, 1875:

Birthday of Robert Frost

Activity: Read several of Frost's poems and pick out effective uses of language which he uses. Discuss why his poems have the tremendous appeal that they do.

Activity: Brainstorm *nature* on the chalkboard. Then have students write personal accounts which tell of an experience that they have had with nature. Frost's poems dealing with nature could then be read and topics can be compared with those listed on the board.

April 2, 1805:

Birthday of Hans Christian Anderson

Activity: Have students read several of Anderson's famous fairy tales and discuss the different ways they would appeal to both adults and children.

Activity: Have groups of students pantomime various tales for the class or for classes of younger children.

Activity: Have students write their own fairy tales and share them with their own class as well as with classes of younger children.

April 3, 1783:

Birthday of Washington Irving

Activity: Have students read *Rip Van Winkle.* Then have students write an account of a futuristic experience they might have if they were to fall asleep today and wake up twenty years from now.

April 8:

Food Day (sponsored by the Center for Science to encourage Americans to improve diets)

Activity: To aid in this campaign, have students develop advertisements and commercials, using various propaganda techniques, to promote improvement of diets. Visual advertisements could be displayed in the halls, radio-type commercials could be aired over the school intercom system, and television-like commercials could be put on at lunchtime.

April 18, 1857:

Birthday of Clarence Darrow

Activity: Have students read *Inherit the Wind* based on the famous Scope monkey trials. Discuss the effective uses of language used by both lawyers in presenting their cases in court.

Activity: Have students form panels or debate teams to discuss the extent to which religion should be discussed and dealt with in today's public schools.

April 23, 1564:

Birthday of William Shakespeare

Activity: Present a biographical sketch of Shakespeare's life and have students read some of his works including sonnets and plays. Discuss why his works have maintained their popularity throughout the years.

Activity: In his works, Shakespeare made many philosophical comments about many aspects of life. Have students explore some of these and use them as discussion and/or writing motivators.

Activity: Modernize Shakespeare by having groups of students rewrite sections of his works in today's language. After sharing the writing with the class, compare the effectiveness of the old and new writings.

Activity: Have students explore some of Shakespeare's works for puns. Posters and bulletins could be made to display the various puns found. Then have students create their own puns and share them with the class.

May 5, 1904:

The first ice cream cone was invented.

Activity: Have students thoroughly describe their favorite ice cream flavors through the senses of taste and sight only. Share descriptions in small groups, enabling group members to offer suggestions for improvements.

Activity: Have students create their own ice cream flavors and present appropriate and appealing names for them.

Activity: As a warm-up activity for creative drama, have students pantomime eating a delicious, yet messy, ice cream cone.

May 20:

Eliza Doolittle Day (to honor Miss Doolittle, the heroine of George Bernard Shaw's *Pygmalion,* for displaying the importance of properly speaking one's native tongue).

Activity: Have students read *Pygmalion* and discuss all references made to the English language. This could be done in conjunction with viewing *My Fair Lady.* The song "Why Can't the English Learn to Speak?" from *My Fair Lady* could also be examined for the attitude it portrays of the speakers of the language.

Activity: Have students form panel or debate teams in which they discuss the extent to which people should have a right to speak their own dialect versus the extent to which speakers of the English language should strive to standardize the language.

Activity: Have the students explore and discuss the differences of British and American English, listing terms which are unique to both (i.e. elevator and lift, policeman and bobby, etc.).

May 31, 1819:

Birthday of Walt Whitman

Activity: Have students read excerpts from Whitman's *Leaves of Grass* and discuss the unique qualities of his poetry. Also, have students discuss Whitman's philosophy of various aspects of life which are mentioned throughout the poetry.

Activity: Have students discuss what good poetry is. Then have them read the Preface to *Leaves of Grass* for Whitman's views of poets and poetry. Discuss his views.

Other special days (following the school calendar) for which you may create language arts activities include:

September 7, 1931
    American Sunbathing Association founded.
September 12, 1910
    Los Angeles Police Department appoints world's first policewoman.
September 13, 1814
    Francis Scott Key writes "The Star Spangled Banner."
September 16, 1620
    Pilgrims set sail on the Mayflower.
September 19, 1888
    World's first beauty contest.
September 20, 1519
    Magellan starts voyage around the world.
September 26, 1774
    Birthday of Johnny Appleseed.
September 29, 1892
    First night football game was played.
October 3, 1899
    Vacuum cleaner awarded patent #634,042.
October 12, 1901
    First secular song published—"Three Blind Mice."

October 13, 1960
   First televised Presidential debate (Kennedy vs Nixon).
October 19, 1781
   End of American Revolutionary War.
October 27, 1904
   Subway opens in New York City.
November 9, 1911
   First neon sign created.
November 12, 1963
   Exotic Dancers League of America is founded.
November 19, 1620
   Mayflower arrives.
November 20, 1945
   Nuremberg trials begin.
November 22, 1927
   Snowmobile awarded patent #1,650,334.
December 5, 1933
   Repeal of Prohibition.
December 10, 1988
   22-foot donut is baked in Florida.
December 11, 1919
   First monument to an insect: The Boll Weevil.
December 16, 1773
   Boston Tea Party.
December 17, 1903
   Kitty Hawk flies 850 feet.
December 20, 1820
   $1 tax is levied on bachelors.
January 1, 1980
   The International Carnivorous Plant Society is founded.
January 3, 1871
   Oleomargarine is awarded patent #110,626.
January 11, 1993
   National Clean Your Desk Day.
January 19, 1825
   The canning process (using tin cans) is patented.
January 24, 1922
   Eskimo Pie is awarded patent #1,404,539.

January 27, 1756
  Birthday of Mozart.
February 1, 1911
  First fingerprint conviction.
February 2, 1929
  First international mail service by dog sled established.
February 8, 1839
  Birthday of Jules Verne.
February 9, 1870
  U.S. Weather Bureau begins observing weather.
February 10, 1933
  First singing telegram is delivered.
February 18, 1930
  The planet Pluto is discovered.
February 19, 1906
  Cornflakes go on sale nationwide.
March 1, 1993
  National Procrastination Week begins (maybe).
March 4, 1634
  First tavern opens in Boston.
March 6, 1475
  Birthday of Michelangelo.
March 10, 1876
  First words were spoken on the telephone.
March 15, 1993
  Buzzard Day is celebrated in Hinckley, Ohio.
March 22, 1882
  Polygamy is banned in the United States.
March 28, 1993
  Teacher's Day is celebrated.
March 29, 1990
  Woodworking class makes 820-lb. yo-yo.
March 30, 1858
  Pencil with an eraser is awarded patent #19,783.
April 1, 1993
  National Laugh Week begins.
April 13, 1860
  First mail delivery by pony express occurred.

April 15, 1993
  National Hostility Day.
April 16, 1947
  Zoom lens is awarded patent #2,454,686.
April 27, 1939
  British military provides servicemen with pajamas.
May 1, 1993
  National Correct Posture Month begins.
May 5, 1891
  Carnegie Hall opens.
May 8, 1993
  Let's Go Fishing Day.
May 10, 1869
  Golden spike completes transcontinental railroad.
May 23, 1785
  Ben Franklin invents bifocals.
May 27, 1930
  Masking tape awarded patent #1760820.
May 31, 1927
  15,007,003rd (and last) Model T was made.

Chapter 12

A POTPOURRI

There are some additional areas on which we would like to share our thoughts. Some are more important than others; all are worthy of attention.

TESTING

Students take many tests in a given year. The testing ranges from the daily pop quizzes, to the unit test, and eventually to the many standardized tests. Too, some districts have developed testing programs based on skill development which are usually carried out in isolation, i.e., not as a part of the curriculum subject matter.

Our concern is for the test-dominated student and for the school curriculum, for it may be that all that is taught is that which can be tested. Most would agree, we believe, that there is much in the English curriculum that cannot and should not be tested. We agree that there may be a place for the test in the English classroom, but we think that there are many other more effective approaches to use. The activities described in this book frequently can be used in place of the test.

Now, what about our students who are in our English classes? How many tests might they be faced with? In any one grade level students may spend days responding to questions that ask about their interests, scholastic ability, aptitude, reasoning ability, and personal adjustment. These, for the most part, are just the standardized tests that are given throughout the local district. There may be statewide testing, too. In addition, the English, math, and social studies departments contribute to the testing program.

In English there is the pop quiz over the homework assignment, the test over the novel, and, of course, the unit and semester exams. Where does that leave our students? We think it leaves them with a warped sense of what learning is all about. Most of what they have been doing has been reduced to a right vs. wrong philosophy. It seems to us that we who test are giving our students a false sense of security. For those who pass, we are telling them that life is a right vs. wrong environment. We all know that it isn't; there are many grey areas. For those who fail, they really have little or no sense of security. They begin to transfer the negative results that they receive from the tests to a negative attitude toward themselves. How many test failures does it take before the ninth or tenth grader simply gives up? This give-up attitude may not occur if we place the students in a success-oriented environment in which they can show us what they can do and not constantly confront them with opportunities to fail.

What do tests do to the English curriculum? Certainly, the standardized or teacher-made objective tests can measure to some extent some aspects of progress in English. They can test reading skills; knowledge of facts about literature—authors, plots, devices; knowledge of grammar facts—parts of speech, spelling, punctuation; editing skills; and study skills. Three questions come to mind: (1) Can we agree as an English profession what is acceptable and appropriate in these areas? (2) Is this information important as it is found on a test or is it more important as it is used in the communicative process? (3) Will students believe that because they can share their knowledge on a test, they will not need to be as concerned about using it in daily communication? For example, it seems to us that students may believe that they are writing well if they can punctuate, spell, and capitalize correctly and use "correct" grammar on a test; teachers can believe so if indeed their students test well in these areas.

Too, it is important to note what the tests often do not include. Will the curriculum continue to emphasize the appreciation of literature, the composing process, the expressive use of language, the speaking and listening processes, the variety and appropriateness of usage and/or dialect forms, and the expression of values? Most would agree that these are very important in an English classroom. Even if these areas are included in the curriculum, will students remember these as important to their lives, or will they want to remember only that information that "will be on the test?"

We have emphasized the objective test whether it be the standardized form or the teacher-made test. There is, of course, another form—the essay test. While there are certain advantages to the essay form, we all know the major disadvantage: it takes much more time to grade. It seems to us, however, that if we are going to test, we should consider this form.

It may be of more educational value, since students may find it easier to respond in areas that are more difficult to evaluate.

In sum, there are many ways to evaluate the progress of students in the English class. The test in whatever form is just one way. We urge you to consider a variety of assessments as you measure the growth of students individually or in groups. Among those suggestions of possible measures include the following:

Teacher made tests and departmental tests
Grading of papers and other work
Self-assessment of students
Reflection of learning by students
Peer evaluation
Questionnaires and rating scales
Interviews
Summaries of conferences

All of these assessments should be placed in a portfolio for the final student assessment. We have described in detail the use of the portfolio in the chapter on teaching writing (Chapter 5), so it will not be repeated here. However, it is important to say that all kinds of alternative forms can be placed in a portfolio by students to show growth of learning over time. While writing is extremely beneficial, other forms such as graphs, audiotapes, videotapes, reading inventories, attitude measures, artwork, and music are also quite beneficial.

EVALUATION

Teachers have used grades for many purposes. Grades reflect to some degree the academic progress of students; they reflect how well or not so well students' social behavior has been in class; and, in some cases, they reflect the motivational element of students. You may have reasons for using grades in each of these areas. We do ask that you consider the following when you reevaluate the use of grades. What does it mean to get an A in English? Does it mean that students have a superior knowledge of the subject matter and can apply it in their everyday lives, or does it mean that students are above average and have used socially acceptable behavior? Perhaps, too, students are average but have always beat the deadline and, therefore, received bonus points which reflect the higher grade. What do business and university personnel believe the grade means? If, in fact, the notation of social behavior can be given on the reporting instrument (grade card, etc.), should this also be included in the academic progress report? These questions do not necessarily elicit a right or wrong response, but they do provide some food for thought as we think about the evaluation process. It seems to us that the importance of grades should be minimized and the importance of learning should be emphasized. If teachers accept this concept, they then must decide on the most effective way to use grades.

How best to report the progress to students on a day-to-day basis is often asked. We are sure we don't have the definitive answer, but we do suggest what has been effective for us over the years.

Daily assignments, creative drama interpretations, classroom discussions, and some group work are graded with participation points. With this point approach, teachers can more accurately acknowledge a task completed without getting into the problem of quality interpretation. If the activity is done, students receive 5, 10, 15 points or whatever the activity is worth. Teachers are not hassled with the problem of giving an A, B, C, D, or F. This also alleviates the problem of assessing the value of a check, minus, and plus if these notations are used.

The range of points is used for larger, more involved assignments in which the quality can be assessed. This range of points can easily be used to evaluate writing that has been revised, end of unit projects, book projects, and essay tests.

Teachers add these points at the end of the grading period and then, at this time, they translate the total points into the final reporting system, usually the A, B, C, D, or F.

HOMEWORK

Teachers and students have struggled with the homework concern for many years. It seems that the motivation of doing homework just isn't there. There are so many outside demands for the student's time that homework is often put off and frequently not completed. There are many reasons for this dilemma; we feel that two are important to be mentioned here.

Extracurricular activities affect students. Schools offer many exciting programs that ask for time: sports, music, drama, hobbies. We school people encourage participation in these activities, too, for we believe they do provide a meaningful experience for students. Work may be considered in this category, too, since it does demand a great deal of time of many students. For whatever reason—school-sponsored activities or work—students frequently set a priority system that often does not put homework first.

A second, and perhaps more important, reason for students not doing their homework is the lack of motivation. Students frequently do not see the need. We think there may be two reasons for this. Frequently, teachers give homework for the sake of homework. Often, there is no need since the concept can be learned during class time. Secondly, teachers don't get the students ready for the assignment. This is especially true when assigning reading material. We have suggested at least one remedy for this problem by using creative drama (see Chap. 4). Students must see the relevance of what they are about to do.

The question of whether to give homework or not rests with the teacher who must evaluate time, curriculum objectives, and teaching and learning theories. We suggest that given the demands on students' time, homework should be kept to a minimum. We do urge, too, that work which is required outside of class be preceded with some readiness activity so that the students have some reason for doing it other than the simple fact that it was assigned.

DISCIPLINE

One of the major concerns of teachers, administrators, and parents is discipline, or the lack of it. Year after year, discipline ranks within the top three topics of concern among parents and teachers. It would seem that discipline is more important than the educational objectives that are implemented in the classroom; perhaps, rightly so. For if there is no structure, no classroom organization, it makes little difference what objectives teachers have. They will be difficult to implement. Our concern here is not whether teachers have it or not but what kind of discipline is in the classroom and how it is achieved.

Achieving discipline through fear and authoritative means lacks the desired focus that should be found in an educational institution. We feel strongly that teachers' attitudes toward students and teaching play an important part in the "control" factor in classroom discipline. We have spoken to that in Chapters 2 and 3 and, therefore, will not repeat the material here. It is important to say, however, that the establishment of an effective classroom climate is one of the most important factors in establishing respect and positive classroom behavior.

In addition to the material suggested in Chapter 2, we offer the following material for your consideration.

Good Lesson Planning

Lesson plans are important, be they daily or unit plans. Planning gives teachers confidence that they may not normally have. We suggest that activities in the plan be challenging to students and yet in reach of the student's capabilities. Discipline problems are most likely to occur when the work involves little challenge and incentive.

Teachers should plan creative lesson plans. Variety can be added to the daily routine by using speakers, films, music, and simulation games. We suggest, too, that teachers have an extra plan on hand for those rare occasions when what is planned cannot be carried out. These can be used if a film scheduled for the day did not arrive or if the students finish their activities sooner than anticipated. We believe the material in Chapter 10 can be very useful for these occasions.

Making Rules

One of the immediate jobs of teachers is to establish with their students some policies relating to classroom behavior. Teachers should not simply list a set of rules for the class without stating the reasons for them or without having the class discuss them. It is important to involve the students (perhaps in a class meeting) in the formulation of the policies of conduct. The following standards should be taken into consideration when making these policies.

1. *Don't make too many policies.* A great many policies may result in a disproportionate time spent in enforcing them. Also, the students are more apt to become confused. If more policies are needed, they can be added as the situations require them.
2. *Make policies comprehensive and broad rather than limited and specific.* The more general the policy is written, the fewer weaknesses will be found in it, thus preventing students insisting it does not apply in certain situations.
3. *State policies clearly.* When policies are written as clearly as possible,

the students are better able to remember them and understand their application.

4. *Policies should be subject to revision.* Because teachers can never predict what new situations may arise in which rules need to be changed or dropped, it should always be clear that they are subject to revision.

Enforcement

Once classroom policies are established, it is then necessary to be sure that they are enforced. In some cases, especially when the students have helped to form the standards, peer pressure in the classroom will see to it that the policies are followed. Unfortunately, however, it is often the teacher who is faced with the enforcement. In so doing, the following guidelines should help in dealing with the responsibility:

1. Be consistent.
2. Don't make promises or threats that will be difficult to keep.
3. Don't punish the group for individuals who misbehave.
4. Avoid ridicule and embarrassment.
5. Reprimand in private.
6. Avoid corporal punishment.
7. Have the punishment fit the individual as well as the infraction.
8. Encourage students to take responsibility for their behavior.
9. Make use of quiet time in the classroom and time-out rooms in the school.
10. Seek outside help when necessary: counselors, administrators, parents.

General Tips for Classroom Discipline

1. It seems to us that if you the teacher keep the students busy with relevant, interesting, and meaningful study, discipline problems will decrease remarkedly.
2. We must constantly remember that students are *people* who are a part of an educational not penal instruction. They command the same respect that any other person would be given. This may be difficult sometimes when they do not have the same kind of respect for you.
3. The key words in good discipline are openness, honesty, and

fairness. If teachers incorporate these qualities in their relations with students, the classroom has a much better chance of becoming a community in which effective teaching and learning can take place.

COMMUNICATION WITH ADMINISTRATORS AND PARENTS

Our efforts in this book have been to provide educationally sound theories and creative activities in the teaching of English. Some of the activities do, indeed, deviate from the traditional approach; therefore, it is imperative that teachers share their classroom procedures with administrators, parents, and patrons of the school district. Actually, this communication should occur with any approach that is used.

Frequently, it is the uninformed persons who question the objectives and approaches used because they simply do not know the entire scope and sequence of the lessons. We in education tend to wait until a problem surfaces before we share what we are doing in the classroom. We believe teachers should take the initiative. Sharing, for example, the theory of teaching writing, the use of creative drama, and the use of the thematic unit cannot but help would-be critics to understand better these components of the English program.

We offer the following suggestions as ways to communicate the English programs to those who may not be informed:

To Administrators:

- Explain in as much detail as possible the various programs you have in the English curriculum. Support your positions with reports of research that corroborate your choices.
- Invite your supervisor to your class so that he/she may see firsthand what your students are doing. Suggest that he/she return for 4 or 5 consecutive days for additional visits.
- Share articles from educational journals which discuss approaches and theories that you are using in your classroom.
- Invite the administrators to attend English conferences at which English classroom practices are being discussed.
- Show off the results! Share your students' work with school personnel.

To Parents:

- Involve parents in your program. Many want to help and you should use as many as you can. The more involved parents become, the more informed they are.
- During back-to-school nights or open houses, share as much information about your program as possible. Encourage questions and respond fully.
- In addition to these school-wide programs, invite parents of your students for after-school discussions of the English program.
- Sponsor an English fair, perhaps in cooperation with other departments. At this time, students are able to show off their work done in class—projects, compositions, etc.
- Establish an English class newsletter to be sent to parents. Descriptions of current activities as well as samples of students work should be included.

FOR ADDITIONAL READING

Cooper, Charles. *The Nature and Measurement of Competency in English.* Urbana, IL.: National Council of Teachers of English, 1981.

England, David; and Flatley, Joannis K. *Homework—And Why.* Bloomington, IN: Phi Delta Kappa Educational Foundation, 1985.

Gotts, Edward E., and Purnell, Richard F. *Improving Home-School Communications.* Bloomington, IN: Phi Delta Kappa Education Foundation, 1985.

Haley, Beverly. *The Report Card Trap.* Whitehall, VA: Betterway Publications, Inc., 1985.

Johnston, Brian. *Assessing English: Helping Students to Reflect on Their Work.* Urbana, IL.: National Council of Teachers of English, 1983.

Purves, Alan. *Common Sense and Testing in English.* Urbana, IL.: National Council of Teachers of English, 1975.

Spargo, Frank. *Changing Behavior: A Practical Guide for Teachers and Parents.* Bloomington, IN: Phi Delta Kappa Educational Foundation, 1985.

INDEX